THE WORLD OF THE EDWARDIAN CHILD

AS SEEN IN ARTHUR MEE'S CHILDREN'S ENCYCLOPÆDIA, 1908–1910

Published by HERMITAGE, 2008

ISBN 978-2-9600047-1-7

Printed and bound in Great Britain by York Publishing Services Ltd.
enqs@yps-publishing.co.uk

To the memory of my parents

CONTENTS

Foreword by Professor Hugh Cunningham *

The twentieth century was heralded at its outset as 'the century of the child'. The hope was that the sufferings children had undergone in the nineteenth century – working in coal mines and cotton factories, or eking out a living on the streets – were now firmly in the past. A bright future beckoned where children would grow up healthy and happy. Science, it was thought, would help bring down the appalling mortality figures for babies and young children. The National Society for the Prevention of Cruelty to Children, founded in the 1880s, would continue its good work of seeking out and putting an end to the cruelties that some parents inflicted on their offspring. Schools would move away from the dull routines of rote learning and would help children to explore their world with new methods of teaching in airy classrooms.

It was in this optimistic world that Arthur Mee had the idea of publishing a Children's Encyclopædia, a kind of Encyclopædia Britannica for children. Many other writers were exploring the world of childhood and reflecting it back to them in these early-twentieth-century years. Beatrix Potter's books began to be published from 1901, J.M. Barrie's 'Peter Pan' was first performed in 1904, Kenneth Grahame's 'The Wind in the Willows' dates from 1908. Mee, like so many other writers for children, starts with his own daughter's questions, those questions that are so often profound – and difficult for adults to answer. One of the most attractive features of the Children's Encyclopædia is the dialogue Mee carries on with readers, answering their questions and encouraging them to 'wonder'.

The Encyclopædia was an extraordinary success. Published first in fortnightly parts between 1908 and 1910, it then came out in an eight-volume bound edition, and was republished many times. The edition in my home, dating from after the Second World War, has expanded to ten volumes, but the format and many of the entries are the same as half a century before. Millions of children brought up between 1910 and the 1960s will have encountered Arthur Mee, their minds in some way influenced by what they read.

Michael Tracy has explored the first edition, the one he was brought up on. You can read his selection of articles as a trip down memory lane, but it will also

---

* Emeritus Professor of Social History at the University of Kent.

prompt important questions about the differences between then and now. Mee and his co-writers have high expectations of what children will read and want to know about. They are confident about their world: Britain is the best country to live in, Christianity is the best religion, science will fuel progress. This world collapsed in the 1960s, and optimism about children and childhood has been replaced by a pervasive anxiety, and some real worries, not least Britain's bottom of the league position in a recent UNICEF survey of children in developed countries.

The ten bulky volumes of the Children's Encyclopædia that sit on my shelves look rather intimidating. I occasionally dip into them, but have never looked at them in any systematic way. Michael Tracy has done us an invaluable service by revealing to us the shape and ambition of the Encyclopædia, and by opening up for us a world of childhood, not very distant in time, that has now vanished. It is both an enjoyable read, with a light but expert touch to the commentary, and a challenge to us to think afresh about childhood.

Author's preface

I was about eight years old, and the year around 1940, when my mother brought home a complete eight-volume set of the *Children's Encyclopædia* – she had a knack of picking up 'bargains' at auction sales. From then on until I reached my 'teens, I frequently dipped into it. Subsequently, it has accompanied me through numerous changes of address. Recently I thought of selling it to make space on the shelf. But first I thought I should look at it again.

I was fascinated by what I discovered. I found many items I remembered, others which I had certainly not read in my childhood. So I started to investigate.

As a child, I had not been much aware of the date of publication: now I realised that it came somewhere between the death of Queen Victoria and the outbreak of the First World War. I became aware that this was a treasury of information on life at that time – not the sort of knowledge that one finds in history books, but something much more real and alive: what questions children were asking, and what they were being taught. And how different their life was from that of children today!

So I dropped the idea of selling the set. Here was a mine which someone should tap! And why not me? – after all, I had written several books and had some experience in historical research, though in a different field.

This book is the result. It has been a substantial task to sift through over five thousand pages, but a rewarding one. I tried also to read around the subject, to become better informed about the Edwardian age, and about the unusual personality of Arthur Mee who was primarily responsible for the *Encyclopædia*. I also found out as much as possible about the other main contributors.

I now know that the *Children's Encyclopædia* was first published in fifty fortnightly instalments, between 1908 and 1910. It was then sold in eight bound volumes, in handsome green and gold hard covers: this is the set which I possess.

It is not arranged in alphabetical order (the name *Encyclopædia* is perhaps misleading) but as a series of articles, approximately the same series in each issue: their titles correspond to those in my table of contents. There is however a very comprehensive and accurate index at the end of the last volume (82 pages in very small print).

The first page of each article has an attractive *art nouveau* border: these have been reproduced here at the beginning of each section.

The articles range from those aimed at very small children, in particular the 'nursery rhymes', to scientific items, some of which would be hard work even for an intelligent teenager. Thus each issue of the *Encyclopædia* would have contained something of interest for children of different ages in the same family, or might have accompanied a particular child as he or she grew up.

Abundant pictures accompany the articles and help to make explanations even clearer than they are in the text. These include photographs, of considerable interest in themselves, mostly black-and-white though some have been touched up in colour (with rather unsatisfactory results to our tastes). Some illustrations are drawings, but many are reproductions of paintings; a few of the latter are attributed to well-known artists but many are anonymous, perhaps commissioned specially for the *Encyclopædia*. A small sample of the most interesting illustrations will be reproduced as we go along.

Half-a-dozen main contributors and others less significant are mentioned, besides the editor himself, Arthur Mee. In so far as it has been possible to find out something about them, this will be indicated.

According to the biography of Arthur Mee by his lifelong friend, Sir John Hammerton (who contributed to the *Encyclopædia*), the work was a success from the first of the fortnightly issues, with sales increasing as the series continued. The work was re-published after the First World War, and there were numerous further editions in the interwar period. The last issue was in 1964, still with Arthur Mee's name on the cover. It had grown from eight to ten volumes. Some of the content was still the same, as was the general presentation (now looking distinctly old-fashioned).

Sir John calculated that total sales throughout the Empire had amounted to over five million volumes, not counting the serial issues which could have been bound by subscribers. It was, wrote Sir John in 1946, 'the greatest force in all the world for enlightening the children of the last two generations'. (He was too hopeful in adding '… and it will continue to exercise that function for some generations to come').

The work was also published in the United States, under the title *Book of Knowledge*, with *The Children's Encyclopædia* as a sub-title. This, according to Sir John, sold at least 3.5 million sets over a 35-year period; as the later editions consisted of twenty volumes, the total number of volumes could have reached 52 million. There were also editions in French, Italian, Spanish, Portuguese, and even Chinese (not, however, German). Given the strongly anglo-centric nature of the work, it would be interesting to know how readers in these countries reacted to it, but that would have to be the subject of another study.

We need to know more about this remarkable man, the editor. Arthur Mee was born in 1875, in a small town near Nottingham, the second of ten children. This was a working-class family. His father was a railwayman who became an engine-driver (Hammerton seems reluctant to recognise Mee's working-class origins, describing his father as an 'engineer': the more accurate description above comes from two other sources – see Bibliography). He was a militant Nonconformist (a deacon in the local Baptist church), an 'upright, earnest citizen'.

Arthur left school when he was fourteen; from then on he was self-taught. He worked first in a bakery; then found a job with the *Nottingham Evening Post* as a copyholder, the lowest rung of the journalistic ladder. Soon he was contributing copy himself. At the age of twenty, he was appointed editor of the *Post*'s sister paper, the *Evening News* (John Hammerton was by then editor of the *Post*). He started sending articles to the periodical *Tit-Bits*, and soon obtained a post on its London staff. Before long, he embarked on a free-lance career, contributing articles to various journals. He also wrote four books between 1900 and 1903, including biographies of Joseph Chamberlain, Lord Salisbury and King Edward VII.

We can pass briefly over his subsequent career. From 1919 onwards he edited the *Children's Newspaper* (which unlike the *Encyclopædia* covered current events): he was still editing it in 1943 when he died, and it continued until 1965.[1] He wrote a number of other books. He became successful and prosperous, though never excessively rich; he built a fine home at Eynsford in Kent. His estate at death was valued at £43,507; his will provided for legacies of some £16,000, but he regretted that because of reduced circumstances (the war?) he could not leave more to family and friends. However this may be, he had come a long way from his Nottinghamshire working-class origins.

Although his own schooling had been limited, Mee always considered education to be vitally important; he had a gift for simple, clear expression, though his style seems unduly paternalistic to our contemporary taste. His biographers state that his moral stance was firmly based in Nonconformist Christianity. There is however no indication that he was a church-goer, and in his will he stipulated that there should be no service at his cremation; indeed, the only religious reference is to 'my faith that all is well and that the Universe is in the hands of God' – a circumlocution which echoes some we shall find in the *Encyclopædia*).

He fiercely denounced alcoholism (he strongly supported the Temperance Movement) and gambling. He took a poor view of King Edward's laxity in moral matters.

He remained consistent to his views throughout his lifetime, despite changing circumstances. This is particularly striking with regard to imperialism: he believed like many others in the white man's superiority (particularly that of the Englishman!) while stressing the duty to improve the lot of the 'lesser breeds'. At the beginning of the century this was an outlook widely shared, but Mee in 1937 was still writing (the closing paragraph of *Salute the King*):

> 'It is not for nothing that the sun never sets on this banner of our ancient land. Out of the historic past it flies, the assurance to mankind that Freedom lives. In its sheltering folds lives one quarter of this troubled world, calm amid storms, free from all terrors, walking unafraid.'

This is a fair sample of his rather grandiloquent style. It is also a surprising statement in view of the growing resentment against British rule in India in particular. Mee died in 1943; four years later, India gained its independence.

Mee's innate patriotism was displayed in the series of books entitled *King's England* (currently being reprinted by the King's England Press) which he edited and produced during the 1930s. These described, often in lyrical terms, England's towns, villages and countryside. Mee himself wrote the first volume, *Enchanted Land*.

We find such views, on Britain's imperial role, on the superiority of Christianity over other religions, on the evils of gambling, etc. recurring throughout the *Encyclopædia*: indeed, since there is no dissent or qualification, such attitudes are implicit. We might now find such ideas quaint or even plainly wrong, but they would not have seemed so to most middle-class people in Edwardian England. They form an essential part of the education which the *Encyclopædia* sought to

---

[1] It is currently being republished online by *Look and Learn* magazine (www.lookandlearn.com).

impart with the general aim of creating decent, honest, hard-working, conscientious citizens.

In the *Encyclopædia* we are not just hearing Arthur Mee's ideas. Certainly, Mee would not have hired collaborators liable to oppose his religious and ethical stance. We cannot know whether or to what extent he intervened in their writing, but consistency of style throughout each series of articles suggests that, having established the general scheme, he left them alone. Moreover, his main contributors were men and women of considerable standing in their own right, and would have felt entitled to express their own views.

The *Encyclopædia* entered a very large number of households and must have influenced the attitudes of many children – perhaps also of their parents – and played a role in the way they lived their lives. With successive editions, this influence probably persisted through the subsequent decades, at least up to the Second World War. Speaking for myself, as I now read through these articles, I constantly hear echoes from my childhood.

It was thus a very significant work. Studying now that first edition, we obtain not only a vision of the life and thinking of the Edwardian period but also an insight into the concepts which, for better or worse, shaped both that and subsequent generations.

I have done my best to provide a balanced and objective account of the *Encyclopædia*. Still, in condensing over five thousand pages into a couple of hundred, choices have to be made all the time: inevitably, these choices reflect what I personally find interesting, significant, or simply amusing. So the reader is entitled to know something of my own background and outlook, which may throw light on the way I have approached this task.

The basic facts of my career appear on the inside back cover. It will be apparent that my experience is very different from that of Arthur Mee and probably most of his colleagues: indeed, an international path such as that which I have trod would have been inconceivable in their time. Further, I believe firmly in the need for international co-operation, European integration in particular. This contrasts with the *Encyclopædia's* assumption that Britain had a right and duty to rule a large part of the world.

After a good grounding at the local State school, I benefited from a privileged secondary education at a well-known Scottish public school, and from there got to Cambridge. This I owe to the encouragement of my mother (with some hard work on my part) through which I obtained the necessary scholarships. Though grateful for what I learnt and experienced at these places, I emerged with a strong dislike of class-based elitism in education. I share with the *Encyclopædia* authors their belief in the vital importance of a good education, but it should be available to all.

I believe that it is a major role of the State to promote equality of opportunity and to provide a welfare safety net for those in need. So I have been attentive to what the *Encyclopædia* has to say (not much) about the conditions of the working classes in their time.

Religion is also a topic on which I should declare my views. In my youth I experienced Christianity in its Presbyterian and Anglican forms. Subsequently, I have had fruitful encounters with Oriental religions and philosophy. I do not accept that any one tradition can have a monopoly of truth. Here too I part company from much of what is said or implied in the *Encyclopædia*.

I suppose that my Irish and Scottish roots (particularly the latter) are also relevant. They have certainly caused me to notice Mee's anglo-centric tendency.

But I live in a different age and a different world: a hundred years ago, the views of Arthur Mee and his colleagues would not have surprised their contemporaries. Who knows what I might myself have thought if I had lived at that time?

So I have tried to avoid judgements based on hindsight, and to convey as objectively as possibly the contents of the *Children's Encyclopædia*, which – despite its limitations, which will be discussed in my Conclusions – was indeed a most remarkable work.

I am much indebted to Professor Hugh Cunningham for his support and for many useful comments. Among other points, the title is his suggestion – much better than the one I had in mind!

My wife Ros, being herself a professional historian, has an encyclopedic knowledge which has often helped to fill in gaps. And I am grateful to friends who have made helpful comments. Researching the background for this book, I have used Internet sources, also the university libraries at Kent and Cambridge and the British Library. Librarians are usually friendly and helpful people to whom a writer owes a great deal.

I have always typed my own work (the arrival of word-processing was a boon) and I have done my own page-setting. Should one give thanks to the creators of computers, software and the Internet, who have made this possible? Maybe; but dependence on such technology reaches a point where one becomes its slave, rather than the other way round. One must then rely on technicians who come to the rescue when something breaks down. Working on this book partly from an Andalucian mountain village, I was much helped by José (I never heard his surname) who installed and maintained my communications system there.

Martin Shoesmith did excellent work improving my scanned illustrations. My long-standing friend Christine Dickert came to my assistance just at the right moment and has carried out a thorough proof-reading, correcting typographical and some factual errors. I take responsibility for any remaining mistakes.

Introduction – The End of an Era?

Sandwiched between the long and illustrious reign of Queen Victoria and the outbreak of the Great War, the Edwardian period seems almost a parenthesis in history, attracting relatively little attention; in many histories it appears as a rather awkward appendix tacked on to discussion of 'the long nineteenth century', to quote the historian Eric Hobsbawm. (See however the Bibliography for various works relevant to the period.)

It was in any case relatively short: Edward VII reigned from 1901 till 1910, when he was succeeded by his son (George V). This was in fact the last period of British history to be known by the name of the monarch. Not that Edward himself made a significant impact. When he came to the throne at the age of sixty, there was considerable doubt about his character, having in his past life indulged in women, food, drink, gambling, sport and travel. On the whole he did not take his kingly duties very seriously, and showed little interest in domestic politics: in his reign, 'ostentatious pleasure' characterised the ways of the court and the leisured classes. But after the strict moral rectitude of the Victorians, this more relaxed attitude was welcome, and Edward was generally popular.

He did appeal to the French public. He was a frequent visitor to France, and a speech he made in Paris in 1903 – in fluent French, without notes – is held to have contributed to the *Entente Cordiale* the following year.

On the other hand, although Edward also spoke excellent German, his relationship with the Kaiser was, to say the least, tense. Wilhelm II apparently adored Victoria, his grandmother, but despised Edward, his uncle. After an Anglo-Russian *entente* in 1907, and when Edward had gone to meet the Czar of Russia in 1908, the Kaiser accused him of being a trouble-maker who was trying to encircle Germany. Not that better relations between the two monarchs would have prevented the Great War – there were far more powerful geo-political forces at work – but this lack of empathy between the sovereigns did not help. Edward got on better with the Austrian-Hungarian Emperor, Franz Joseph, but still did not succeed in dissuading him from the alliance with Germany which in the end made the war inevitable.

Hobsbawm has described the 'Age of Empire' from around 1875 till 1914 as 'an era of unparalleled peace in the western world'. Nevertheless, in Britain, the Edwardian period was by no means exempt from political and social strife. The Boer War of 1899–1902, ending in an inglorious victory, had divided the people. It contributed to a growth of radical thinking and to the overwhelming success of the Liberal party in the election of 1906.

In that Parliament the Liberals had an overall majority which enabled them to govern alone, and brought to the fore such prominent politicians as Lloyd George and Winston Churchill. The increasing militancy of trade unions reinforced the recently-formed Labour party: the first Labour MPs were elected in 1906, and after two elections in 1910 their support was needed by the Liberal government.

Women had begun to demand greater recognition, including university education and above all voting rights. With the founding of the Women's Social and Political Union by Mrs. Pankhurst in 1903, the suffragette movement became militant. There were mass meetings with ugly scenes, leading to arrests, imprisonment, hunger strikes and forcible feeding. By the outbreak of war, not much concrete progress had been made.

Home Rule for Ireland was another major political issue. Despite much debate and some attempts at compromise, involving the partition of the country between Ulster and the rest, this too remained unsolved, a running sore that erupted in the following years.

The nineteenth century had seen great scientific and technical progress; Britain had become 'the workshop of the world'. This continued in the Edwardian period, though other nations, notably Germany, were now catching up. A dense network of railways covered most of Britain (see illustration), and train speeds were not much less than they are on many lines today. Motor-cars had made their appearance, with the first Motor Show in 1903 at the Crystal Palace: there were 8,500 private cars in 1904, the number doubled in the following year and exceeded 200,000 by the end of the period. The first electric underground trains ran in London in 1904; the last horse-drawn bus had disappeared there by 1911, and motor-taxis had begun to outnumber horse-drawn cabs.

The illustration 'busiest street in the world' (Mansion House Street in London) shows a chaotic mingling of pedestrians, horse-drawn and motorised vehicles: the caption suggests that the need for a rule of the road was only beginning to be perceived.

Electricity was beginning to penetrate the homes, with electric lamps replacing gas and oil. Electric motors led to innovations such as the vacuum cleaner (cumbersome machines at first, for the use of the servants). The gramophone with flat disks was replacing the wax cylinder, and many records became available, capturing for posterity the voice of Caruso and the music of other great artists. The telephone was spreading to more and more homes.

Wireless telegraphy permitted long-distance messages, even across the Atlantic and to ocean liners. The latter, powered by the new turbine engines, could now cross the Atlantic in five days.

In 1903 the Wright brothers had made the first flight in a heavier-than-air craft, and in 1909 Bleriot flew across the Channel; there was intense interest in this new form of travel – with keen Franco-British rivalry – although airships with gas-filled balloons seemed at least as promising.

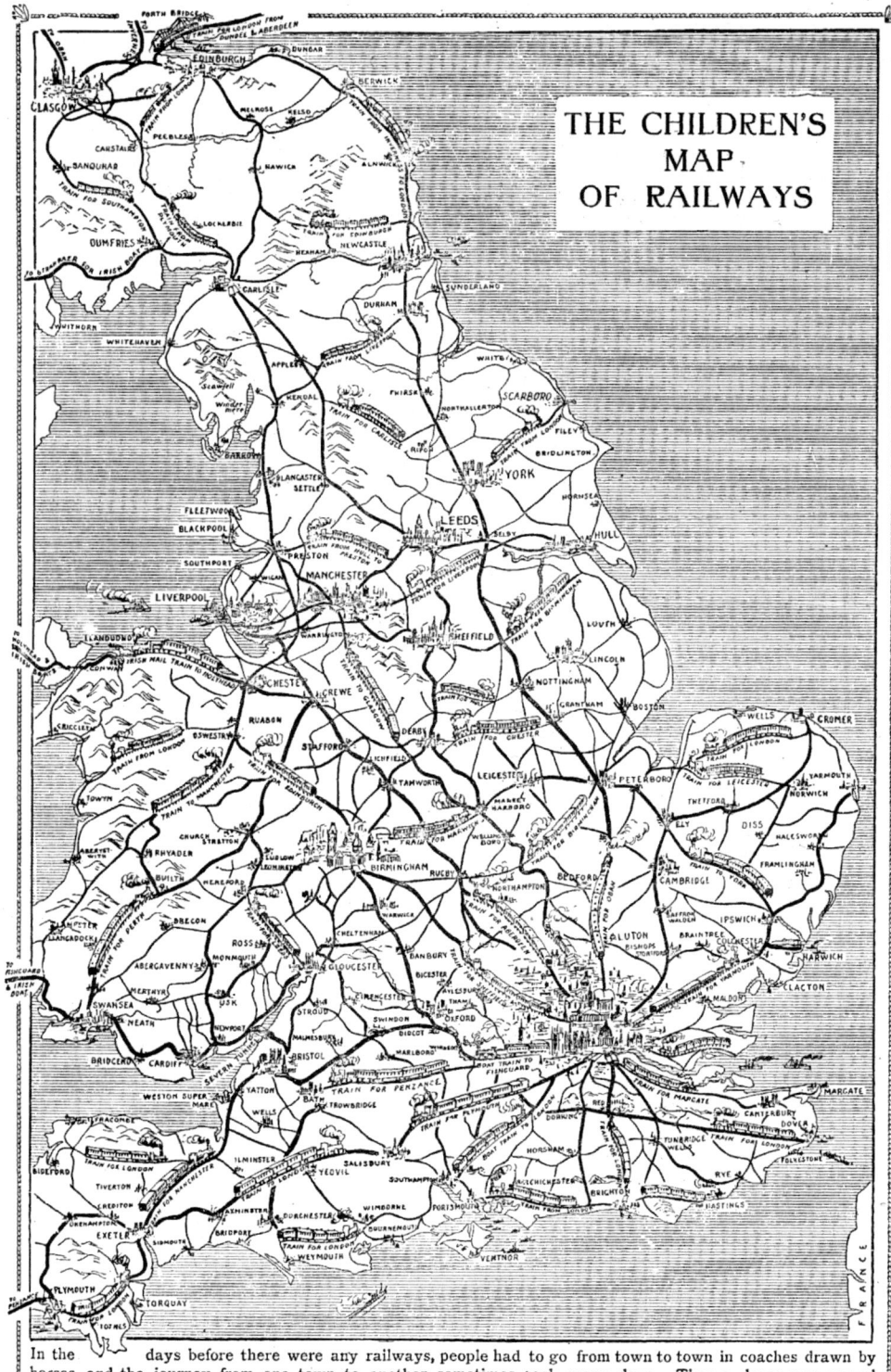

THE CHILDREN'S
MAP
OF RAILWAYS

In the   days before there were any railways, people had to go from town to town in coaches drawn by
horses, and the journey from one town to another sometimes took many days.   Then a clever man named
George Stephenson made an engine to go by steam, and since then railways have been laid all over England.
There are more than thirty thousand miles of railways in England, and thousands of trains are always running.   There are still some little villages without railways, but the railway is not very far away, and we can
leave London after breakfast any morning and be in any part of the country we want to go to at bed-time.

THE BUSIEST STREET IN THE WORLD

When we see a street like this, in the heart of a busy city, we understand the need for some rule of the road. Were omnibuses and carts allowed to go to the right or left as they thought fit there would be hopeless confusion, and all traffic would be at a standstill. The street shown here is Mansion House Street, in the centre of the City of London, which is said to be the busiest thoroughfare in the world. Eight or nine different streets meet here, and many thousands of vehicles pass to and fro every day. The pictures in the following pages show us the dangers to be avoided in the streets, and teach us the rule of the road, so that we may avoid these dangers. In America and on the Continent the road traffic passes to the right instead of to the left.

4302

INTRODUCTION

The British Navy was the most powerful in the world, though here too Germany was catching up: in response the first 'Dreadnought' – a super-powerful battleship – was launched in 1906. The Navy guarded an Empire 'on which the sun never set'. Investment by Britain in the colonies and in America far exceeded foreign investment by any other country.

There were few qualms of conscience about imperialism: indeed, bringing civilisation and Christianity to 'lesser breeds' was regarded as a duty. The 'public school' system was geared to producing leaders to manage and rule the colonies, India in particular, and to educating the male children of colonial families; Sandhurst trained the officer corps. (In the case of India, some upper-caste Indians willingly adopted British ways, even sending their boys to English public schools, and cricket became a national sport.) Baden-Powell founded the Boy Scouts movement in 1907; he had considered calling them 'Young Knights of the Empire', and his sister wrote a book called *How Girls can help build up the Empire*. Kipling was closely interested in the movement.

In 1908 the Olympic Games were staged at the White City in London; British athletes won 56 gold medals (as against 22 for Americans). The same year saw a major Franco-British Exhibition.

Intellectuals pondered on the difficulties of reconciling traditional religious teaching with the findings of science, in particular growing knowledge of the nature of the universe and the origins of the earth, and – following Darwin – the theory of evolution. The Church of England was being forced onto the defensive.

The benefits of material progress were enjoyed by a large and prosperous middle class, who looked forward confidently to continued scientific, technical and economic advances. Some in government were aware of mounting dangers. But for most people, this did not seem like 'the end of an era', on the contrary. They were not to know that Britain, along with Europe and indeed the whole civilised world, was heading for catastrophe.

As we look back, the Edwardian era seems a last moment of relative peace, of continued progress in all fields, of unshaken confidence in man's destiny – in all of which Great Britain was expected to continue to play a leading role.

That is the context in which the *Children's Encyclopædia* was published in 1908–10. As will be seen below, it reflected this widespread confidence. With some exceptions, which will be pointed out as we go along and in the Conclusions, no troublesome issues of the kind mentioned above appeared in its pages. One would not expect a book aimed at children to dwell too much on such problems, but we might feel that they were being excessively shielded in their 'state of innocence'.

We should bear in mind that we are reading a work produced by and destined for relatively well-off society. It is unlikely that the *Encyclopædia* found its way into many working-class households (or, for that matter, into Catholic and rural Ireland). It does provide us with a remarkable insight into the life and attitudes of those fortunate classes – from which, of course, came practically all those who ruled the nation and the Empire. We can admire the breadth and quality of the subject-matter and the clarity of the explanations; and we may regret our loss of the sense of peace and security imparted to the children of those families, in what was perhaps the last era during which such an attitude was possible.

Poverty and riches

Those fortunate classes, however, probably made up only about one-seventh of the population. We should be aware of the conditions in which the greater part of the population were living. By the end of the nineteenth century, Britain had become a predominantly urban civilisation, with three-quarters of the population living in towns. Conditions had improved from Dickensian times, but were still squalid in many of the industrial cities. The working class suffered from low wages, long working hours and the virtual absence of any welfare provision. Conditions in urban slums were grim; in the country, for the families of landless labourers, they were not much better. The destitute were still relegated to 'workhouses', in hopeless conditions.

Given a dearth of official statistics on living standards, two surveys were particularly significant; both were undertaken on the initiative of their authors. Starting in 1886, Charles Booth (a wealthy ship-owner) carried out with numerous helpers a remarkably detailed investigation in the poorer areas of London. The results were published in 1903, and he concluded that:

> 'There is struggling poverty, there is destitution, there is hunger, drunkenness, brutality and crime... There is a great sense of helplessness: the wage-earners are helpless to regulate their work and cannot obtain a fair equivalent for the work they are willing to give; the manufacturer or dealer can only work within the limits of competition; the rich are helpless to relieve want without stimulating its sources.'

This was followed up by a study in York carried out by Seebohm Rowntree (of the chocolate firm, and a Quaker). He obtained similar results, published in 1906.[1] Putting the two surveys together, he found 'a startling probability that from 25 to 30 per cent of the town population of the UK are living in poverty'. Since three-quarters of the population was urban, he suggested that this could represent a third of the total population.

Both surveys found that urban poverty was associated with poor nutrition, inadequate housing, low standards of health and high infant mortality. Other studies showed that poverty was even greater among agricultural labourers (cf. Hattersley, 2004).

Further work by Chiozza Money – a Liberal Member of Parliament – based mainly on taxation statistics, concluded (1906) that 'nearly half of the entire income

---

[1] The slum area of York investigated by Rowntree is now a site for small industries, among them the premises of York Publishing Services where this book is being produced.

of the UK was enjoyed by one-ninth of its people'. He also found that more than half of its land area was owned by only 2,500 people.

These studies caused C.F.G. Masterman – also a Liberal MP and in 1910 Under-secretary in the Home Office under Winston Churchill – to write (1909, p.228) that England had:

> 'a civilisation containing many of the elements of human welfare and enjoying a widespread happiness and personal comfort. Such comfort appears as somewhat unjustly divided between class and class. A main body of adequately rewarded and satisfied workers are set between the unnaturally wealthy on the one side, and on the other the unnaturally poor'.

To call this 'an error of distribution', as he did, seems an over-cautious way of describing the situation.

During the Edwardian period, a number of reforms were implemented. Working hours were increasingly regulated and minimum wages introduced in some industries, notably mining. An old-age pension scheme came into force in 1909.

A national insurance scheme for unemployment and health was enacted, but the means of financing it led to a constitutional crisis. A budget proposing major tax increases on wealthy landowners was blocked by the House of Lords, where the Tories held the majority. This was a constitutional crisis which Edward VII left to his son: the Lords capitulated only when George V was persuaded by the government to declare that if necessary he would create enough new Liberal peerages to pass the measure.

Child education and welfare

In Scotland, the principle of education for all dates back to the Protestant Reformation in the sixteenth century: John Knox held universal education to be essential (Protestants should be able to read their Bibles). In the early seventeenth century every parish was required to set up a school, to be financed by a tax on local landowners. Already by the end of that century a considerable proportion of the population was literate, and the education system continued to develop at all levels. Schooling for all children between five and thirteen was made compulsory in 1872; in 1883 the leaving age was raised to fourteen. School fees in the public system were abolished in 1890, and by 1902, when a Scottish Education Act was passed, there were already four hundred schools providing some kind of secondary education.

In England and Wales, the process took much longer, with education mainly controlled by the Church of England. Until 1870, those parents who could afford it sent their children to fee-paying institutions, mostly church schools (chiefly Anglican, some Catholic and Nonconformist); the really rich might have a tutor or governess to teach them at home. In that year, the first major Education Act – opposed by the Church – provided for school boards to establish new elementary schools where existing voluntary provision was insufficient; these would be financed by a local education rate and grant, with small fees. The Act was thus aimed mainly at working-class children; wealthier parents were expected to continue making their own arrangements. The boards were elected by rate-payers, and board members included working-class men. Religious instruction could be part of the curriculum but had to be non-denominational.

In 1880 attendance was made compulsory between the ages of five and ten, after which pupils could be exempted to work part-time if they had attained a certain level. In practice attendance remained irregular, even after legislation in 1867 and 1889 restricted child employment and their hours of work. In 1891 grants were made available to schools which abolished fees. So by the turn of the century, a national system of compulsory and free education was in place.

The 1870 Act had led to the building of new 'Board schools', mostly an improvement on the pre-existing establishments. Even so, their premises were often inadequate and their equipment was limited. The quality of teaching left much to be desired: most training was done within the schools through a 'pupil-teacher' arrangement, which meant that teachers came from within the system and perpetuated the existing methods. Teacher training centres gradually came into existence: the first was in Liverpool in 1876, and by the end of the century over half of the pupil-teachers were receiving part of their training from such institutions. Still, in 1905, the Chief Inspector of Schools described elementary teachers as 'uncultivated and imperfectly educated people who were for the most part creatures of tradition and routine' (cf. Hattersley, p.260).

The methods included frequent corporal punishment, often severe; this applied also to the private, fee-paying schools. Walvin (1982, p.60) wrote that 'the world of the Edwardian child remained circumscribed by the threat, and often the reality, of a sound beating'. This tends to be confirmed by the anecdotal evidence collected by Thompson (1975) and Arthur (2006). A somewhat different picture emerges from the chapter 'Willingly to School' in Jonathan Rose's work (2001): interviews conducted in the late 1960s with people born between 1870 and 1908 suggested that most had good memories of their schooling. Even so, about a third felt that corporal punishment had been too severe.

A new Education Act in 1902 established a national Board of Education and a network of local education authorities, with powers to set up and finance both elementary and secondary schooling. Secondary schooling, however, was not compulsory, and fees were normally charged; though some free places were made available, the main beneficiaries of this secondary education were children from the lower middle-classes, with few coming from unskilled worker families.

The new Board issued in 1904 a Code for Public Elementary Education: the aim should be to 'strengthen character, develop intelligence and arouse interest in the ideals and achievements of mankind' (quoted by Hattersley, p.257)).

However, classes remained large; learning by rote was prevalent, and mainly concerned the 'three Rs' – reading, writing, arithmetic - which for many working-class parents seemed sufficient. Otherwise, English literature was the subject receiving most attention. History, geography and languages were taught very superficially if at all.

In England and Wales, other reforms included legislation in 1906 allowing local authorities to finance school meals – it was recognised that many children from poor families were handicapped by poor nutrition at home. Also, as childhood diseases – measles, whooping-cough, scarlet fever, diphtheria etc. – were widespread, medical inspection was authorised in 1907, but this was not systematically followed up by proper treatment.

The Prevention of Cruelty to Children Act had been passed in 1889, in the same year as the NSPCC was formed. The Children Act of 1908 was a major plank in the reform programme of the Liberal government and its provisions reflected current concerns. It introduced further legislation against cruelty and neglect; sought to prevent smoking by anyone under sixteen; prohibited children under fourteen from public bars and made it an offence to give alcohol to children under five; made it illegal to send persons under sixteen to prison, providing instead for authorised detention centres; and abolished the death penalty for young persons (see Annex).

We shall find in the *Children's Encyclopædia* only a few allusions to these matters. Taking note of them, however, helps us to appreciate the significance of Arthur Mee's work in the field of education, and indeed in its general attitude to children. This was in line with the reforms of the previous years, but which were only slowly being felt in the state system. For Mee and his collaborators, children were to be respected, learning should be made interesting; and the range of subjects covered in the *Encyclopædia* far exceeded that which would have been found in most schools.

It would be good to think that the benefits penetrated somehow to the children of the poor: that, however, is doubtful. We shall return to these points in the Conclusions.

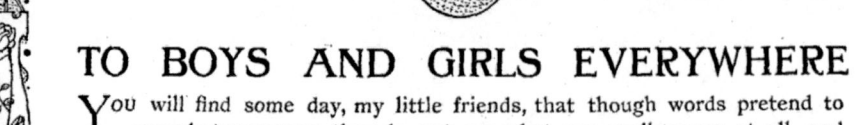

TO BOYS AND GIRLS EVERYWHERE

YOU will find some day, my little friends, that though words pretend to say what you mean, they do not say what you really mean at all, and I do not know of any words that can tell you all I want to say to you and all that this book means to me. Yet it is your book, and the story of it belongs to you; and here it is.

SOMEWHERE, in a corner of the world that a mother knows, is a little lonely girl, the gentlest little fairy who ever opened her eyes to see the sun. When Master Jack Frost wakes up from his sleep and drives the children in, our little fairy rides on her rocking-horse to Fairyland, or rings the bell on her toy shop door and pretends to sell things to somebody who is not there, or puts her dolls to bed long before it is time, or tells her bear the strangest stories that ever were heard. When the sun is high in the sky, she sets to work with her spade to turn the earth upside down, or talks to the fairies in the trees, or begs Robin Redbreast to come down and be friends.

AND, though Robin does not come down to her because bad boys with stones and catapults have made him afraid of all things that have hands, our little maid has friends in every flower that grows, in every wind that blows; and at night, as the great sun goes to his bed in the west, and the dark creeps over the world; as the days begin and end, as the weeks go by, and the months roll on, and the years begin to come, her little mind grows great with wonder, and she finds that behind the world and its play, behind all that she can see and hear and feel and know, is Something that she does not see and hear and feel and know, Something great and powerful that she cannot understand.

AND so there comes into her mind the great wonder of the earth. What does the world mean? And why am I here? So the questions come, until the mother of our little maid is more puzzled than the little maid herself. And as the questions come, when the mother has thought and thought, and answered this and answered that, until she can answer no more, she cries out for a book: "Oh, for a book that will answer all the questions!" And this is the book she cried for.

THAT is how our book began to be. Let us think that we are sitting by the fire, little and big children everywhere, with story-tellers and wise men to talk to us. If we ask for stories, we shall get them. If we are very, very little people and ask for little tales and rhymes, we shall get them too. If we are growing up to wonder how the world was made, and how the flowers grow, and why the sky is blue—or if we are bigger still and go to school—we shall find that all we want to know is in our book. Such a big book must have a big name, but you will learn to say it easily, and you will know when you grow up that it is the only name that would really do. The name is the biggest word in all the book, for all that wise men know is written here so that we can understand.

IT is a Big Book for Little People, and it has come into the world to make your life happy and good. That is what we are meant to be. That is what we must be. That is what we will help each other to be.

Your Affectionate Friend,   ARTHUR MEE

ARTHUR MEE'S GREETING

The *Encyclopædia* opens with an address by the Editor to his young readers (reproduced opposite). They are his 'little friends', and he signs himself as 'Your Affectionate Friend'. He seems to be aiming the work at quite young children, although he does refer to 'little and big children everywhere'. It was no doubt Arthur Mee's choice that the first illustration in the work is the pretty child of Joshua Reynolds 'Age of Innocence' (below).

In fact, as will be seen, much of the *Encyclopædia*'s content is quite advanced. Several of the contributors – particularly those writing on scientific subjects – undoubtedly aimed at an older age-group (who might not have appreciated Mee's talk of Jack Frost and fairies).

THE AGE OF INNOCENCE

This famous picture was painted by Sir Joshua Reynolds about 150 years ago, and now hangs in the National Gallery in London. The children's faces at the bottom are from a famous sculpture of singers in the Cathedral at Florence.

However, Arthur Mee's enthusiasm is transparent. On a further page, he explains 'to all who love children all over the world' his purpose in producing the *Encyclopædia*. It is 'the first attempt that has ever been made to tell the whole sum of human knowledge so that a child may understand'.

In implied criticism of current methods, he declares that it does not seek

'to cram the mind of a child with things that children do not need to know... It conceives the bringing up of a child as the supreme task in which we can engage, but it has no sympathy with those who would set a child down at a desk almost before it can run... It has come to bring more joy to childhood, believing that true joy of life comes from sympathy and understanding.'

The *Encyclopædia*, he says, is based on

'the finest ideas of education that have ever been expressed in English, set forth in a book which Herbert Spencer gave to the world now nearly fifty years ago.'

(The reference is probably to Spencer's *Principles of Psychology*, 1855).

The *Encyclopædia* should be 'a gift to the nation; a thing of measureless value to parents and teachers; a treasure for children to which they may come whenever they will; and inspiration to childhood which will make these precious years a time of happy building-up'.

Mee's introduction also includes a colour picture (reproduced) entitled 'Your little friends in other lands'. Again, these are small children. We should note the order of precedence. The children in the front row of the procession are American, French, Italian, Spanish and Greek; other white races follow; then come Turks, Arabs, Egyptians, Indians, Chinese and Japanese; near the back are South Sea Islanders, Apache Indians; and finally Hottentots, Negroes and Pigmies. This is the first indication of the assumed superiority of the white races, which we shall find recurring throughout the *Encyclopædia*.

At the same time, the title 'little friends' announces another theme: that the other races, though inferior, deserve respect.

YOUR LITTLE FRIENDS IN OTHER LANDS

THE STORY OF COMMON THINGS

WE shall read in this part of the book the story of many interesting things we see and use every day. We shall learn of the wonderful way in which a cup of tea comes to our breakfast-table—all the way from India. We shall see how we get our letters—all the way across the sea. We shall learn how a newspaper is made, and how a book is printed; how the train carries us by land, and the ship by sea; how a balloon rides in the air; how a camera takes a picture; how the piano makes music for us; how we can talk to friends far away; and a thousand other strange things which are wonderful and yet true. The first story tells us how a lighthouse is built in the bed of the sea.

HOW A LIGHTHOUSE IS BUILT

By MANY WRITERS

ONE of the most wonderful things to think of is the way in which men have been able to make light when darkness creeps over the world. A great city lit up at night is a beautiful sight to look upon. Have you thought, when you have been in the dark, how difficult it must be for the sailor to find his way at sea when the moon is not shining and the stars have shut their eyes? We cannot put lamps everywhere in the sea as we do in the streets, yet there are dangerous rocks which would wreck a ship if the captain did not see them. On these rocks, then, and at dangerous parts of the sea coasts, men build lighthouses, with lanterns that throw a great light over the dark water, to help the sailor to find his way and keep his ship out of danger.

THE LONELY OLD MAN ON CAPE MATAPAN

One dark night, many years ago, a ship was sailing on the sea near the coast of Greece. It was so dark that the captain could not see how to guide the vessel, so he made up his mind to stay until morning brought the light to let him see where to steer.

Soon after he had stopped the vessel, someone cried out: "I see a light!" There, far away, was a tiny light, like a dim, distant star, twinkling in the blackness that hung over the sea.

"I know now where we are," said the captain. "We are near the big rocks of Cape Matapan. A kind old man lives there all by himself. When he hears the noise made by the engines of a ship, he knows that the ship is in danger of running on the rocks. So he lights his little lamp and waves it, just as he has done now, to show us where we are."

And now, having got to know where he was, the captain was able to start the ship again, and steer away safely.

There are many places where ships are in danger. There are hidden rocks; there are great cliffs where they may run ashore at night; there are great banks of sand just beneath the water where they may stick fast. The ships have to be guarded from these dangers. But we cannot have men running down to the water's edge with lamps wherever these dangers are. Instead of that, we build great lighthouses, whose light can be seen far over the sea.

BUILDING A HOUSE AMID THE ANGRY WAVES

These lighthouses are built in all sorts of places. Some are on the land; some are built out in the sea on rocks, over which the waves are often sweeping. Others are built on sand. These are hard to build, because, before the foundations can be laid, great piles of timber have to be driven down into the soft sand, so as to make a firm base for the lighthouse.

Men who build lighthouses are so brave and clever that if they could

1. FAMILIAR THINGS

This was not the first section to appear in each issue, but it makes sense to take it first since it gives us a good picture of the typical surroundings of a child growing up in the first decade of the nineteenth century.

These articles are ascribed to 'Many writers', which is unsurprising since they cover a very wide field. They differ from other sections in that there is relatively little text: usually, after a brief introduction, explanations are given in illustrations, each with a short explanatory caption. Usually these are extremely clear. Only a small sample of pictures can be reproduced here.

The objects described come in no particular order. They include items of food (bread, sugar, salt, fruit, etc.), clothing (cloth, fur, shoes…). In each case the article explains where the materials come from and how they are processed. In cases where the raw material is produced abroad, the pictures give children a good idea of the processes involved – cultivation of sugar-cane and of cotton, salt mines and so on.

Other household objects include clocks (illustration reproduced here), pens and pencils, cutlery, china, glass, sponges, bricks, pianos, bicycles, etc. Telegrams and wireless telegraphy were recent inventions that must have been causes of wonder to children at the time; some striking drawings are reproduced.

Pumps would have been a familiar object in houses dependent on a well: their operation is illustrated and explained. Moving further away from the home, we find gaslight, trains, lighthouses and lifeboats.

There are several pictures on the building of the Forth Bridge (completed in 1890). Three are reproduced here: they include a remarkable demonstration of the cantilever principle, and well as dramatic photos of a caisson being sunk in the Forth Estuary. Other pictures show the completed bridge.

Two pictures from the article on coal are reproduced. The first is one of a series showing miners at work deep in the pits; the second shows a well-dressed family sitting around a coal fire in a comfortable, spacious room; the contrast is striking.

The printing process is described and illustrated in some detail, using the production of the *Children's Encyclopædia* as an example: 'The beginning of this book' is reproduced here.

Another series of articles take us into the countryside, showing many different types of grass and trees. Here, lacking colour photography, all the pages including illustrations are printed in light green. Writing about trees, the author grows lyrical:

> 'In silence, in perfect stillness, the beautiful leaves of a tree drink from the
> air, and sweeten the twig, the branch, the great trunk, and the spreading

roots deep under the earth, with the invisible nourishment of the air. This
work is part of Nature's marvellous chemistry…' (p.3183)

In a further article on trees, the same writer (presumably) sees an opportunity
for patriotic inspiration in the oaks of which Nelson's fleet was built, describing
how at Trafalgar in 1805:

'Oaks of England bore him in their arms when in a divine moment of inspiration he made himself England, and spoke for England to his sailors.
Can we not hear the voice of English oaks in these words?' (p. 3440)

Certain other topics can hardly be regarded as 'familiar', but are also of much
interest. **A Little Talk on Sculpture** (pp. 4159–70) starts with ancient Egypt (the Sphinx
and the great statues near Thebes of Amenhotep III) and continues with Greece (the
Venus of Milo, the Laocoon, the Parthenon frieze). After the 'Dark Ages' comes the
Italian Renaissance with Pisano, Ghiberti, Donatello, Michael Angelo (*sic*). Then
sculpture became 'more tasteless, too ornate, and too extravagant'. The greatest of
modern sculptors is Rodin (the 'Citizens of Calais' is illustrated), though

'our younger sculptors in England are doing beautiful work… These men
are thinking more for themselves, and are copying old work less than
was formerly done.' (p. 4161)

A Little Talk about Pictures (pp. 4585–94) is a parallel brief survey of art
history, again with illustrations (black-and-white). It refers to Byzantine mosaics,
then jumps to thirteenth-century Italy with Cimabue and Giotto; then we find da
Vinci, Raphael, Michael Angelo (*sic*). Velasquez, Rubens, Van Dyck, Rembrandt are
discussed. Among English artists, there is mention of Hogarth, Sir Joshua Reynolds
('the greatest painter of children'), Constable (his painting of Salisbury cathedral is
illustrated); and finally Turner, 'who painted the sun and the skies, the sea and the
meadows, ships and harbours, and castles and rivers with astounding beauty and
poetic feeling'. One feels how much the author would have enjoyed colour
photography if it had been available. (There is more about painters under **GREAT
LIVES**.)

An article in the last volume deals with **Monuments** (pp. 5003–5). It begins with
Stonehenge, and Cleopatra's Needle in London. The author does not hesitate to
express his opinions: the Albert Memorial in Kensington Gardens is 'bad in every
way'; the Nelson Column is 'too high for the statue'. Going further afield, there are
illustrations of the Sphinx and the Great Pyramid; Roman triumphal arches –
'proportions extremely fine' – compared with the *Arc de Triomphe* in Paris – 'very bad
… top-heavy'.

Finally, an article in volume seven is devoted to **The Rule of the Road** (pp.
4299–4313). The opening sentence gives cause for thought: 'Since motor-cars
became common in this country, the number of accidents upon our roads has
increased terribly.' Firm instructions follow as to how children should behave
when walking on a footpath, crossing the road or riding a bicycle. These are
reinforced by illustrations, including one to cyclists on 'The right way to pass a
horse in a lane'. I am reproducing a page which particularly attracted me as a
child, because of the pictures of open-top tramcars: this page is much thumbed!

HOW THE WHEELS GO ROUND

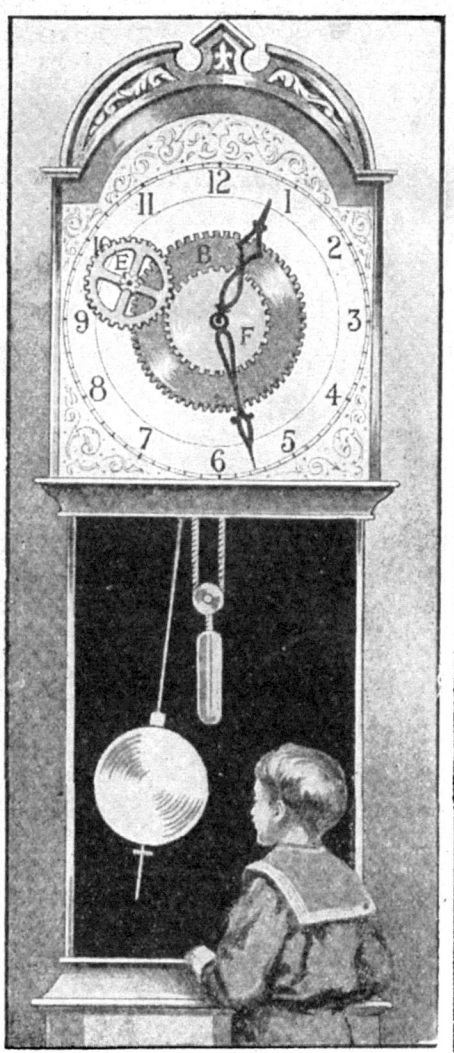

This picture of the inside of a clock shows us how the wheels go round. It is not the pendulum that makes the clock go; it is either a weight or a spring. In this grandfather's clock it is a weight. The weight is on a cord which passes round a broad wheel, called a barrel, marked A in the picture. The heavy weight pulls the cord downwards, and the cord, being wound round the barrel, pulls the barrel round. The edge of this barrel has teeth which work into the teeth of another wheel, marked B, so that both wheels go round. This second wheel causes the top wheel, marked C, to go round, and so all the wheels are set to work. But if that were all, the wheels would run round too quickly, and they must be made to run slowly and regularly. At the top is a curved piece of metal with a catch at each end; it is called the escapement, and is marked D. This swings to and fro, and every time it swings, it catches the top wheel and prevents it from going round more than one tooth.

This picture shows how the wheels make the hands go round. The three wheels shown in front of the clock, marked B, E, and F, are really behind the face. B, E, and F are necessary for the hands. Wheel F goes round once every hour, and as the minute hand is fixed to it, the wheel carries the minute hand round with it. Now wheel F touches wheel E with its edge, making it go round also. E is a double wheel, having near the centre a small wheel fixed to it with only six teeth; it is really on the other side of wheel E, but is shown in the picture in front for clearness. Each tooth in it fits into a tooth in wheel B, thus making that wheel go round. As wheel E goes round once in an hour, the six teeth in its centre carry round one-twelfth of wheel B, which has seventy-two teeth. The hour hand is fixed to wheel B, so while F is going once round, it makes wheel E drive B one-twelfth of its journey. Thus wheel F, with the minute hand, turns twelve times while wheel B, with the hour hand, turns once.

MESSAGES THAT FLY THROUGH SPACE

Here we see the latest invention in telegraphy—the wireless system. We tap a key and send a current of electricity along a wire. From the end of this wire the current springs into space and flashes across the sea.

If we want to send a wireless message from Ireland to Cape Breton, on the other side of the Atlantic Ocean, we tap our key, and the message flies through the air, covering the 2,000 miles journey in the sixtieth of a second.

THE END OF AN ELECTRIC JOURNEY

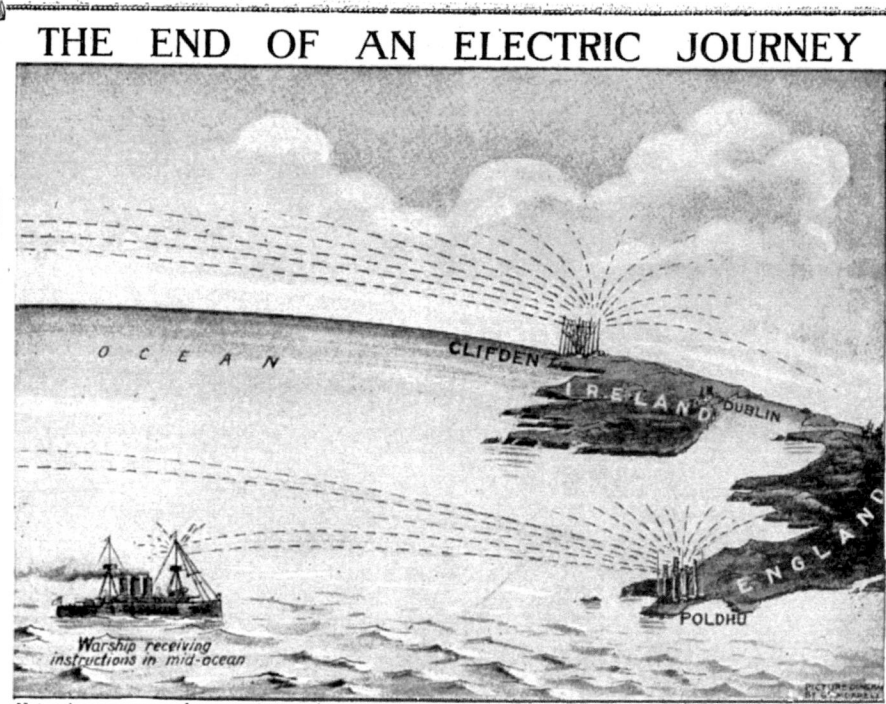

Not only can we send our messages from the Cape Breton station; we can receive messages as well. If we get news for somebody on the sea. we can receive it at Cape Breton and telegraph it out to the ship.

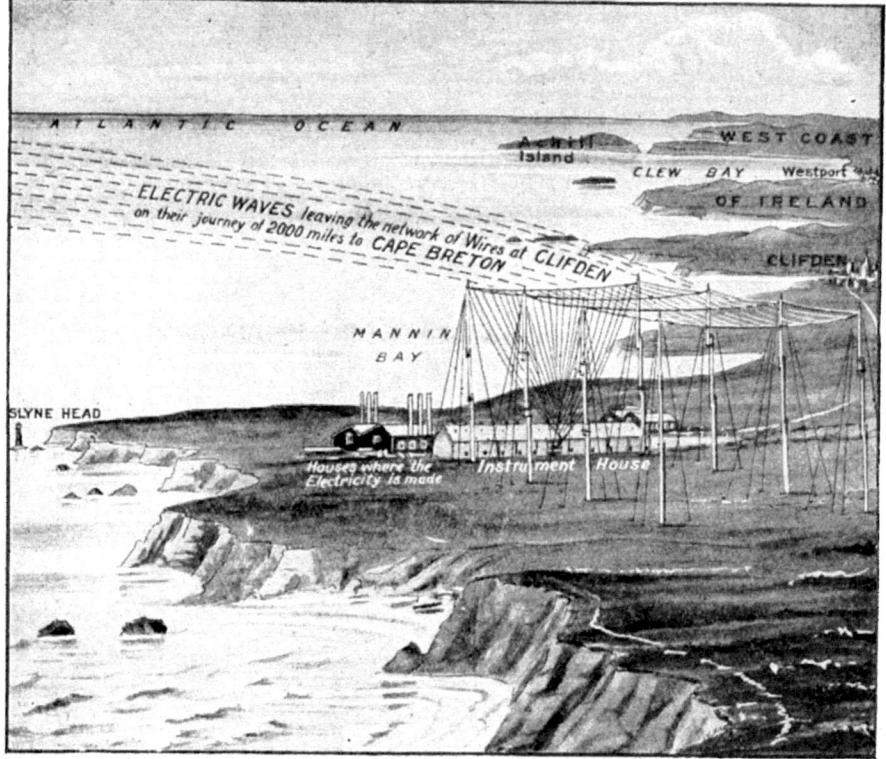

Of course, though we call it wireless telegraphy, we have wires at the receiving and despatching points. High posts are erected at the instrument houses to catch the waves as they fly to us from those who send the message.

3529

THE BEGINNING OF A GREAT BRIDGE

This shows us how the weight of a bridge is distributed; it illustrates what bridge-builders call the cantilever principle. These two men are sitting on chairs, each holding two sticks. The outside sticks are fastened to weights, and cannot move. The inner sticks are fixed to the chairs, and from their tops another stick is stretched, bearing a weight of 112 pounds. Yet the men feel no weight, and they represent two pairs of cantilevers.

This is a caisson, like a great hollow chamber, inside which men can work to set up the foundations of a bridge. The caisson is here floated into position for the building of the Forth Bridge. The huge steel tubes reach down to the bottom of the water, and men work inside them without danger, as if in a workshop.

This shows the caisson in position, sinking in the water. It is about 70 feet wide at the bottom. Though open at the top, it has water-tight floors inside, and at the bottom there is a chamber 70 feet wide and 7 feet high, lighted by electric lamps, in which the men, breathing air sent down in tubes, can work safely.

1827

WHAT IT IS LIKE DOWN A COAL-MINE

Down in the mine there are roads like this, along which trucks take the coal from where the men work to the foot of the shaft. Great timber props are placed in position to prevent the roof falling in.

And at last we sit round the fire enjoying the sunshine that was buried in the earth millions of years ago. Coal fires are so good that it seems strange to us that they should once have been forbidden.

THE BEGINNING OF THIS BOOK

When the writer has set down his thoughts on paper, and the editor has prepared it for the printers, it is then passed on to be set up in type. In the small picture on this page the master-printer is marking the copy for the boy to take to the man at the machine. This machine is the most wonderful thing in printing. It almost thinks. By pressing down keys as we do at a typewriter, or a piano, the man at this machine sets the words in metal lines. Almost as fast as a man can think, this machine puts his thoughts into solid metal. The machine is called a linotype, because it sets up lines of type. The pictures on the next two pages show us how it works.

THE NEED FOR CARE IN BUSY STREETS

Our public roads are becoming more and more crowded with fast-travelling vehicles, and this renders it necessary that all who use our highways should understand "the rule of the road," so as to save themselves from danger and avoid causing accidents to others. The general custom is for vehicles using the roads to keep to the left, and in crossing a road we must always be careful when passing behind a tramcar going in one direction to keep a sharp look-out, like the children in this picture, for a fast-travelling car coming the other way.

The custom is for fast traffic to keep to the middle of the road and slow traffic to be on the "near" side, which is the left, or footpath, side. If we are walking on the edge of the pavement, it is dangerous to step off and walk in the road, as, although we may look out for fast motors, we may lose sight of a slower cyclist riding near the kerb.

4303

I WONDER WHY

ALL our lives we are asking questions; all our lives we are saying to ourselves, "I wonder why." Why is it dark at night? Where do I go in my sleep? How do I remember? To all of us come such questions as these, and as long as we live, however wise we grow, such questions will come. The questions will never stop as long as the world lasts, because out of the answer to one question another question grows; and so, all through the world and down all the ages of time, children and grown-ups have been saying to themselves, "I wonder why." All through our book we shall find the answers to our questions, but in this part we shall find questions about many things which we particularly want to know. We learn, first of all, how men know things that happened long ago, and how they have gathered up all the knowledge that is in the world. Then we come to the questions asked by children, and any child who sends a question to the editor of this book may have it answered in this place.

HOW WE KNOW THESE THINGS

By THE WISE MAN

ONCE upon a time there was a Wise Man who declared that he could answer every question, and there came to the Wise Man a little child. The little child asked the Wise Man questions all day long, and the next day she brought with her another child. All day the Wise Man sat with the children in the woods, and the First Child, thinking to puzzle the Wise Man, asked him this question: How many boys and girls are there in all the world?

The Wise Man waved his wand and the children fell asleep. When they woke the woods were full of children. From one end of the wood to the other the children reached in a great and beautiful procession; for miles and miles, north and south and east and west, there was nothing to be seen but boys and girls, and every boy and girl was happy.

Then the Wise Man said to the First Child: "This is the number of all the boys and girls in the world." And the First Child said to them: "This is the Wise Man who will answer all the questions." Then over the faces of the children there came a great wonder, and every child in the world came to the Wise Man and asked him questions. And as the Wise Man answered them there came over the faces of the children a greater wonder still, for the answers were so wonderful that the children went on for ever asking questions, and the wonder of them never ended.

The Wise Man told the children the story of the world as it is told in this book. The story of the great earth-ball on which we live, how through all the ages of time boys and girls have come into the world, have grown up into men and women, and have built up great countries and made the earth yield up its fruits—all this, and all the story of things that happened before the boys and girls were born, the Wise Man told them. And none could guess how he became wise, though all the children wondered; and the Wise Man, seeing the wonder in their eyes, told the children how he knew these things.

Once upon a time, he said, there were not nearly so many people on the earth as there are to-day. We cannot tell exactly what happened then, because it is so very long ago; but we can make-believe that all the people lived in one small part of the world all by themselves. They were like a big family living together in the same house. By-and-by the family grew bigger; more boys and girls began to come, and at last the house became too small for them to live in. So some of them had to go out and find another home. They wandered up and down over the earth, and

2. WONDER

This section can be regarded as the core of the work. As already mentioned, Arthur Mee was prompted to launch the *Children's Encyclopædia* by questions put by his daughter: so this section consists entirely of questions and answers. The author is given as 'The Wise Man'. No doubt Mee himself wrote some of the answers, and probably supervised the others; those of a scientific nature may have been handled by Dr. Saleeby, who wrote the series on **EARTH** and **LIFE**, and the two authors of **NATURE** may also have been involved. Possibly other contributors, not mentioned among the writers of the *Encyclopædia*, were called in too.

In many cases under **WONDER**, we find brief answers on matters which are dealt with more thoroughly in those other series; perhaps to some extent they influenced the treatment there.

That this question-and-answer process was dear to Arthur Mee's heart is evident from the introduction to some of the instalments in which he refers to himself as 'The Editor', inviting children to send in questions and thanking them for doing so. Some of the topics in the first volume are rather abstract, sounding as if they had been planted by the authors, but by page 477 the Editor is writing that 'The questions grow more puzzling than ever as the children find the Wise Man able to answer them'; and on page 505 instructions are given (apparently because parents or other adults had been putting in questions, and that was not the idea):

> 'From now on we are to have real questions from real boys and girls who read this book. They should be sent on postcards to the editor of the *Children's Encyclopædia*, who will give the best of them to the Wise Man to answer.'

By volume 5 we start getting photographs of 'boys and girls who received the highest awards for their questions'. Looking at these pictures – one is reproduced here – they seem to be aged between about ten and fifteen. Many questions are quite advanced and lead to correspondingly sophisticated answers, though the presentation always remains clear and precise. Other questions are delightfully naïve and could only have come from quite small children.

Any parent knows how difficult children's questions can be – even simple ones which nevertheless defy adult logic, and especially if they come when one is busy with some other task. One can imagine in such cases the busy parent saying to the child: 'Why don't you send it to the *Children's Encyclopædia*?' The eight volumes contain over a thousand questions with answers; they are listed in a special index which covers six pages of tiny print. The number of questions received was certainly much greater: already by Volume 5 the figure of 40,000 is mentioned.

VIDA ANDERSON   DOUGLAS SHAW   ENA RUSSELL

VIOLET EDWARDES   HENRY NANCARROW   GERTRUDE JAMES

These are the six boys and girls who received the highest awards for asking questions in the Wonder Book. The number asked was from 30,000 to 40,000, and a full list of those answered appears in the index.

The questions come in no particular order, presumably as they were received: so in any one issue there is a miscellany of topics. Here is an example, taken at random, of the items in just one of the fortnightly issues (pp. 1985–93):

'Why do we count in tens – Why are all our fingers not the same length? – Why have we finger-nails and toe-nails? – Why does a moth fly round and round a candle? – Why are some people dark and some people fair? – Why is the sky dull when a storm is coming on? Where does the spring-water come from? – Where do plants get their salts from? – Why does wood rot away? – If we throw up a ball and go forward why does the ball fall at our feet? – Why do onions make our eyes water? – How does the milk get into cocoa-nuts (sic)? – Why are we taught at school to use our right hand and not our left? – Why does a river curve and twist instead of running straight? – Why do the beds of rivers change? – Why cannot we make a real vacuum? – Why is it easier to swim in salt water than in fresh? – Why have we to develop photographs in a red light? – When water goes bad, why do colours come over its surface? – What is beauty?'

Clearly it is impossible in this review to do justice to such extensive coverage. I shall cite samples of questions throughout the work, following a rough classification, moving from the naïve through the practical and scientific to some which raise moral and abstract issues. So, starting with the naïve, we have for example:

'Why is Granny's hair grey? – Why do we have two eyes? – Why does the fire go out? – Can the flowers see? – Is there a man in the moon? – Who lighted the volcanoes? – Why is medicine nasty? – Could the sky fall down? – Why does sea-water not make fishes thirsty? – Why do we not laugh when we tickle ourselves? – Are there such things as ghosts?'

In such questions we can hear quite small children wondering about things they see and feel around them. This is not to say that adults would find the answers easy, but in the *Encyclopædia*, every question is treated respectfully and gets a thoughtful answer.

Many such answers deserve attention, as the writer takes the opportunity to make a substantial point. A few examples follow (the first demonstrates that humour is not excluded).

'Why does a cat always fall on its feet?'

'One answer to this question is that its feet are the best part of it to fall on, but the real puzzle for us is how does the cat manage to get its feet lowermost... It has been argued that the cat manages to turn itself by the use of its tail. If that be so, of course, Manx cats, which have no tail, ought not to be able to fall on their feet, but they are able... All we can say is that somehow, by moving one part of its body or another, the cat controls its fall in order to fall most safely. It is so clever of the cat that we are not yet clever enough to find out how it does it.' (p. 1573)

'Can we fall off the earth?'

'We cannot fall off the earth because the earth holds us to itself by means of its attraction. The earth is so big that its power of attraction is great, and if we wished to escape it altogether we should have to use some other power sufficiently great to succeed in opposing the pull of the earth.' (p. 1062)

'Why cannot we feel the earth going round?'

'We are going round with the earth, and, as we are moved around with it at exactly the same rate and in exactly the same direction, we notice nothing... The real lesson we can learn from this question is that the only kind of movement which we can feel is relative movement – that is to say, movement of one thing as compared with another.' (p. 1578)

'Why can't we see in the dark?'

'Seeing and hearing depend, first of all, on there being something there outside of us – a particular kind of wave – and secondly, on our being able to feel that something... That is why we cannot see in the dark, because there is no light, and it is only light that we see... When we do 'see the table', we really see the light coming from it.' (p. 1433)

'Is it bad to sleep with the moon shining on us?'

'It is not bad to sleep with the moon shining on us, but it is bad to believe nonsense. ... All notions of this kind are really remnants of the old astrology, which ascribed all sort of influences to the heavenly bodies, and thought that lunacy – the word from the Latin *luna*, meaning the moon – was caused by the moon. Moonlight is only reflected sunlight, and, though it is very feeble in proportion to its brilliances, it is valuable, just as sunlight is.' (p. 3380)

Most questions are quite practical, and get precise answers. Sometimes there is an illustration to help, though this series contains relatively few pictures. One illustration reproduced here shows, with explanation, why wood floats though iron sinks; and how nevertheless an iron ship can float because of the air it contains.

A full-page set of illustrations shows how a camera (a cumbersome piece of equipment at the time) takes a picture, and how this corresponds to the functioning of the human eye. There are several drawings showing the main working pieces of a motor-car – the great novelty of the Edwardian period; the first of these is reproduced here.

In these very early days of air travel, gas-filled balloons were carrying passengers: a Zeppelin which could carry twelve people is photographed flying over Zurich. But the commentary to another picture reproduced here points out how big and cumbersome balloons have to be, and suggests that 'the successful machine will be more like a bird.'

Heavier-than-air craft were in their infancy. There are photographs of several early machines, including the one made by the Wright brothers. Accompanying text explains how the wings are made to catch the wind, thus enabling the aeroplane to fly like a kite.

WHY WOOD FLOATS AND WHY IRON SINKS

Wood floats because it is full of tiny quantities of air, and so is lighter, or less dense, than the water. A stone, or a lump of iron, has no air in it; it is denser than the water, and therefore it sinks. An iron ship floats because it is hollow and full of air, so that *as a whole* it is lighter than the water. If we filled it up solid with iron or stone, or if it cracked and so let the air escape from it and the water come in, it would sink, as shown in the second of these pictures

WHY AN IRON SHIP FLOATS

Such pictures bring home to us the tremendous changes that have occurred during the twentieth century. In particular, the *Encyclopædia*'s vision of future air travel looks utopian: it is more like a ship, with passengers standing on an open deck looking down on small landing platforms. (The author has not realised that to carry so many people, a plane would have to fly much faster to get the necessary lift, and would certainly need much more powerful propulsion than that shown.)

Likewise the prediction of a 'gyrorail' as the 'railway of the future', though not an unreasonable idea, has not been fulfilled. On the other hand, a bicycle (not reproduced here) looks very little different from those of today.

HOW THE CAMERA TAKES YOUR PHOTOGRAPH

These pictures show us how a camera takes a picture, why it takes the picture upside down, and also how the eye is like a camera in this way. The boat in this picture gives off rays of light, which strike in all directions. Some of these rays go out towards the camera, and, as light always travels in straight lines, never crooked ones, all the rays that can be seen from the lens of the camera travel straight up or down towards the lens. Inside the lens they continue travelling in the same direction, and at last they meet and cross, so that the lines of light given off by the top of the boat strike the bottom of the photographic plate, and the lines given off by the bottom of the boat strike the top of the plate. The small picture on this page shows a way in which any boy or girl can find out how the lines of light cross so as to make an image upside down. Take a white cardboard box without the lid, and prick in one side a small hole with a pin. Hold the box, say, under a gas-jet, so that the gas will reflect through the hole. The hole will then act as a focus of the rays, which will enter the box through the hole and cross, so that the inside of the box, where they fall, will reflect the gas-jet, which will be upside down. The bottom picture shows us that the eye acts in the same way as the camera, but a very wonderful thing happens in the eye that no man quite understands. When the photographer finds that his picture is upside down, he turns the plate the other way and everything is right. But what wonderful thing is it that turns the picture printed inside the eye the right way up? The rays of light stamp themselves upon the retina of the eye as seen in this picture, and the nerve of the eye carries them to the brain. What happens there nobody knows, but

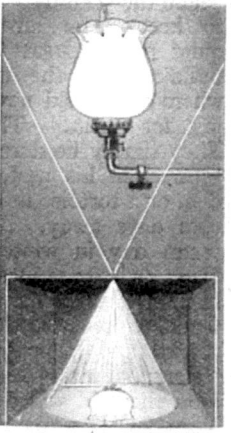

when the brain brings together these rays of light so as to make a clear picture, the picture is the right way up. The picture is printed on the retina of the eye upside down, but our brain puts it right in the millionth part of the twinkling of an eye, and this is, perhaps, as great a miracle as anything that ever happened.

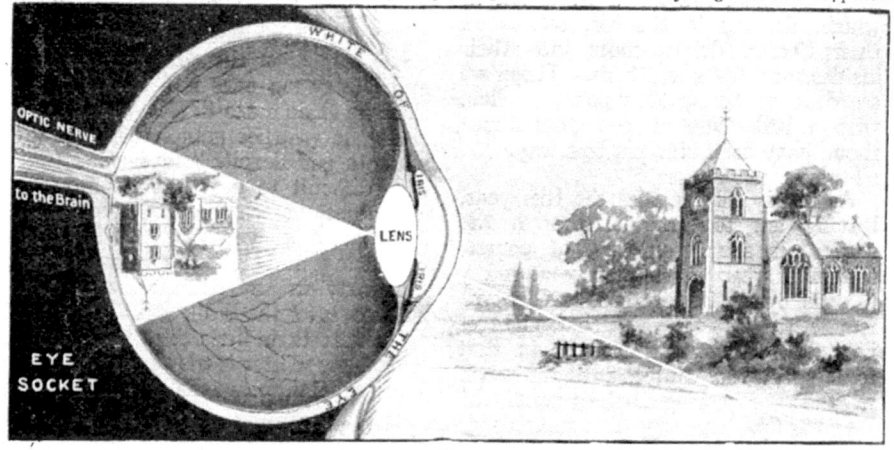

WHAT MAKES THE MOTOR-CAR GO

When we look inside a motor-car the works seem hopelessly puzzling, but, wonderful as they are, they do quite a simple thing. Let us here suppose that we have cut our car right in half, from end to end, so that we may see inside. The fly-wheel is shown facing us for the sake of plainness; it is really fixed the other way—the opposite way to the ordinary wheels. Now let us look at the letters. A is the inlet valve, open ready for the gas to rush in. B is the exhaust valve, through which the used-up gas rushes out; it is shut here. C is the sparking plug and its electric wires, which fire the petrol gas. D is the current of air and petrol gas going up to the inlet valve. E is the piston, which has to be forced up and down in the cylinder. The arrow on the piston shows the way the piston goes.

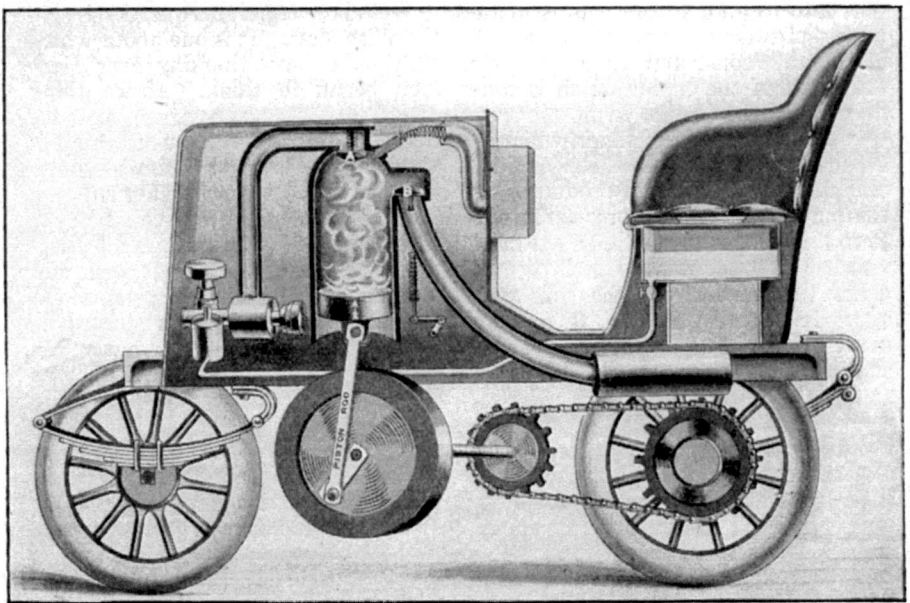

Petrol oil is forced from the tank under the seat into what is called the carburettur, marked in the first picture. There it is acted upon by a spray, which breaks up a drop of petrol into atoms and makes it into gas. This gas is mixed with air. The fly-wheel is set going by turning a handle in front of the car, and as it goes it works the piston, pulling it to the bottom of the cylinder. As the piston goes down, the gas causes the inlet valve to open, as in the top picture, and gas and air rush in. The piston, worked by the force of the fly-wheel, rushes back, and as it goes up it compresses the gas into the smallest possible space, closing the inlet valve so that the gas cannot escape.

HOW MEN ARE LEARNING TO FLY

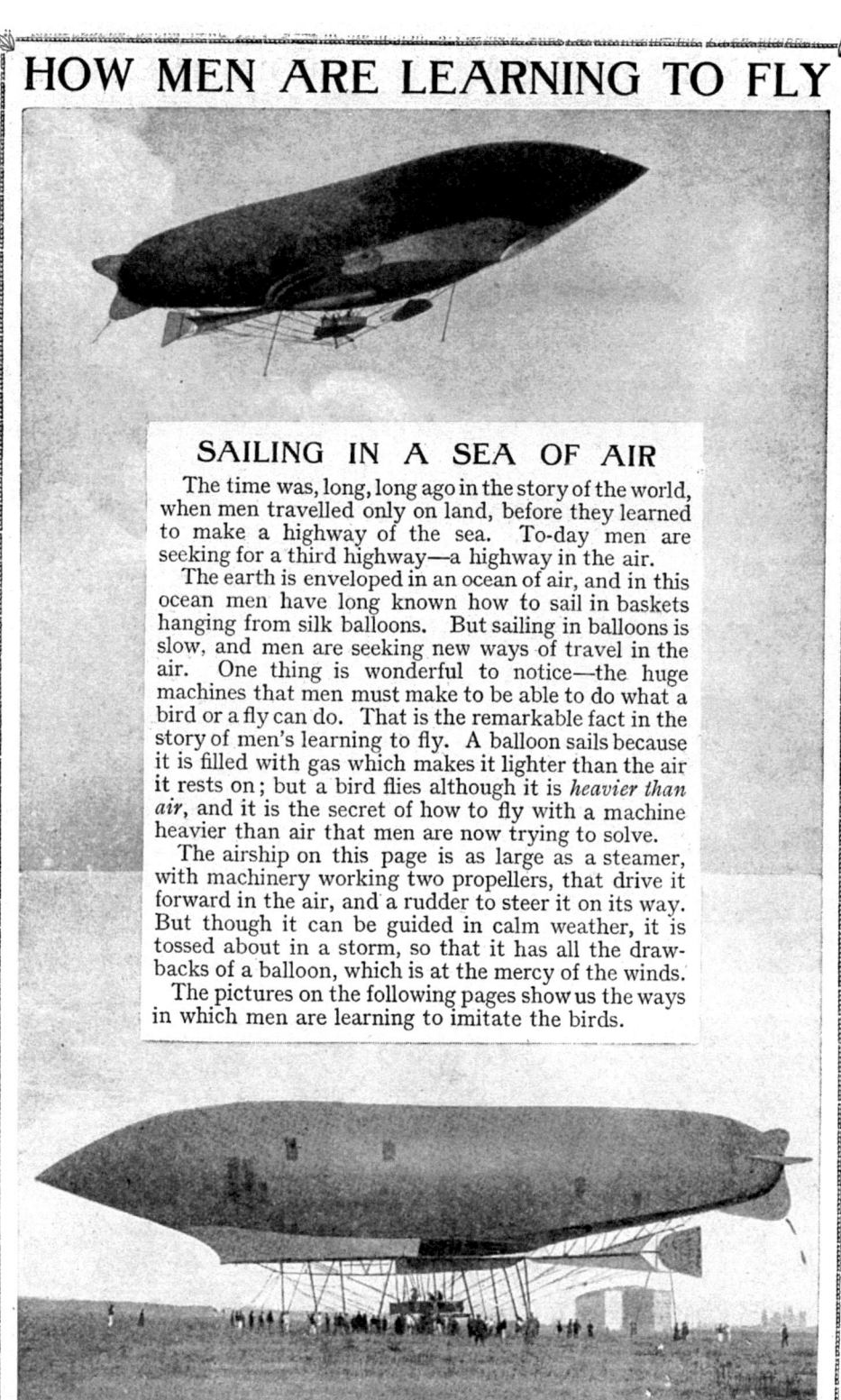

SAILING IN A SEA OF AIR

The time was, long, long ago in the story of the world, when men travelled only on land, before they learned to make a highway of the sea. To-day men are seeking for a third highway—a highway in the air.

The earth is enveloped in an ocean of air, and in this ocean men have long known how to sail in baskets hanging from silk balloons. But sailing in balloons is slow, and men are seeking new ways of travel in the air. One thing is wonderful to notice—the huge machines that men must make to be able to do what a bird or a fly can do. That is the remarkable fact in the story of men's learning to fly. A balloon sails because it is filled with gas which makes it lighter than the air it rests on; but a bird flies although it is *heavier than air*, and it is the secret of how to fly with a machine heavier than air that men are now trying to solve.

The airship on this page is as large as a steamer, with machinery working two propellers, that drive it forward in the air, and a rudder to steer it on its way. But though it can be guided in calm weather, it is tossed about in a storm, so that it has all the drawbacks of a balloon, which is at the mercy of the winds.

The pictures on the following pages show us the ways in which men are learning to imitate the birds.

THE BEST AIRSHIP EVER MADE BY MAN

From the simple machine shown on the opposite page, the Wright brothers have developed this marvellous aeroplane, here seen sailing splendidly high above the trees. While it has been improved in some respects, the main idea is still the same. Instead of one aeroplane in front there are two, and the rudder is also double, while in the centre of the lower of the two great wings is a powerful little motor to force the machine forward. To go long journeys in an airship like this the rider need only clear the tops of tall trees or houses. This gives it a great advantage over a balloon, which must soar far higher, as it is difficult to keep a balloon at exactly the same height, even a slight change in the atmosphere from hot to cold immediately altering the level of the balloon.

2693

WHEN MAN HAS CONQUERED THE AIR

There will, no doubt, be many improvements in flying machines once men have agreed that the aeroplanes are the best means of sailing in the air. The machines will, no doubt, be made smaller than at present, and all sorts of things will be done to enable them to carry as many passengers as possible, and to come easily to rest at stations. Large platforms will probably be erected as we see on the left of this picture, and beneath the airship long springs may be placed like those used on sledges, so that the great machines may fly up to their stations and drop slowly down on to the platform, where passengers will get out and descend to the ground by elevators.

2694

THE WONDERFUL TRAIN THAT IS COMING

In this picture we have a vivid and realistic picture of what the railway of the future will be like. Remarkable results must follow the invention of the "gyroscope" train, which is the application to the railway of that interesting toy, the gyroscope, which all boys know is the most wonderful of tops. Exhaustive experiments have already been made with a large car, and the "gyro-car," that runs on a single rail, has fulfilled all that its inventor expected of it and claimed for it. Not only will enormous speeds be reached by trains of this kind, but the gyroscopes will keep the train so steady that we shall be able to write while travelling, or even to play billiards.

Many questions deal with aspects of astronomy, reflecting the wonder felt by any child looking at the sky at night, and perhaps recent and ongoing discoveries. Here is a sample from various issues of the *Encyclopædia*:

'What keeps the stars in their place? – Will the sun ever cool down like the earth? – What was there in place of the earth before the earth was formed? – What makes an eclipse of the sun? – Do people at the poles spin round like a top? – Is the earth spinning more slowly? – What is the sun made of? – Does the earth look like a star to other planets? – What keeps the stars in their place? – Do all things move in space? – How many worlds are there?'

The answers are generally clear and precise, and for the most part could hardly be improved upon today. Here are a couple of examples:

'Why is it warm in summer, cold in winter?'

'We might think at first that perhaps the earth is nearer the sun in summer than in winter… We know that the earth does not move in a circle round the sun, but in a sort of oval path called an ellipse. But the fact is that … it is nearest the sun in winter and farthest in summer, in the Northern Hemisphere… That our distance from the sun does not make the seasons is plain when we remember that in our winter it is summer in Australia. It is warm in summer because then the sun's rays strike the earth more directly; the sun rises higher in the sky, as we say, and that means the same thing… In winter the sun's rays have to pass very slantwise through the air, and so lose a great deal of their power. The reason for the difference between summer and winter … is that the earth is tilted on its axis, the line running from the North Pole to the South Pole.' (p. 3032)

'How does the moon cause the tides?'

'The moon is made of matter, and so is the water of the sea. All matter everywhere pulls, and is pulled towards, all other matter everywhere. We call this gravitation. So far as the whole earth is solid, the whole earth, and the whole moon, are affected by this pull; but as part of the earth is ocean, and as water is not rigid, it can be, and is, specially affected by gravitation. The water opposite the moon at any time is pulled up towards the moon; and as the earth is turning all the time, this really means that a mighty heaped wave of water travels over all the oceans, day and night, in response to the pull of the moon…

'The sun also makes tides on the earth; but the power of gravitation lessens very quickly as the distance through which it acts increases. Thus, though the sun is vastly bigger than the moon, it is so far away compared to the moon that its influence on the ocean is comparatively small… When the sun and moon are pulling on the same side of the earth, they help each other; and the tides during a few days will be very high and very low as the water flows and ebbs.' (p. 1675)

This explanation was not quite complete, and prompted a further question from some astute young reader:

'Why are there two tides a day?'

'This is a very puzzling question, to which very few people know the answer. The earth only spins round once in a day, and the moon pulls the water up towards itself on the side of the earth next the moon, making what we call high tide. Anyone would think, then, that there must be only one high tide a day. But the moon not only pulls up and heaps up towards itself the water on the side of the earth that is next it at any given moment; it also pulls the earth towards itself away from the water on the other side of the earth, the side farthest from the moon... So when it is high tide anywhere, it is also high tide on the other side of the earth. This must mean that we get two high tides in twenty-four hours...' (p. 3978) [1]

Inevitably, later in the series, someone asked:

'Shall we ever be able to get to another planet?'

The 'Wise Man' (p. 4119) was not hopeful. It would never be possible to fire an object like a cannon-ball (as Jules Verne envisaged) fast enough to go so far; a flying-machine could not work because there would not be enough air for the machine to work against; and passengers, even if they could take enough air with them, would have to travel millions of miles through the coldness of space. The ability of rockets to operate in space had not been foreseen.

In contrast to the usual scientific precision, the following question has the author at a loss:

'What set the sun on fire?'

'The sun is not "on fire" in the same way that an ordinary fire is. We are certain of this for two reasons; first, because of the high temperature of the sun, burning, or combustion, could not occur... and second, because it has been proved that the sun must long ago have burnt itself out if its heat and light were obtained from burning.... We are bound to look to something other than burning to account for it all. The question where the sun gets its power from is most important. Heat must be produced by the atoms striking one another as the sun shrinks under the action of its own gravitation... it is now thought that probably most of the sun's power is got from inside its own atoms. And they received their power, first of all, from the Author of all the power in the universe.' (p. 4437)

---

[1] It is indeed surprising that this question is rarely asked – despite the visible evidence – and even more rarely answered correctly: this is still the case even with most Internet sources! The *Encyclopædia*'s explanation is in fact broadly correct.

Not infrequently, such theological explanations appear, apparently as a last resort where science provides no adequate answer to a difficult question. Here is another case in point:

> **'What is the ether?'**
>
> 'If we understood the ether, we should have they key to almost every puzzle we find in Nature. At present we know very little about it, but we are sure of certain facts. The ether is everywhere... It cannot be seen... it has no weight, yet it is the cause of weight, in a sense, for weight is due to gravitation, and it is through the ether that gravitation acts. And we believe that matter is really made of the ether – that the electrons of which the atoms of matter are composed themselves consist of things in the ether which we can only dimly picture to ourselves as knots or lumps of ether. Yet, though we do not know how, there is now really no doubt that the ether is the universal mother of all matter, and of all material things; it is the element of elements, and we cannot pierce behind it to anything, but to the Author of all that is.' (p. 2798)

One can sympathise with the writer, for this is a dilemma that has occupied the greatest scientific minds since Newton: how can waves of heat and light and the force of gravitation travel through apparently empty space? The concept of the ether had emerged in consequence, but since no-one could identify or define it, it remained an unsatisfactory solution. The topic recurs frequently in the section of the *Encyclopædia* on **THE EARTH** – see later chapter.

There are very few cases where the answers provided in the *Encyclopædia* appear incomplete or wrong in the light of subsequent scientific investigation. One instance, however, is a recurring preoccupation with the 'shrinking' of the earth. The following is just one example:

> **'Is the earth getting smaller?'**
>
> 'We are certain that the earth is shrinking smaller, because we know that it is slowly losing heat and getting colder, and if it does this it is bound to shrink. We suppose that the great cause of earthquakes is the shrinking of the inside of the earth as it cools, so that the crust on which we live is left not sufficiently supported.' (p. 4548)

In fact, shrinking of the earth, if it is still occurring, is a negligible factor (some very recent observations from satellites have indicated that the Earth's circumference has shrunk by about half a centimetre in a year). Later discoveries relating to 'continental drift', with the consequent pressures where underground land masses collide, provide a much better explanation for earthquakes.

Perhaps because items in the *Encyclopædia* had set its readers thinking, some abstruse questions start to appear, in particular the following, where the writer seems to abandon any attempt at a scientific answer (but who could do better?):

> **'What is at the end of space?'**
>
> 'This is a question which we can answer out of our heads. We find, directly we begin to think of the end of space, that there must be more

space beyond it. It is impossible for our minds to think of the end of space. In the same way, we cannot think of the beginning nor yet of the end of time… We are bound, by the very nature of our minds, to think of space as infinite, and of time as infinite too. *Finis* is Latin for end, and infinite literally means unending.' (p. 4114)

On the other hand, the writer deals very adequately with the following tricky question:

'What happens to the light when it goes out?'

'We have to think of light as a kind of energy, a kind of disturbance full of power that is made in the ether. It is a thing that travels at a tremendous speed, and it is not capable of being still… If there is to be steady light in any place, there must be a steady source of light to produce it. When we darken a room we cut off the source of light.

'But this question is a most important one, and people often forget to ask it. Nothing is lost, and the energy or power that made the light is not lost, even though the room is quite dark. If we could trace it, we should find that it had been transformed into other things; it is transformed into heat, which we find in all the matter which it strikes; … it is also changed into the power which starts chemical changes, as, for instance, when carpets and curtains gradually fade under its influence.' (p. 3432)

Turning to other fields, the question **'Why do we dream?'** gets a reasonable answer:

'The brain has many parts, and some part of it may be asleep, while another part is awake and active… Most of the brain, especially the highest part of it, is asleep in a dream, but parts of it are awake, and these, unguided by the highest powers of the mind, work on the materials of past experience, especially recent happenings… No dream has any meaning about the future.' (p. 2685)

There is no mention of the 'sub-conscious': the concept had only recently been advanced, and Freud's early work would have been little known in Britain. [2]

The question: **'What is pain?'** (p. 3092) gets a rational answer in terms of nerve-cells; however, it steers clear of the deeper issue: '*Why* is there pain?' That no doubt would have led into dangerous theological territory: how is pain to be reconciled with a benevolent God?

On the other hand, a question about **alcohol** gives the author(s) an opportunity to emphasise a favourite topic:

'It is now clearly proved … that alcohol stops the action of the nerve-cells which it affects; and the constant rule about its action is that it always first affects the highest nerve-cells, those which are newest in the history of the race; and after them it affects lower types of cells in

---

[2] The concept was first advanced in France by Pierre Janet in 1889. Freud's *Interpretation of Dreams* appeared (in German) in 1900 and his *Essays on Sexuality* (likewise) in 1905.

their order… When too much of it is taken, [alcohol] destroys the nerve-cells and causes the overgrowth of the substance that lies between them. This means the eventual destruction of the mind.' (p. 4343)

The mention here of cells that are 'newest in the history of the race' is no doubt a reference to the theory of evolution. Darwin and his *Origin of Species* are discussed in the section of the *Encyclopædia* entitled **MEN AND WOMEN**, and the series on **LIFE** and on **NATURE** trace the evolutionary process as far as the apes. Here we have an implicit recognition that humans have evolved too. But it is nowhere suggested that humans may descend from a type of ape. Probably the authors felt that this was too controversial, with uncomfortable implications for Christian doctrine, and best not mentioned to children.

A question on **'materialism'** first gets an obvious definition: 'The belief that matter is the all-important thing, and that mind is of less or no importance.' But the author takes his point further:

'It is materialism to worship supposed pieces of the true Cross, or to care very much where Jesus Christ was born, and to forget His words when He said: "For what shall it profit a man, if he shall gain the whole world, and lose his own soul?" ' (p. 4439)

The author points out other errors arising from a materialistic outlook, and ends, curiously, by attacking the notion that 'the question of national exports has only to do with cotton and coal, and not with the sending of our best youth of both sexes to the colonies or America or abroad, and leaving the poorer specimens to the heart of the empire'. This seems to contradict statements elsewhere in the *Encyclopædia* about the white man's duty. It also reflects current concern about physical and moral degradation among the urban working classes. This preoccupation had largely motivated the 'eugenics' movement, which was active at the time of the *Encyclopædia*. [3]

An unexpected question, showing that the readership certainly included some mature youngsters, is the following:

'What is Positivism?'

'Positivism is the name of a kind of new religion invented by a remarkable Frenchman called Auguste Comte… Comte believed that the only kind of real knowledge we have is simply our knowledge of

---

[3] Cunningham, in *The Invention of Childhood*, p.179, observes that such deficiencies caused concern that Britain might become uncompetitive in a world where Darwin had shown that only the fittest could survive. Darwinian evolutionary theory provided an apparent justification for the conquest by white men of other races; in fact, in *The Descent of Man*, Darwin himself had written that 'the civilised races of man will almost certainly exterminate and replace the savage races throughout the world'. To some, this even suggested the possibility of scientific breeding of humans. This was a live issue in Britain and America around the time of the *Encyclopædia* (cf. Hobsbawm, also J. Kevles, *In the Name of Eugenics* (1995). Dr. Saleeby, author of the articles on **EARTH** and **LIFE**, was known as a prominent advocate of eugenics at the time of the *Encyclopædia* – see comments in those chapters.

things around us… His religion included a great deal of regulation of human society, and very careful education of the young. It is often called "the religion of humanity"… Positivism contains many beautiful and noble elements, but not in one case out of millions does it satisfy human nature.' (p. 5249)

We know (cf. Maisie Robson's biography, *op. cit.*) that Arthur Mee was no royalist. The following question gets a firm response:

'Why were kings in the old days cruel?'

'Now kings know that their only "divine right" is to be kingly men…'
(p. 5022)

To complete this survey, here are a number of questions which raise moral and philosophical issues. Again, the 'children' who put them must have been well into their 'teens.

'What is beauty?'

'We call anything beautiful which gives us pleasure, and that depends as much upon ourselves as upon what is outside us… Nothing is beautiful or ugly in itself, but "thinking makes it so".' (p. 1993)

'Where do thoughts come from?'

'We know certainly that the thoughts depend on the brain… but it is not thought itself… There is a something which thinks, a something which knows. We cannot feel it, or see it, or cut it up… I can only reply that thoughts come from the thinking substance – the Something that thinks.' (p. 1365)

'Will the children rule the world?'

'It is really true that the children of today will rule the world tomorrow… All individuals are mortal, and the destiny of the world, the ruling and the being ruled, is all in the hand of the children… That means that "a mother is the holiest thing alive", that history is made in the nursery, that the bringing up of children is the noblest, the purest, and the most necessary work in the world. And it is the most difficult, just because the human being is so wonderful and complicated in the nature of his mind and his body…

'The writer has two little daughters. He knows that the highest thing a woman can be is a mother, a maker of the life of mankind. He hopes that they one day will have children; and he lives and works to teach all who will listen, so that the children of to-day, and their children, may live in a better world, where no child starves, or cries, or works, or dies, or is afraid, or cold, or lonely.' (p. 2879)

Here the writer – it cannot be Arthur Mee, who had just one daughter[4] – gives an interesting answer, but also reveals his thoughts about the role of women.

---

[4] In fact, it sounds like Dr. Saleeby, who had strong views on the domestic role of women, though he did favour education for girls.

A thoughtful question gets a thoughtful answer:

'Why do we not get all we want?'

'Some people do get all they want, at least for most of their lives, though the time comes for almost everybody when he wants to get well, and cannot. Now, if we study what happens to these people who get everything they want, even without having to work for it, we find that it is very bad for them. It is quite certain that we, and every part of our bodies, and every power we have, are naturally meant to work, to fight against difficulties; and it is better to fight, even if we do not conquer, than it is not to fight at all.

'One of the reasons why history records so many wicked and degraded kings is, that these were people who, all their lives, got everything they wanted. Every living creature that gets everything it wants given to it without striving is apt to become weak and degraded.

'Many sensible grown-up people who have lived careful lives, and have had a fair chance in the world, know that they get all they really want. No doubt they would like to have more money than they have, or, if they are a higher kind of people, more wisdom that they have, yet they know that if they work they will get enough for their happiness, and if wise people have that, they do not worry themselves by wishing for more.

'Children do not know what they can get, and what they cannot get. So all children, more or less, cry for the moon, as we say, not knowing how far away the moon is. As they grow up, they learn that it is not worth while to worry about things they cannot have, but that it is much better to work hard for the things they can have.' (p. 3433)

A similar question later on gets a somewhat different response:

'Why are we never satisfied?'

'There are a certain number of people in the world who are satisfied. They are to be found more especially in the East; but among the more active races of mankind it is scarcely possible to meet any one who is satisfied… But it is one of the highest marks of human nature at its best that it always goes on, and that, whatever it attains, it always sees that there is something better beyond…

'We often speak of the Founder of Christianity as "gentle Jesus", but no one since the world began was ever more fiercely dissatisfied with evils and shams than He was, and his followers should be like Him in this respect.' (p. 5170)

Here, the reference to people in 'the East' who are satisfied is interesting, suggesting an awareness of other traditions (Buddhism?) that is not often found in the *Encyclopædia* (see however the article on Buddha under **GREAT LIVES**). But the qualification is quickly made: these are not the 'more active races'…

The following response sounds more complimentary about Asia, and contains some profound thoughts:

'Ought we to be afraid to die?'

'No animal is afraid to die, but that is because it does not think of the future, and cannot know what death is. A child does not naturally fear to die, though we can easily teach it to be afraid. For ages past many men have made it their business, for one reason or another, to teach people to be afraid to die. This applies only to our part of the world. In mighty Asia, where the greater number of all mankind is still to be found, men are not afraid of death. But in our part of the world they are, and for two reasons.

'The first is that we are usually taught that death is very painful. This is false. As a rule, the only painless part of a painful illness is the death that ends it. Dying is no more painful than going to sleep... Then men fear to die because of "the dread of something after death". Only the wisest of us, those who believe in their hearts what they profess to believe with their lips, know that "To the good man no evil thing can happen", as Socrates said before they poisoned him. Another great and good man, Spinoza... said many words of eternal wisdom and truth: "The free man thinks of nothing so little as death, and his wisdom is a meditation not of death, but of life".' (p. 4745)

The following two questions (from the last volume) provide a fitting conclusion to this chapter:

'Is there a reason for everything?'

'It is indeed the first of facts that there is a reason for everything... We are apt to be foolish in these matters, for we admit the cause of a thing when we see it; but when we do not see it we are apt to deny that a cause was there at all... The first and greatest belief of science is that causation is universal... Every effect is the cause of further effects... And so, if we think, we shall soon see that we must go back to the First Cause and All-Reason, the Cause of causes, whom men have come to call God.' (p. 5248)

The last sentence can be read in several ways. Is this once again the device of a *deus ex machina* to resolve a dilemma which defies rational explanation? or another example of the tendency to promote Christian faith among young minds? or perhaps, in the cautious form of expression, an attempt to express the mystery of existence in a more universally acceptable form?

In his answer to the last question which we shall quote, the 'Wise Man' takes the opportunity to make some points which do not seem immediately relevant (the cruelty of bull-fighting in Spain...) but also expresses his deepest convictions.

'Must all things end?'

'We can think of a hundred things that end for us – such as, for example, a storm which comes to an end as far as we are concerned, though we cannot say that the rain really ends, because the storm may have gone somewhere else. There are other things which we may allow to end or not, because we can control them. There are many cruel things in the world which men might bring to an end if they would, such as bull-fighting in Spain, or the cruel treatment of drunken children by parents in England.

'We know that nothing can be utterly destroyed, and so we know, therefore, that nothing can be utterly ended. But the form and shape of everything may end... The very earth itself may cease to be as we know it now... But the earth can never be destroyed, however much its form may change. This book may end, in the form in which we hold it in our hands; but the thoughts this book has put into our minds, the feelings that have grown, perhaps, in our hearts as we have read it, will remain and influence our lives.

'Of one thing let us be sure for ever – that goodness never ends, that all this beautiful world, this wonderful life of ours, was not created by God to exist for a few years and then to die. The changes of Nature are sometimes more than we can understand, and the last change that we know, the sleep that we call death, is the strangest of all. But it is a sleep, and not an end.' (p. 5247)

THE STORY OF THE ANIMALS

NATURE, a wise man said, is the mother of us all. By Nature we really mean the whole of life—everything that is not made by man. But many natural things, such as the sun and moon and the earth itself, come into other parts of our book, and here we shall read of the two most important things in Nature—Animal Life and Plant Life. There were plants on the earth before the animals came, but it is better to begin with animals, and our book of Nature tells us first the story of the animals, and then the story of flowers and trees. We shall not tell our story as grown-up people do, with big words and strange names; but we shall learn all that we need know now about animals and flowers. The beginning of our story tells us of the wonderful things that live in the world with us, and the huge monsters that once lived upon earth and have now passed away.

NATURE'S WONDERFUL FAMILY

By ERNEST A. BRYANT

WHEN we are kept awake at night by the noise which cats in the garden make, perhaps we wish that there were no such things as cats. Let us suppose that all the cats were sent out of this country. We know that our houses would soon be swarming with rats and mice. But something far more strange than that would happen. Soon, nearly all those beautiful wild flowers called heartsease would fade away and die. We should have scarcely a heartsease left. That would be because the cats were gone.

What does the cat do to make the heartsease grow? Nothing at all. It never touches a heartsease if it can help it!

Well, why would the heartsease die if the cats were to go away? Because, if the cats went away, they could not catch the field-mice. Soon there would be so many field-mice that they would eat up all the nests of the humble bees in the fields. Now, the humble bees are the little friends which make the heartsease grow. The heartsease has a sweet juice which the humble bees love. The humble bees fly into the heartsease to drink this juice, and in doing so they carry in with them from other plants a dust, called pollen, which the heartsease needs to make its seeds. If it does not get that dust the heartsease must die. Therefore, if our gardens are to have this pretty flower, we must have cats to keep the field-mice from eating all the nests of the humble bees. The cats do not kill all the field-mice. That would not do. They prevent the mice from becoming too many. Then, though a few mice do eat nests of the humble bee, there are still enough bees left to bring the yellow dust to the heartsease.

That is a little thing which clever men were a long time in learning. We ought always to remember it, because it shows how Nature has to plan so that the world may go on in the best way for us. When we think of the world, we think of a great place where men and women and children live. But the world was not made simply to be a home for men and women and children. If there were no living creatures but ourselves, there would be a great many empty places in the world. There would be a great deal of work left undone. There are places in the world where we cannot live.

But Nature does not like empty spaces. She must have living creatures everywhere, in earth and sky and sea. And she has life everywhere.

Our eyes are not strong enough to see all the tiny things which live. If our eyes were as strong as the strongest magnifying glasses, we should see that the air we breathe is

3. NATURE

The series of articles on **NATURE** is in two parts – animal life and plant life – each with its own author.

Ernest Bryant wrote the items on animal life. He is frequently mentioned by Sir John Hammerton in his biography of Arthur Mee. Like Arthur, Ernest Bryant had been on the reporting staff of the Nottingham Daily Express; later, he was a frequent visitor to the latter's house in Kent; he was Mee's 'intimate friend and colleague throughout his life'. He is described by Hammerton as 'a student of bird life' and 'a knowledgeable person on wild nature'. He would thus have been a natural choice for this section of the *Encyclopædia*. He was one of the legatees in Mee's will.

There is no record of any other writings by him, and he does not appear in the *Dictionary of National Biography*.

I. Animal Life

The articles on animal life cover practically all kinds of mammals (wild and domesticated), reptiles, birds, fish and insects: these take up the first six volumes of the bound edition of the *Encyclopædia*. These descriptions are precise and often detailed: together with the very complete index at the end of the work, they would have provided a valuable source of reference.

We need not go through all this descriptive material, but a few examples will indicate how the author makes it interesting. Thus, an article on **Animals living in the Sea** (pp. 1081–91) explains that whales are mammals, as are seals, walruses, porpoises and dolphins. Manatees and dugongs, it is suggested, gave rise to the legends about mermaids, because when feeding their young they hold them between their flippers so that the heads of mother and baby are above the water… (These 'sea-cows' do indeed belong to the species 'sirenia'.)

Discussing reptiles – which, it is pointed out, began in the sea but emerged on earth long before man – the author explains how once there were giant creatures, and flying reptiles:

> 'Serpents and crocodiles such as we have in the world today are bad
> enough, but they are mild creatures compared with these terrible giants
> of long ago.' (p. 1217)

Once, monstrous crocodiles flourished where London now stands. The sphenodon, which now lives only on small islands near New Zealand, is a 'living fossil': a relic of millions of years ago, with the remnant of a third eye still visible on top of its head. [1]

On snakes (p. 1373–82), the author mainly describes the species found in tropical countries and explains the difference between those that kill by poisoning and those that crush their prey. There is mention of the tricks of snake-charmers in India. Readers are reminded of the danger from vipers in England and Scotland. (The author does not say whether their absence in Ireland is really due to St. Patrick…)

An article on sea-fish (pp. 2531–40) deals mainly with species caught for food: cod, herring, halibut, hake, mackerel, plaice, sole, etc. In view of our contemporary dearth of these species, resulting from overfishing, it is worth noting the remark that cod 'swarm in enormous numbers off the Dogger Bank, in the North Sea, and to a still larger extent off Newfoundland'. Herring too were caught in 'vast numbers'; fish are 'very important to the food supply and wealth of the country'.

Two articles (pp. 2815–26 & 2941–50) recount the life of bees and wasps and ants in a manner so vivid and interesting that one would like to reproduce them in full. The writer stresses the extraordinary skill and organisation of these insects and asks: is this intelligence or instinct?

> 'The story of the bees is like a fairy tale. They are creatures of the sunlight; their food is of the sweet nectar and nourishing pollen of the flowers…
> They have their queen and their princesses; they have their willing slaves; they have their lazy idlers.' (pp. 2815–16)

As for the ants,

> 'Great men place them next to man himself as the wisest of all created things; their life-story is the most extraordinary in the whole book of Nature… They are superior because they live together in cities as human beings live; because they construct wonderful dwellings; because they divide their labours among themselves as we do; because they cultivate crops, and store food in barns; because they keep cows and milk them; because they keep pets.' (p. 2941)

The story of the butterflies and moths is also eloquent. Here is the passage about the moment when the chrysalis is transformed:

> 'In that state it lies like a dead thing for days and days. We see nothing from the outside beyond the dull, horny cover, which is about as interesting as an empty shell. But within that covering a miracle is being performed. The body of the caterpillar is being remade while we wait. It may take only a fortnight if the weather is warm at the time. At the end of that period the chrysalis will open at the top end; the top ring will come off like a lid, and a lovely moth or butterfly will creep out…' (p. 2988)

---

[1] This unusual piece of information is quite correct. The sphenodon (or *tuatara*, in Maori) is now a protected species on some New Zealand islands; in England, specimens can be seen in Chester Zoo. The 'third eye' is apparent only during the first few months of the animal's life. (Cf. *Wikipedia*, under 'tuatara'.)

There is an unusually good colour illustration, and fifteen species of butterfly are mentioned: of these, six are today rare or extinct in Britain. [2]

There are many articles describing the various species of birds, and in discussing **Birds of the Ocean** (pp. 1625–32) another eloquent passage appears:

> 'The sea-birds are in some ways the most wonderful of all living creatures... They swim as lightly as corks in the deepest seas, in the fiercest storms. They dive like fish. To crown it all, they fly with an ease and grace which nothing else can match... The powers of these birds make man feel that Providence, when it made him lord of the earth and the waters, was very mindful of the needs of the inferior creatures.' (p. 1625)

The author tackles the question of bird migration (pp. 2209–18). As the weather gets colder in autumn and food grows scarce, some bird species fly from the north to warmer lands. How they do this, and how they find their way back, often to the exact spots where they had nested in previous years, was still a mystery. Some people, the author tells us, say that the birds fly with the wind, which blows them south in the autumn, and they come back to us 'when the spring breezes, sweeping over England, carry the scent of our fair land into the heart of Africa'. A poetic explanation! but the author recognises that it is not sufficient; the secret of their navigation remained unknown.

These are examples of descriptive passages taken almost at random. For our purposes, it is of particular interest to review the treatment of certain major themes.

One of these consists of what we would today call 'ecological balance'. The point is made already in the first page of this series (reproduced above), which demonstrates why cats are necessary to the little flowers called 'heartsease' (wild pansy). This is not a very good example (for cats are mainly domestic animals), but there are better ones, such as the following passage:

> 'Nature so planned that her various workmen should have so much liberty and no more. She never meant rats and mice and voles to become too many; there were the owls and other birds, and polecats and the common cat, and the foxes to keep their numbers down. When we destroy these, and leave our little enemies too much scope, we interfere with the plans of Nature, and we must pay the penalty.' (p. 792)

The sparrow provides the occasion for another lesson on the need for natural balance. Sparrows are so numerous as to be a nuisance in public places, and they eat a lot of the farmers' grain.

> 'It is around the sparrow that the great debate as to the value of birds centres... Numerous clubs exist in the country solely for the slaughter of the poor sparrow... But when we resolve to destroy one of Nature's

---

[2] These are the Camberwell Beauty, Large Copper, Large Tortoiseshell, Glanville Fritillary, Purple Emperor, Swallowtail - cf. www.butterfly-conservation.org.

families, let us look back at what has happened to other people who have done a similar thing. The Government of Maine, in the United States, carried out the slaughter of the sparrows some time ago, and in the following year, through there being no sparrows, the caterpillars multiplied so enormously that they not merely ate all the leaves of the fruit-trees, but actually killed the trees themselves.

'A similar thing happened in France. Therefore, let none of us take any share in trying to prove that men's ideas as to what should live and what should die are wiser than Nature's laws.' (p. 2218)

Indeed, man interferes with Nature at his period. An article on **Animals that work for Nature** (pp. 275–87) says that the lion may seem a cruel creature, for it eats other animals: yet if there were no lions, tigers or other flesh-eating beasts, then all kinds of deer, cattle, sheep, goats and rabbits would have multiplied to such an extent and eaten so much vegetable matter that the beautiful places where they lived

These pictures show us some of the strange creatures that have passed away, and help us to understand the story of animal life from the first thing we know about it. Once all creatures lived in the sea, and the first of all were only soft things like jelly, with no bones.

These creatures had the sea to themselves for a very long time, and slowly they grew into separate families, unlike those which had gone before. Proper fishes began to swim about, and some of them lived in shells. Then on the land great forests grew, and a new kind of animals came.

The first crocodile appeared now, but this age is important because great trees grew, drinking in the sunshine for thousands of years, and then fell, to be buried in the earth, and to lie there millions of years until they turned to coal. That is how coal began.

In the sea great fish-lizards grew, four times as long as a man, some with necks like snakes. There were great sea-serpents, fish with skins almost like iron, and huge animals that could live either on land or sea.

Some of these creatures could fly and swim, and some could eat off tree-tops. The first birds came, and flying dragons. It has taken millions of years for these strange things to become the beautiful birds we know.

HOW THE ANIMALS CAME INTO THE WORLD

On the land the great monsters were growing up, and the mastodon, like a giant elephant with four tusks, fought the savage tiger with teeth like swords. There were bats in those days, and a strange little animal walked the earth which we may, perhaps, call the first horse.

The little sloths we see to-day have descended from creatures like that clasping a tree on the right of this picture. The giant sloth lived when the hippopotamus and elephant began, when there were horses with many toes, and animals like tortoises bigger than a man.

Slowly the world grew into the kind of place it is to-day, and the animals became more like those we know. Bears lived in the caves, and the woolly rhinoceros and the savage hyena roamed the earth with the mammoth, like a giant elephant with long hair.

At last came man, the lord of all the animals. The first men lived in trees and caves, with the wild animals about them, and it has taken thousands of years for men to learn how to build houses, and tame animals, and make fires, and write books like this to tell us what a wonderful place the world has been, and how much more wonderful still it is to be.

SOME OF THE GREAT MONSTERS OF THE PAST

would have been turned into deserts.

This, in fact, had happened around the Mediterranean, where man had killed off most of the predators, allowing goats and sheep to become too numerous. 'Wherever the white man makes his home, the lion and tiger have to leave'. And when forests are destroyed, the climate too is ruined.

The other major theme is evolution, and this runs throughout the series. Darwin is not explicitly cited here (he is discussed elsewhere in the *Encyclopædia*), but his influence is evident. Already in the first article, on **Nature's Wonderful Family** (pp. 25–32) the evolutionary concept is emphasised:

'The story of the animals makes us wonder if Nature tried all sorts of patterns before she made up her mind what sort of creatures should live in the seas and on the land... It has taken millions and millions of years to make the birds and animals the wonderful creatures that they are today'. (p. 26)

Life began in the oceans, and only gradually took shape on land. The story is told here in a series of pictures. These and other pictures of pre-historic creatures in this article would certainly have imprinted on a child's mind the successive stages of evolution. Drawings of the horse in different eras also make the point clear.

How did evolution work? The first explanation we find reads as follows:

> 'Those animals that improved themselves, and made their lives fit the world around them, increased and prospered and developed; those that did not adapt themselves to the conditions about them died out. The animals that survived developed better brains than those that died, and mated with other animals of better brains, and the offspring of these had better brains still. Little by little the animals with better brains developed into new kinds of animals; those that did not improve, that could not keep pace with the changes in the world around them, died out.' (p. 917)

The emphasis here on brain-power can be questioned: physical prowess is at least as important for many species. Also, the mating process remains unexplained. Still, this gives some idea as to how natural selection might work. [3]

Another illustration of the theme comes in **Animals with wonderful coats** (pp. 3407–16), which tells us about the camouflage (or 'protective mimicry') used by many creatures to blend in with their surroundings – such as polar bears, lions and tigers, and many insects. How did this come about?

> 'Somewhere in their family history there must have been definite acts of selection – deliberate choice by females of mates whose shape and colouring made them most like their surroundings. The result has been that their successors have become more and more like the leaves, and twigs, and moss, among which they make their dwellings… The insects that are best protected in this way are the insects that have the best chance of escaping hungry enemies, and so of rearing families of their own.' (p. 3415)

The evolutionary process gets further explanation with an article on **Birds of Beauty** (pp. 1737–48). A bird does not make up its mind to wear rich plumage.

> 'The appearance of birds is brought about by long ages of change, by the slow working of natural laws.'

In a flock of birds, if some have plumage which conceals them better from enemies, these have a better chance of surviving; and their offspring will be like them. Moreover:

> 'It is the way of the female bird to mate herself to the handsomest among her suitors, like the princesses in the story-books; so that each generation of birds tends to become stronger and more handsome'. (p. 1737)

---

[3] For a good summary of modern understanding of natural selection, taking into account genetic science (which has of course greatly advanced since the time of the *Encyclopædia*), see: www.globalchange.umich.edu/globalchange1/current/lectures/selection/selection.html
The important point is that there must be 'heritable variation' for some trait, and 'differential survival and reproduction associated with that trait'. But variations do not arise because they are needed: they arise by random processes governed by the laws of genetics.

We hear a little about the mating display of the male paradise birds. The actual role of the male and what happens in mating is still left unexplained.

In fact, even in this series on animal life, the *Encyclopædia* remains coy about the reproductive process. An item on river fish (pp. 2675–84) tells us about the wonderful life cycle of the salmon, describing in particular the struggle of adult fish up the river of their birth, to breed. The males fight terrible battles and many are killed, yet 'when all the battles have been fought, or even while they are going on, the female makes her nest and lays her eggs'.

An intelligent child might have wondered what the males are for and why they fight, but this is not explained.

Discussing bees, the author refers to courtship rituals and even to 'mating', so the role of the male does get mentioned, though never fully explained. The queen bee's role is to fill the hive with eggs, and 'the drones only exist that the queen may choose a mate from one', but the connection between these events is not explained.

Among the ants, 'on a bright day in summer the young queens and the handsome males (which, at this stage, have wings) come out of the nest and sail away into the sunlight: it is their wedding day'.

The male cicada, we are told, makes its loud chirp (by rubbing its wings together) in order to attract the females.

Among the spiders 'the males are small, and are more often than not eaten up by the females after the wedding-day: in fact, they may be gobbled up even before the courtship is over'.

An attentive young reader who wondered just what happened on these 'wedding-days' would not have found the answer here.

The last article on animal life – **Nature's Great Family** (pp. 3675–82) – summarises the history of evolution that has been taught in the previous items. Man, it emphasises, is part of that family; we are not descended from monkeys, but from creatures from which the monkeys also descended (which is correct).

Another article on **The Animals most like Men** (pp. 579–586) describes the apes and monkeys. Their bodies are similar to those of men; but there the likeness ends:

'The apes have brains like those of a tiny child, but they are as much below the savage in brain power as the savage is below you.' (p. 579)

The author has frequently referred to 'Nature' or 'Providence', suggesting that some higher power has ordained the evolutionary process; he has not, however, referred specifically to 'God'. In his last article on **Nature's Great Family** (pp. 3675–82), he tackles the vital issue: how does all this fit in with the Bible story? He gives a prudent answer: 'The Bible story is true, but the Bible does not teach science, and it must be read intelligently in the full light of truth as we know it'.

When the Bible says that God made the world in six days, those 'days' may have been ages too long for the human mind to understand. 'Man would pass through many stages before God made him perfect... God gave man a soul.'

Animals, the writer says, do not have souls; but he does not sound entirely convinced, admitting: 'When we see a bad man and a faithful dog, we feel it a shame that the brutal man should have a soul and that the animal should not.'

We find a tendency to consider Man as not only the culmination of evolution but as the central element around whom the rest of Nature revolves. The second article in the series (pp. 131–139), on **Animals that serve Man** (horses, oxen, donkeys, mules, elephants, camels and others), makes this explicit: 'Once upon a time the animals lived in the world alone. Then came man, and by his wonderful mind conquered the animal world'. And a little later, in **Some very strange beasts**, we are told:

> 'Ants perform very good service in the world, but they have become so numerous that they are a plague to mankind; and therefore we have strange animals that live by eating ants... They are Nature's outposts, placed, as it were, to keep the way open for Man.' (p. 995)

The author recognises, however, that there is a wide gap between the highest and lowest forms of human life. Among the former he cites Pasteur, Ruskin, or great musicians and painters; at the other extreme are the 'cannibals' and other 'savages': once these people were higher in the scale of human civilisation, but have degenerated (he does not explain how).

II. Plant Life

Edward Step wrote the articles on plant life. He produced many books on nature, including insects, shellfish, trees and above all flowers, published from 1896 till 1940. Those on flowers were beautifully illustrated, some if not all by Mabel Step (his wife?): in particular a 'pocket guide' entitled *Wayside and Wayside Blossoms*, published in 1905 (i.e. three years before the appearance of the *Encyclopædia*). Today, we can see some of these pictures in their original beauty: illustrations from Step's first work of 1896, *Favourite Flowers of the Garden and Greenhouse*, have been reproduced on Internet sites: www.finerareprints.com and www.printspast.com
In the *Encyclopædia*, the illustrations of plants are numerous, but consist exclusively of photographs in black-and-white (attributed to a Mr. Edward Connold). Maybe there were copyright obstacles to the use of the Steps' own paintings.

This series begins with general explanations of the life cycle of plants. We are attracted by their flowers, yet these, it is pointed out, are just the means to an end: their pollen, carried from one plant to another by insects, enables the plants to produce seeds and thus to reproduce themselves.

Seeds can travel long distances, carried by the wind or by birds, or even by humans on their clothing. We hear of cases where humans have deliberately taken seeds from their homeland to a country where the plant did not previously grow; sometimes this was a mistake, as in the case of the Scotsman who introduced thistles to Australia!

Like animals, plants face a fight for life. Their enemies include slugs, insects, birds and beasts which eat their seeds, kill their seedlings or damage the full-grown plants. The greater the danger a plant has to face, the larger will be the number of seeds it produces. Then there is not room for all the seedlings to grow, and only the strongest will survive. If we visit an oak-wood in May or June, we can see many seedling oaks; but very few of them will be alive by the end of the year.

Different species have different needs, and this determines where they grow – i.e. their habitat. Often their choice is due to their degree of thirst: plants with thick leaves – including the evergreens and cacti – allow less water to evaporate, so can live on drier soils. It may also be due to the amount of light and heat they require, so we find different species at different seasons of the year.

Plants also flower at different times of the day: this can be due to the presence at those times of the insects on which they depend for their pollination. Their hours can be so regular that the great Swedish botanist, Linnæus, made a floral clock with plants which opened their flowers one after the other.

The amount of light in different places also plays a large part in determining which plants grow there. Not many plants can grow in a pine-wood, partly because of the thick carpet of dead pine-needles, but also because not much light can penetrate at any time of the year. Likewise in a beech-wood in summer, the leaves cut off much of the light, but in winter and spring the plants can do well: so in spring we find wood anemones, bluebells, violets, etc. The leaves of oak-trees let more light through, so there we can find many more wild flowers in spring and even in summer.

Such explanations, and many more, aim to encourage interest and observation among the young readers.

> 'When we are out of doors, in the garden or the fields, we must look at all the kinds of flowers we can find, and must take note of their shapes and colours, and see where they grow, and what kinds of insects are settling upon them. Then we shall become interested in all the flowers and learn to love them.' (p. 3952)

These general explanations are followed by a series of articles on different habitats, where the main themes are further developed and plants are described, often in some detail. Britain, we are told, has some two thousand plant species, which can be classified into about one hundred families. In eleven articles, with around twenty plants described in each, the author covers not just all the familiar species but a considerable number of lesser-known ones. [4]

The descriptions come in a series of articles corresponding to a variety of habitats: hedgerow, meadows, cornfields, woodland, heath, downs, mountains, streams, bogland, seaside and finally garden.

---

[4] Trees are not covered in the series on **NATURE**: they are discussed in three articles under **FAMILIAR THINGS**.

This enables the author to illustrate further the concept of habitat. In meadows, for example, we find few annual plants, because with grazing and cutting for hay they do not get much chance to flower and seed; but perennials with strong roots can do well as the soil is not interfered with (as any farmer knows from his constant struggle against thistles!) In arable land, on the other hand, ploughing disturbs the roots of perennials, while annuals growing from seed, such as poppies, can flourish.

Each article has five or six full-page illustrations, each page showing photographs of four plants. The quality is poor, which must have been frustrating to the author; without colour, their usefulness as aids to recognising the plants seems limited. One example is reproduced here: it shows daffodils and three less obvious flowers. The captions under each picture are instructive: here we learn that 'butcher's broom' is used to keep rats and mice away from meat, while 'spurge-laurel' and 'dog's mercury' are poisonous.

The text makes up for the technical limitations of the illustrations: never just a descriptive catalogue, it always has something interesting to say.

So this series of articles offers a comprehensive and interesting survey of Britain's plant life; it must have provided both a useful reference – subject to the limitations of the illustrations – and an incentive for readers to take an intelligent interest in the nature around them.

THE BUTCHER'S BROOM

The butcher's broom is so called because butchers used to preserve meat from rats and mice by covering it with this plant. The small greenish-white flowers are succeeded by bright scarlet berries that are very attractive.

THE SPURGE-LAUREL

The yellow-green flowers of the spurge-laurel, that grow in clusters, change into bluish-black berries, so poisonous that quite a few are sufficient to cause death. The bark is often used by doctors to make a lotion.

THE DAFFODIL

Where the daffodil is found it grows in great abundance, and the poet Wordsworth wrote of this flower, "ten thousand saw I at a glance." Country children are fond of "going daffying," as they call daffodil-picking.

THE DOG'S MERCURY

Dog's mercury is poisonous, and cattle know this, for they will eat all the herbage round, but leave this plant severely alone. It is a very common weed in the woods, but is unattractive, its flowers being small and green.

ALL ABOUT YOURSELF

THE greatest wonder in the world is Life. What is it that makes us move, and breathe, and feel? Nobody knows that. But there is a greater wonder still than breathing and moving and feeling. Even animals can do these things. What is it that makes us think, and love, and hate, and pray? Nobody knows. It is the world's great mystery, which no man yet has ever known. The world is a beautiful place filled with living things, and men and women and boys and girls are the masters of creation. We can measure the earth, and we know what the sun is made of, but we do not know the wonder of ourselves—what makes you YOU, what makes me ME. In this part of our book we shall be told all that we can know about the great mystery of Life.

LIVING THINGS AROUND US

By DR. SALEEBY

OF all the interesting things in our wonderful world none are more interesting than the living creatures we find everywhere around us.

They are our own friends and relations. If we think of the moon, beautiful but dead, a great splendid tomb, we shall see what a difference there is between the moon and our own earth, which is the mother of all living creatures. No doubt there were once living creatures on the moon, too. If there were no animals, there were at any rate some plants. But the moon has now grown cold; she has lost all the air that she once had such as our own earth has now; she has not even a drop of water left, and so all the plants that once lived upon the moon are dead now, they and their children. How different is the earth! Life fills the seas, covers the dry land, and flies in the air above. Everywhere there is life and movement, and birth, and

death, and new birth; always and everywhere there is life and more life. These are the most interesting facts of the world we live in, and we must ask ever so many questions about them. For instance, what is the difference between a living thing—like a fly, or a rose, or a child—and a thing that is not living or that never has lived—like a stick, or a stone, or the gravel or clay in the garden? Then again, what are the different kinds of living things? How is it they are so different? An elephant is very different from a piece of moss, yet an elephant is much more like a piece of moss than it is like a piece of flint. How is this?

The business of our lives is to ask questions, to try to answer them, and to act and live in obedience to the answers; and after we have answered these questions, there remain many more to puzzle us. We know that living creature, die,

How can we tell whether a thing is alive or not alive? What is the difference between a living thing, like a boy or a rose, and a thing that is not living, like a stick or a book?

4. THE CHILD'S OWN LIFE

This section, like the following one on **THE EARTH**, was written by **Dr. Caleb Williams Saleeby**, 1878–1940. He qualified in medicine and practiced in Edinburgh and London; but he soon became a freelance writer and journalist – in fact, a very prolific one, with strong views on many subjects. By the time of the *Encyclopædia*, he had already published, in particular, *Cycle of life according to modern science* (1904) and *Health, strength and happiness* (1908): material from the latter in particular found its way into this *Encyclopædia* contribution.

At this time he was mainly known as an advocate of eugenics: in 1907 he had been influential in launching the Eugenics Education Society, and in 1909 he published (in New York) *Parenthood and Race Culture* (this can be found on *www.questia.com*). Here, he described eugenics as being based on selection for parenthood, which determines the nature, fate and worth of living races.

Later, he moved away from eugenics and did not publish any more on this subject after 1921, though he continued to write on health matters in particular. During the First World War he was an adviser to the Minister of Food and argued in favour of the establishment of a Ministry of Health.

Like Arthur Mee, he was a keen temperance reformer; he also campaigned for clean air and the benefits of sunlight (he founded a Sunlight League in 1924). He was an effective public speaker, and addressed audiences all round the world in support of his favourite causes.

There is no full biography of Dr. Saleeby (his early eugenic associations may have discouraged potential investigators); the above information comes mainly from the *Dictionary of National Biography*.

This section starts with the origins of life and its evolution, but while the series on **NATURE** relates to animal and plant life, this – as the title indicates – aims to explain in simple terms the anatomy and functioning of the human body. (Scientific names like biology or anatomy are avoided, though often the explanations seem quite demanding of the reader.)

The first article aims to make clear the distinction between living creatures and inanimate objects. The main criterion mentioned for life is movement, which leads to some difficulty in explaining that plants too are alive. The author avoids referring to ability to grow and – above all – to reproduce, which seem more significant characteristics: perhaps this would have led into questions about sex, which the *Encyclopædia* studiously avoids.

Articles in the first volume go on to discuss the origins of life. After the earth had cooled down sufficiently, the first simple living organisms must have arisen in the sea. At some point, probably helped by the tides, marine creatures emerged on to the land, developed lungs and became established. In the sea, progress was limited (fish have not changed very much over a long period of time). Land animals had much more opportunity to evolve into higher forms; one reason is that air-breathing animals can get as much oxygen as they need for their activities.

All this is made interesting, told as a story. It is pointed out that by digging down through deeper-and-deeper layers, we can discover the successive stages.

> 'As time goes on, the great fact is that low and humble forms of life are giving place to higher forms.'

Humans are the highest form of life:

> 'As we go on increasing (in numbers) we take the place of low and humble forms of life, and, indeed, we make all other forms of life serve ours, including even the life of the sea.' (p. 618)

A picture of the 'Animal Ladder' (reproduced) makes clear this evolution, showing an ape at the top of the line of mammals. Logically, man should appear next – the caption points out that in this line 'man came later, and higher still' – but perhaps this would have been too controversial.

Despite the assertion in the first article that 'We know that all things, living and dead, have come from God, who sustains them from everlasting to everlasting' (p. 18), this exposition – like that in the series on **NATURE** - is firmly Darwinian. The progress of archaeology and palaeontology during the twentieth century has of course filled in many details, but the broad outlines described here in the *Encyclopædia* have not changed.

The main element lacking is an indication of the vast stretches of time over which life evolved, and the very recent appearance of *Homo sapiens*, which of course makes it more difficult to assert that Man is the purpose of Creation. [1]

Indeed, intelligent readers must have wondered how these explanations could be reconciled with the book of Genesis. However, there is no attempt here to resolve this apparent conflict between science and religion.

A further article emphasises the vital role of sunlight: where there is no light, there is no life. The function of the 'green stuff' in plants is explained (words like chlorophyll and photosynthesis are avoided): it enables plants to take up carbonic acid gas from the atmosphere, converting it into carbon for their growth and releasing oxygen back into the air. Some of this is quite difficult material: well beyond the capacities of the small child of Mee's imagination.

------

[1] It is now generally held that the Earth was formed 4500 million years ago; the first bacterial life began 3800 mya; the first fish appeared 480 mya and the first mammals 220 mya. Primates emerged 60 mya, the earliest species of genus *Homo* 3 mya, and *Homo sapiens* only about 150,000 years ago. See *inter alia* Stringer and Andrews, *The Complete World of Human Evolution* (2005).
While I was writing this chapter, the journal *Nature* published (on 6th April 2006) the finding in the Canadian Arctic of the fossil named 'Tiktaalik', considered to be the 'missing link' between fish and land-based vertebrates; it is dated at some 375 mya. One imagines that this news would have delighted the *Encyclopædia* author…

THE ANIMAL LADDER OF LIFE

All living creatures had their far-off beginnings at the bottom of the ocean. This picture makes clear the later steps in the ladder of life—the steps taken since the making of the backbone, which the first creatures had not. The oldest backboned creatures are the fishes. Above them are animals that live on land and in water. Then there is a split. On the one side the land-and-water animals gave rise to the reptiles, and these gave rise to the birds. On the other side the land-and-water animals gave rise to the mammals. Man came later, and higher still, in this last line.

728

The author points a moral, typical of the *Children's Encyclopædia*:

> 'So if you are a little boy you might do worse, when next you run out into the garden, than take off your hat to the sun above you and the grass upon which you tread. Though you are, beyond words, more wonderful and greater than them, and though they are so wonderful themselves just because they make little boys possible, yet who will dare to deny that even little boys owe them wonder and awe and love?' (p. 365)

Volume 2 begins by pointing out the essential difference between animals with a backbone (it avoids the term 'vertebrates') and those without. It then embarks on a series of articles on the tiniest forms of life, containing many points which should have stimulated the interest of the readers, including the not-so-young. The author says that to study life, we need to begin with the simplest forms, i.e. single-celled, which moreover would have been the first to appear on the earth (or rather, in the sea).

We can only observe such creatures through a microscope. There is detailed description of how the amoeba lives, moves and divides. The author also explains how microbes multiply by division, and in conditions which suit them they can do so at a very rapid rate. We should not think of microbes as being necessarily our enemies. In fact, since they live on food from other creatures, including dead matter, they perform a vital role as scavengers.

> 'The work of microbes is the greatest instance I know of the economy of Nature… There is no wholly wasted life in the world, for there are always microbes ready to take the dead creature's body and prepare it, so as to be useful for future life, which may be better and higher life.' (p. 887)

Efficient sewage treatment makes use of microbes. They are also involved in the process of tanning skins. And of course they are required for turning milk into butter and cheese. Some microbes can convert nitrogen from the air into food for certain crops, e.g. peas, and this is the basis for the rotation of crops.

But of course, microbes are also responsible for disease: in particular, for consumption (tuberculosis), which – the author says – kills 50–60,000 people in England every year, including many babies. This, he adds, is largely due to people living in crowded, unsanitary conditions; those who live in the open air and get plenty of sunlight are much less at risk.

There are some diseases which we cannot catch twice, so in these cases vaccination is a means of prevention, though this is mentioned here only in the context of smallpox. [2]

Yeasts too consist of single-celled organisms, and the author points out how useful this is in making bread. It turns sugar into alcohol, which is also a very useful substance in many arts and industries. It is 'a splendid fuel'. Interestingly, the author

---

[2] The possibility of smallpox vaccination had been discovered in the eighteenth century by Edward Jenner, and by the time of the *Encyclopædia* was compulsory in England.

declares that it is far cheaper than petrol: 'most people expect that before long alcohol will be used to drive motor-cars, and also to work engines.' (p. 889)

But alcohol, when we drink it, is a poison, which in time causes disease in every part of our bodies, especially the brain... It also prevents us from protecting ourselves again microbes. This leads into a characteristic *Encyclopædia* diatribe:

> 'We find the microbe of consumption in abundance in public-houses, because many people who suffer from consumption spend much of their time in public-houses, and there the microbe attacks people who are made ready for it by alcohol. Especially does this apply to children, and there are far too many little children in England whose playground now is the public-house floor, covered with microbes. But men are fighting to stop this, and are going to stop it soon.' (p. 889)

All living creatures are made of cells, so these are the abode of life. Anticipating subsequent research, the author observes: 'If we could learn the secret of the cell, we should have the secret of life' (p. 1003). Protoplasm is the living stuff found in every cell; it always contains carbon, oxygen, hydrogen, nitrogen and phosphorus, and other elements besides, in compounds different from those found anywhere else.

Moving on to human anatomy, the author discusses the role of the red blood cells, carrying oxygen from the lungs throughout the body, and of the white blood cells, which act as 'scavengers' destroying microbes. With reference to Harvey's discoveries, and with a useful diagram, he explains the circulation system, with the heart pumping blood out through the arteries, to return through the veins.

This leads to practical advice about how to stop bleeding: below the bleeding point in the case of a vein, but if the blood is brighter and instead of oozing comes in spurts, that means an artery is involved, so pressure must be applied above the bleeding point. There is detailed explanation of the functioning of the heart itself: the roles of the left and right chambers, and of the auricles and ventricles. [3]

There is more practical advice about the importance of breathing through the nose, not the mouth, as the nasal passages filter out dirt.

> 'There are few more important lessons for health than this lesson... All over England there are unfortunate children who suffer from frequent colds and sore throats, and so on, simply because they have something the matter with their noses, which could easily be put right.' (p. 1635)

Further, it is important to give the diaphragm free play in breathing: many women wear their clothes too tight!

An article entitled **Fresh Air and Healthy Lives** (pp. 1787–9) points out that without fresh air, there is not enough oxygen, and the blood becomes overloaded with carbonic acid. Everyone should sleep in a bedroom with a window open. Bad ventilation of school-rooms is one reason why children cannot attend to their

---

[3] This seems quite advanced material for child readers. I certainly missed these explanations, which might have been useful to me much later in life!

lessons. Many shop assistants are pale and tired, and a large number die of consumption, simply because the air is not often enough changed.

> 'Some day the law of the land will lay down definite rules as to the
> quality of the air in shops, and workshops, and factories, and so on.'
> (p. 1788)

Other articles deal with the skin, the sweat-glands (which regulate body temperature), hair and nails, and the teeth. Sugar can be bad for teeth if they are not kept clean: powder is best, and can be made from carbolic powder and precipitated chalk, bought a pound at a time... But sugar is a very valuable food for children, who need the energy.

The process of digestion is explained: its starts with the saliva in the mouth, so it is important to chew food well, and continues in the stomach and the bowel, which is a very long, coiled tube. The useless part of the food is disposed of every day by healthy persons: 'not a subject that people think it suitable to talk about much' but still an important subject of study.

The skeleton is described, with its bones and ligaments: there are illustrations showing the bones of the legs, arms and hands, and of the hip joints.

In humans, as compared with the apes, the skull has grown forwards to accommodate our larger brains: and there is an illustration comparing this development as between an 'Australian native', a negro and a European ('the highest type of man'). We might find this scientifically dubious and unacceptably racist. The author does add, rather condescendingly, that:

> 'we have no more right to despise these people than we have to despise
> any other creature that God has made...' (p. 2542) [4]

A further article covers muscles, tendons and nerves.

A number of articles go on to consider food, containing the carbohydrates, fats and proteins which are the 'fuel' for our muscles. Milk is the perfect food, providing all the elements we need.

> 'We spend too much time in trying to make good soldiers out of boys
> who did not have enough milk when they were children, boys with bad
> teeth and crooked bones and narrow chests.' (p. 2794)

There is a reference to Japan, where people are 'small and stunted', because they drink very little milk.

But milk can also contain microbes, in particular those which cause 'consumption'; so it must be milked by clean hands into clean pails, then cooled immediately and packed into bottles sealed with cotton-wool.

---

[4] There had been much interest in 'craniometry' during the nineteenth century, spurred on by Darwinism; the white races, having apparently larger skulls and hence bigger brains than others, were thought to be more intelligent in consequence (reasoning which would also imply that men are more intelligent than women...). Later, similar reasoning was also employed to justify Nazi racist doctrines. Few scientists today would support this argument. But we have here a rather distasteful hint of Saleeby's eugenic convictions.

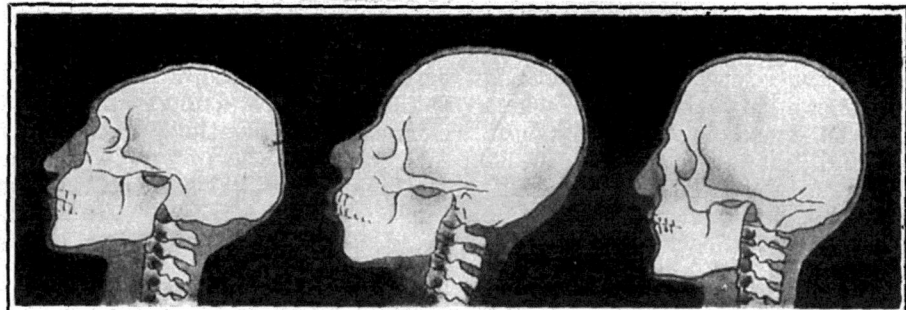

In animals the skull is all behind the face. These pictures show how in man the skull has doubled over in front to make room for the brain. The first is the skull of an Australian native, the lowest type of man, the second of a negro, and the third of a European, the highest type of man.

Bread is 'the staff of life', the basis of Western civilisation. It is superior to rice, which has more starch and less protein, and that is linked to the relatively *'slow life'* of the East... But the white population is outrunning the supply of wheat: Britain is dependent on imports from America.

> 'It is practically certain that before many of the children who read this book have grown up there will be no more wheat coming from America, because America will need every grain of the wheat she grows for her own use.' (p. 2923)

This was a Malthusian-style prediction which totally neglected the potential for yield increase. But the author declares:

> 'It is our national duty not merely to grow wheat where we can, but to grow it as intensely as we can.' (p. 2925)

Economic theory, it seems, was not Dr. Saleeby's strong point. Here he seems unaware of the Ricardian theory of comparative advantage.

Maize, much used in America, is cheap and nourishing. Oats, grown mainly in Scotland, contains a lot of fat and is therefore suitable for people in a northern climate.

> 'The strength and vigour of the Scotsman at his best, his vigour of brain and body, and his capacity to withstand his climate, probably depend in no small degree upon the excellence of oatmeal as a food and its richness in the very substances most needed in such a climate.' (p. 2926)

However, there is a reminder of the risk of physical degeneration:

> 'The younger generation in the big Scottish cities, largely fed on starchy bread and jam, are promising to become, very soon, about the smallest nation on the face of the earth.' (p. 2927)

Man is very adaptable: our teeth, unlike those of most animals, are suited to every kind of food; and a mixed diet is best. However, our appetites are no longer to be trusted: we eat more than is good for us, and we take things which the natural appetite would not care for at all (such as mustard, pepper and vinegar).

An article entitled **The Real Value of Food** (pp. 3109–13) advises us to 'obey Nature'. Unfortunately:

> 'In spite of all we spend on education, we are not yet teaching ourselves or our children the great lessons of Nature – the mighty mother of all real wisdom.' (p. 3111)

Should we eat meat? is it right to take life for the purposes of food? Some religions teach that this is wrong. The author suggests that, since all creatures are mortal, the important question is how the animals are killed (one might add, how they are kept).

He goes on to discuss whether we really need meat. Some flesh-eating animals, such as dogs and the big cats, are quick and intelligent, in contrast to slow grass-eating animals like cows and sheep. But the higher apes are even more intelligent, and their food consists of fruit and nuts. Vegetarians in Britain have shown it is possible to make athletic records and to turn out 'splendid and vigorous works of the mind' without eating meat.

So children should not be forced to eat meat if they do not like it; milk, eggs (no mention of cholesterol), fish, wheat bread are to be recommended.

Nor should children be encouraged to drink tea and coffee: they do not need such stimulants. Cocoa, however, is admissible, especially as it is usually taken with milk and sugar; likewise, chocolate is a 'splendid food', and if children's teeth are properly cared for, there is no need to worry about the sugar content. No condiments are good for children, except salt.

There is, as one would expect, a long discourse about the danger from tobacco: the nicotine in the smoke is a poison. Yet a 'vicious circle' is set up: the smoker initially feels restful and contented, but soon becomes restless again so that the body demands more. Anyone who regularly inhales tobacco smoke is bound to spoil his voice sooner or later, though many grown-up people smoke without any sign of harm. (There is no mention of cancer risk, identified much later.)

The author admits that he has smoked for fourteen years without a break, but has just stopped without much difficulty (one wonders if he kept this up...). It is best not to learn to smoke at all. Boys are encouraged to smoke because they are told 'to be a man'. This is the occasion for the author to make a strong moral point:

> 'The real mark of a man is not that we should smoke, or drink, or shave, or be six feet high; the real mark of a man is to be ourselves, to do things or not to do things because we think so fit; and the mark of not being a man... is to do things because other people do them.' (p. 3320)

Very recently – in 1909 – a law had been enacted (this was the 1908 Children Act – see Appendix) which, the author says, would do something to protect children from themselves and from foolish people in this respect: any child under sixteen found smoking in the street or in a park must be stopped by the policeman or the park-keeper, and tobacconists will be punished if they sell cigarettes to children.

Drink, however, is the big enemy: an entire article is devoted to **Alcohol, the Enemy of Life** (pp. 3491–5). It causes loss of self-control, and leads to disease, death, insanity, poverty, crime and cruelty to children. Spending on alcohol totals £160 million per year, a huge amount compared to the cost of building just one of the biggest and newest battleships, i.e. under £1.5 million. (This is a remarkable comparison, for which the author does not cite his evidence.)

The Children Act of 1908, besides its regulations concerning tobacco, had stipulated that no alcohol should be given to children under five, and that those under fourteen must not be admitted to pubs. The author points out that a recent study in London had shown that over forty per cent of infants drank alcohol more or less regularly. He also claims that tiny children had often been taken into public-houses, where by crawling on a floor infected by spittle they picked up all sorts of germs, including those causing consumption.

Subsequent articles return to anatomy, with explanations – often detailed, sometimes verbose – of the brain and the nervous system; the functions of sight, speech, hearing, smell and taste.

The Master of the Body – the title of a further article (pp. 4731–34) – is the mind, which is not just intelligence or intellect but involves many sensations, including instincts, habits and feelings. This subject had been studied two hundred years previously by John Locke, who concluded:

> 'Nothing is in the mind that was not first in the senses, and the whole of our knowledge and ideas and beliefs depend upon two things, and two things only: sensation, and reflection upon what the senses tell us.' (p. 4732)

This, the author says, gives us the key to real education: if we want the best possible mind, we must do our best for the senses. This causes him to launch into a passage which is worth quoting in full, for it expresses well the general philosophy of the *Encyclopædia*:

> 'This means that we shall begin to care little about teaching facts and ideas, arithmetic, language and such things, to small children, and that we shall begin by saying to ourselves that our first duty is to the child's senses. These are the avenues of knowledge, and the mind is made out of them. It is therefore wicked folly to attempt to teach a child history or geography when it is half deaf for lack of attention to its throat and nose and ears, or half blind for lack of spectacles that are suited to its eyes…
>
> 'When we have the child before us with healthy senses, our next duty is to train it; it must be taught to see differences between things; it must learn to appreciate beauty of colour and form. We must take great care that the child sees beautiful things…
>
> 'Children should be trained to recognise the tone of different musical instruments, and to know when a piano is in or out of tune. They should learn to recognise the notes of birds and the other sounds of Nature… Such a child will be happier and healthier… The foundations of that child's mind have been rightly and solidly laid.' (p. 4733)

This leads into an article entitled **How to Remember** (pp. 4807–10). The process is said to involve three steps: an impression is made on the brain, we recognise what we remember, and we recall it.[5] Learning by heart is easier for young people; older people tend to lose short-term memory.

The author strongly criticises education methods based on learning by heart: 'No kind of learning by heart increases the brain's power of retaining things'. In fact:

> 'What we call education, which is sometimes just the opposite of real education, very often means that we injure the brain and spoil the memory at the very time that we think we are training it. School hours are often too long; no child should attend to one thing for so long as an hour... Light, and especially air, may be defective. Foul air means foul blood... and foul blood means that the brain also is being fouled and poisoned. Our great business, therefore, in taking care of our memories when we are young, is to lead healthy lives as much in the open air as possible...' (p. 4809)

In the next two articles, entitled **What happens when we think** (pp. 4939–44) and **How to think** (pp. 5025–28), emphasis is placed on 'association' of ideas and sensations, by likeness or by contrast. Great thinkers and artists are able to go on to create new concepts, works of art, music, etc. It is important to fill our minds with things worth having, and to avoid foolish talk and wicked things.

> 'There is no better treasure than a mind well filled with beautiful, true, and valuable memories of noble things seen, noble sounds heard, noble ideas, great poetry, recollections of friends, and so forth.' (p. 4941)

We must seek truth, which may not be what we want to believe. The intellect can be influenced by other parts of the mind: what we feel often decides what we think, and this can have unfortunate consequences.

> 'We want to win, for money or for glory or for spite; we are fighting another country, and we want to prove that we are right; or we are fighting for our class or our church against people who dress rather differently, or who arrange their service rather differently in their places of worship... We are driven by some interest which is not interest in truth, and that decides where we get to. This upsetting of the judgement by feeling ... is one of the most important facts in the life of mankind, and accounts for half the facts of human history.' (p. 5028)

Fortunately, there have been some men – the author cites Newton and Darwin – who are real lovers of truth, and they are the great thinkers of the world. [6]

---

[5] There is here a lengthy metaphysical discourse, which seems to have been influenced by the writings of Herbert Spencer, particularly his *Principles of Philosophy* of 1855. Spencer contended that the human intellect had slowly developed as a response to its physical environment.

[6] This is somewhat too favourable to Newton, who besides his great scientific contributions also devoted much of his time to alchemy. This fact was known before the date of the

Knowledge in itself does not make us wise or good; our emotions and instincts also decide our deeds. Fear is one of the great emotions: it may act by preventing action, and it has always been used by masters and governors of all kinds to control the people subject to them. Very important also is the fighting instinct, and the anger that goes with it; it is powerful among males, but occurs with females too, especially when they have young to protect. Indeed the paternal or maternal instinct is strong in humans, and leads to generosity, pity, unselfishness.

> 'What we need today … is men of good will; and the great business of real education and the real bringing up of children is to try to make them into men and women of good will. That is what we mean when we talk about training character, and the importance of character-making is that character, and not intellect, makes our conduct.' (p. 5132)

The last article in this series is entitled **Our Lives and the Nation** (pp. 5281-84). The author quotes Aristotle: 'Man is a social animal'. A nation is a whole, the 'body politic': it has men to guide it, soldiers to guard it, doctors and nurses to protect its health. All are dependent on each other. Rich men must not seize all the wealth. It is an injury to the social body to set religion against religion, or class against class, or school against school. Further, in some distant day:

> 'Men will learn that what is true of one nation is true also of the whole of the nations which we call mankind. They will learn that just as to oppose one part of the body against another is to injure it or to destroy it, just as strikes or labour wars, in setting one class against another, injure the social body, so wars between nations injure that mightiest body of all which we call humanity.' (p. 5284)

As has been pointed out, Dr. Saleeby, the author of these articles, was a prolific writer on a variety of scientific subjects. In this series on **LIFE** he has ranged over a wide area: on most topics he probably reflects contemporary knowledge quite accurately (a minor exception has been noted where he strays into the field of economics).

Sometimes verbose, but usually clear and interesting, he does not hesitate to give his opinions, so that these are not just science lessons but include practical advice and moral recommendations – with some of which we may not agree, but which undoubtedly reflect the views of the *Encyclopædia* contributors in general, and probably of most educated people of his era.

Dealing with anatomy, he is of course within his professional medical sphere; likewise in his recommendations on diet and other health matters. As we have seen, this advice covers a number of items: the importance of breathing through the nose, of chewing food properly, of fresh air in schools and factories, of not wearing tight clothes; he even has ideas as to how cows should be milked properly

---

Encyclopædia, but probably did not fit the desired image. See Michael White, *Isaac Newton – The Last Sorcerer* (London 1997).

(one wonders if many farm families received the *Encyclopædia*) and how to make one's own toothpaste!

It is interesting to find a thorough discussion of vegetarianism, with arguments on either side which remain basically valid today: his own conclusion is that children do not need meat.

His objections to tobacco are unsurprising, and his attack on alcohol abuse corresponds to the general line taken by the *Encyclopædia*. This is quite un-compromising: there is nowhere even any tolerance for the pleasure of drinking a good wine, but of course children would not have been expected to drink wine in any case.

Beyond such recommendations, one can glimpse features of the Edwardian age. The importance of fresh air in homes, schools and workplaces was probably not widely recognised; nor were the principles of good nutrition (but is this any better today?). He cites a study showing that alcohol was commonly given to small children: since this was one target of the 1908 Children Act (see Introduction) we can take it that the problem was real. We are also given a sordid image of small children being allowed to crawl around on pub floors, catching tuberculosis from men's habit of spitting.

His account, near the end of the series, of the workings of the mind, is relatively difficult to follow and has been only briefly summarised above. (This again raises the question of the target audience: certainly not under thirteen or so.) He appears to have been much influenced by Herbert Spencer.[7] As already pointed out, Freud's work was as yet barely known in Britain, and though the author stresses the role of emotions, there is no mention of the sub-conscious.

Dr. Saleeby's strong criticisms of current education are particularly interesting. Apart from stuffy class-rooms, he objects to long hours, too much learning by rote, and emphasis on dry facts rather than the appreciation of beauty. Like Arthur Mee and other contributors, he obviously felt that the *Encyclopædia*'s purpose was to remedy such omissions: hence his final recommendations on seeking truth, on character-building, on the individual's duty in society, and on tolerance for other classes, religions and countries.

In his next series on **THE EARTH**, we shall note that he avoids any suggestion that a scientific account of the nature of the universe and the origins of the earth may conflict with the belief in God as the Creator. The same applies here: his explanation of the origins of life and its development in scientific terms does not seem to leave much room for a divine purpose, but no such dilemma is apparent. Yet from his other works, it is fairly clear that Dr. Saleeby was not a religious believer.

It has been pointed out that Dr. Saleeby, at the time of the *Encyclopædia*, was well-known as an advocate of eugenics. On the whole, his ideas on this subject do not intrude too much upon his contributions here. In *Parenthood and Race Culture: An Outline of Eugenics* (published in 1909, i.e. during the work on the *Encyclopædia*), he had much more to say. He stressed the importance of 'selection for parenthood

---

[7] As previously noted, Spencer's *Principles of Psychology* was published in 1855.

as determining the nature, fate and worth of living races, which is Darwin's chief contribution to thought, and which finds in eugenics its supreme application.' This selection should be based upon 'the facts of heredity... Our end is a better race... The choice for Great Britain today is between national eugenics and the fate of all her Imperial predecessors from Babylon to Spain'.

In particular, parenthood by the 'unworthy' should be discouraged: this was aimed at those with congenital diseases and disabilities, but he did not indicate who should designate those concerned.

Women had a special role as future mothers, so their education was particularly important. They should be well educated to be good parents, but only up to a point: if they were too well educated they might not want to be mothers... Later, in *Woman and Womanhood* (1912), he objected to those who were 'deserting the ranks of motherhood and leaving the blood of inferior women to constitute half of all future generations'.

These ideas are linked to his concept of evolution, on which he is firmly Darwinian. However, like the authors of **NATURE**, he does not fully explain the principle of 'natural selection'. He too is probably hampered by the *Encyclopædia's* systematic avoidance of any mention of sex, no doubt considered unsuitable for young minds. Indeed, it is remarkable that this entire series on **LIFE** contains no explanation of the process of reproduction. (Contrast some current encyclopedias for children – see note at the end of this book – which do deal with this matter, some quite explicitly.)

It is also notable – this too is characteristic of the *Encyclopædia* – that although man is recognised to follow apes in the evolutionary ladder, it is not suggested that there is any direct link.

For Saleeby, mankind stands at the pinnacle of evolution, and the white race is the highest form of humanity. As elsewhere in the *Encyclopædia*, this racism is explicit, though slightly tempered by the recommendation that we must respect the 'lower' breeds. His insistence on the supposed superiority of the white race as compared to all others is supported by dubious 'craniometry'. Even though he tells his readers not to despise other peoples, such statements would have made a lasting impression on young minds, justifying the contemptuous treatment of 'natives' by so many colonialists.

For us, after the experience of Nazi racial policies, it is difficult to view eugenics dispassionately. And in its present-day form of genetic engineering, the topic remains highly controversial (see, for example, the current *Wikipedia* article on eugenics). Dr. Saleeby had good intentions, but – like many others of his time – he did not foresee the abuses to which eugenics could lead. Later he did break with the eugenic movement, and did not write on the subject after 1921.

WHAT THIS STORY TELLS US

WE have learned already that the earth is round like a ball; we learn now that the great earth-ball is always spinning. If you could throw a ball into the air which would spin round and round like a top, and travel through space without ever stopping, the ball would be doing what the earth is always doing. Nothing seems so still as the earth on which we stand, but that is because it moves so smoothly. The earth is really moving faster than the fastest train; but we cannot tell that it is moving because it moves so quietly and smoothly, and everything moves with it. It is this movement that makes day and night. The sun does not rise nor set; it is the earth passing in and out of the sunlight that makes day light and night dark.

THE EARTH IS ALWAYS MOVING

THE first thing that we are inclined to say when we are told the earth moves is that we do not feel the earth moving, but the answer to that is easy.

CONTINUED FROM PAGE 10

When you are in a train in a station, you sometimes cannot tell whether the train is moving or not, except, perhaps, by looking at another train standing at the other platform, and sometimes you think your train is moving, until you see that the platform is quite still. It was the moving of the other train that made you think *your* train was moving. So it proves nothing to say that we do not feel the earth moving with us. If you are travelling in a train, or on a boat, or in a balloon, or on this great earth of ours, you have only two ways of judging whether you are moving or not. One is by feeling the movement under you, and the other by noticing that things outside seem to be moving past you.

Now, certainly we cannot feel the earth move under us, but this is simply because the movement is so smooth. When you are inside a very big boat, you cannot tell whether the boat is moving if the sea is smooth. If you shut your eyes in a balloon on a calm day you cannot tell that it is moving—often you cannot tell even if your eyes are open. When we feel that a 'bus is moving under us, that is only because its movement is jerky. Every time the 'bus moves a little more slowly, our bodies go on moving forward at the old rate, and then are

slowed up with a jerk; then, when the 'bus goes on a little faster, our bodies are left behind a little, and then are jerked forward. So we know that the 'bus is taking us where we want to go.

The more smoothly the 'bus travels, the less can we feel its travelling. Now, of all the things that men can travel in, the balloon is said to be the smoothest, because when the air is quiet you cannot feel its motion at all. It is better than travelling in the best steamer, the newest electric train, or the finest motor-car. But really the smoothest thing to travel on is *the earth itself*, which we are all really travelling on all the time, no matter whether we are swimming or walking, or flying in a balloon. The best proof of the smoothness of the earth's motion is that no one has ever felt the earth moving. Sometimes a little bit of the outside of the earth moves by itself, and then people feel it. That is called an earthquake, and is quite different. No one has ever felt the movement of the earth as a whole.

What would happen if the earth suddenly stopped moving? If suddenly the earth *did* stop moving, as a 'bus pulls up sharp, or as you pull your arm up sharp when you throw a ball, what would happen to us? When a 'bus stops suddenly, all the passengers are jerked forwards. When you pull up your arm sharply to throw a ball, it is thrown forward ever so far. The earth is going so fast that, if it were suddenly to stop moving, all the loose

5. THE EARTH

This series, like the previous one on **LIFE**, was written by Dr. Saleeby: see the note about him at the beginning of that chapter. The title again reflects the general policy in the *Children's Encyclopædia* of avoiding – or at least postponing – words that might seem difficult to children. In fact, it deals with major fields of science: astronomy, chemistry, physics, geology, etc., without establishing firm barriers between them.

Each article is quite lengthy – typically 5–8 pages. The articles follow, on the whole, a coherent sequence, so with a few exceptions the same order can be adopted here.

The first article – **The Big Ball we live on** (pp. 5–10) – responds to the sense of wonder felt by any child looking at the skies, especially at night, or wondering about the movement of the sun and moon. It explains that the earth is not flat: that it is round – demonstrated by a charming illustration – and that it spins on its own axis daily, causing the alternation of day and night. It also moves around the sun in the course of each year. There is brief reference to Galileo (he gets fuller treatment later on).

The Sun and his Children (pp. 233–242) describes – with illustrations – the other planets: their size, and their distance from the sun. Eight planets were known, including the earth, the furthest from the sun being Neptune (Pluto was discovered in 1930, but astronomers have recently decided that it did not count as a 'planet'). Comets and shooting stars are explained. The real stars are not planets but other, distant suns far beyond our solar system.

How the Earth was made (pp. 393–7) suggests that the solar system was once a 'nebula', like others that can be observed, and that under the effect of gravitation (brief reference here to Newton) the matter it contained gradually clustered together to form the sun and the planets. So the earth would once have been 'a great glowing globe of gas' – it still retains a very hot core. At some point the moon would have been thrown off from the spinning earth. The concept of the 'big bang' as the origin of the universe was of course not yet known, but these are already challenging ideas, bound to provoke further reflection.

The Shaping of the Earth (pp. 475–483) carries the story further, describing how the 'crust' of the earth has been moulded over time. It emphasizes a shrinking of the earth as it grew cooler, causing folds which became valleys and mountains. (This theory was prevalent at the time: the phenomenon of 'continental drift' and of its consequences where continents collide – 'plate tectonics' – was not yet known.) The earth is not quite round, but flattened at the Poles, on account of the spinning of the earth. The tilting of the earth in its orbit around the sun explains the seasons.

The Fire that feeds itself (pp. 705–8) refers to the discovery of radium. This article seems somewhat out-of-place here, perhaps because it was prompted by current discoveries. It refers especially to findings of radium in many parts of the earth by an Englishman, R.J. Strutt; the pioneering role of M. and Mme. Curie is also recognised. Radium appears to be 'all the time making heat out of itself' so may be 'a means of making heat which will probably not be exhausted for ages'. It may even be responsible for keeping the earth warm, offsetting the general cooling process (a dubious proposition).

The dilemma as to how this property can be reconciled with the law that nothing can be made out of nothing is tackled in a much later article. There it is suggested that the heat emanating from it results from the breaking-down of its atoms, and predicts that:

> 'The time will come – perhaps not for hundreds of years – when mankind will be able to tap this energy inside the atom, and use it as a source of heat – to drive ships and to do work of every kind.' (p. 4323)

This article ends with a lyrical passage, written in the first person, about the power of the human mind. It is pointed out that no-one has yet reached the North or the South Pole, nor has climbed to the top of the highest mountains, so there is still much to be learned about the Earth.[1] However:

> 'I want you to distinguish between what man can do with his body, and what man can do with his mind... Every day the mind is teaching us more about the earth... Though it makes mistakes and cannot do all that we would like it to do, the mind is far more powerful, and its eyes can see what the bodily eyes have never seen... And though we die, the work of our minds, if it is good and real, does not die...

The earth is not flat like a table, but round like an orange. We know this by the way a ship comes into sight at sea. At first we see only smoke.

Then we see the top of the mast, as if the ship were climbing up the side of a hill.

Then the front appears, and we see the vessel rising higher and higher

HOW WE KNOW THE EARTH IS ROUND

---

[1] A later article (in Volume 7 – see under 'Countries') mentions that the American explorers Captain Peary and Dr. Cook had just claimed to have reached the North Pole: this was in April 1909. In fact this was not authenticated. Amundsen reached the South Pole in 1911. Hillary and Tenzing Norgay climbed Everest in 1953.

If the earth were flat we should see the whole of the ship at once, not the front of it first and the rest of it bit by bit.

But we do not see it that way. We see the ship rising as if it were sailing up the other side of a ball.

At last the ship is over the circle, sailing clear on the top of the ball.

HOW WE KNOW
THE EARTH IS ROUND

'Dead men and women have done most of the works by which we live now; and we, too, can help men and women who are yet unborn. Animals cannot tell what they have learnt to their children; we can. And so we learn the truth, and how to forget the untruth, and that is progress.' (p. 792)

One could hardly find a clearer expression of early twentieth-century optimism!

What the Earth is made of (pp. 793–5) returns to the main theme. It points out that matter consists of solids, liquids and gases. It stresses – a recurring theme – that 'nothing is made out of nothing, and nothing returns to nothing' (p. 794). Subsequent articles explain the nature of 'elements', such as carbon, consisting of atoms of one kind, and 'molecules', such as water (the formula H_2O is introduced), consisting of more than one element. This is in fact an introduction to basic chemistry; later on, the use and significance of equations is explained (e.g. $CaCO_3 = CaO + CO_2$), and there are explanations about the difference between acids and alkalies, organic and inorganic chemistry and so on.

But the impulse to point a moral is never far away: when the salt molecule is explained one finds the statement: 'Some of us think that the tax on salt in India is a cruel and wicked thing, since people must have salt or die' (p. 1389) – a point to be remembered when in due course we come to the articles dealing with Britain's imperial role in India. [2]

We find a reference to 'electrons' in the composition of atoms – said to be a discovery in the previous twelve years – and a discussion as to whether atoms can be divided; this question is taken up more fully later on. There is the provoking thought that there is as much room between electrons in the atom as between planets in the solar system; it is not yet known what force

the atom as between planets in the solar system; it is not yet known what force

---

[2] Gandhi's march to collect salt from the sea in protest against the tax occurred in 1930.

keeps the atoms together, though positive and negative electricity are thought to play a role (protons – in fact the negative charge – and neutrons are apparently not known). All this is 'the question of questions for this branch of science to-day'. (p. 1555)

In Volume 4 we return to astronomy, with **Worlds in the Skies** (pp. 1939–49). There is reference to ancient beliefs: alchemy and astrology are described as 'unreal science', contrasted with the discovery by Copernicus that the sun, not the earth, is the centre of the solar system.

This prompts a discussion of scientific method:

> 'First come the facts, and then comes the meaning of the facts... If you do
> not know what the facts mean, it is better to say so and to go on looking for
> more facts, rather than to pretend that you know what they mean.' (p. 1942)

Galileo, who invented the telescope, was persecuted and silenced by the Inquisition, being made to declare that his discoveries were false. Giordano Bruno realised that our sun is in fact a star, and that all the other stars are also suns.[3] He taught that

> 'these little points of light were suns, like our own, perhaps vastly bigger
> and more important, and that probably there were planets circling round
> them with living creatures, perhaps as intelligent as men, or even more
> intelligent than men, upon them'. (p. 1944)

The following articles go into more detail about the sun: its size, its great heat, sun-spots, how eclipses permit us to observe it. Then the moon is described, with illustrations to show what its surface is like.

The Wonder of Time and Tide (pp. 2279–83) explains the gravitational pull of the moon, and how tides are greatest 'spring tides' when sun and moon are pulling in the same direction. It is suggested that the action of the tides must slow down the spinning of the earth, so that the earth's day must very gradually become longer.

We come now to the first mention of the 'ether'.

> 'The planets and their moons, as they move, are moving through
> something. That something is not the air, for the air is the outer part of the
> planets or moons that have an air, or atmosphere. It is the ether. We are
> perfectly certain that the ether really exists, and we already are beginning
> to learn just a little about it.' (p. 2283)

This raises the question whether the ether must not slow down movements of bodies passing through it, even if just a little. In this case, the argument goes on, the solar system might some day become just 'one dead round ball'.

We return to firmer ground with **The Sun's Family of Worlds** (pp. 2423–9) which describes the planets in greater detail, and with **Comets, Meteors and Sky**

---

[3] A somewhat doubtful assertion. Giordano Bruno was a sixteenth-century philosopher who did indeed adopt the positions of Copernicus, but was not himself an astronomer. He was burnt at the stake for his 'heretical' views in 1600.

Dust (pp. 2495–2501). Some comets return to the neighbourhood of the sun only in thousands or hundreds of thousands of years: this is compared to the length of life of mankind upon the earth, which 'cannot yet be as much as 500,000 years'. (pp. 2498) [4]

In **The Stars as we see them** (pp. 2609–17) we learn about constellations, with maps of the stars at each quarter of the year. It is estimated that there are about 100 million stars. This article finishes with another provoking thought: 'Our universe of stars probably has a boundary; but there may be an infinite number of other universes in other parts of space'. (p. 2616)

The next article explains how 'spectrum analysis' can tell us the chemical composition of the stars – they contain elements found on earth, but in varying proportions – and also detect changes in a star's light, and thus indicate its motion. Recent discoveries by 'a famous German astronomer' and 'an English astronomer working at Greenwich' suggest that there may be 'two great drifts of stars, which are moving in opposite directions to each other' (p. 2718). The concepts of the 'big bang' and of the 'expanding universe' were still some half-century ahead.

The Making of other Worlds (pp. 2861–6) sets out current knowledge about nebulae. Once thought to consist just of clouds of rarefied matter, more powerful telescopes had shown some at least to be groups of very distant stars. But there are also real nebulae, consisting of gas and nothing more. Photographs of some spiral nebulae suggest that suns or stars are being formed in them.

There is proof that gravitation is at work among the stars: therefore there is the possibility of collision. In that case their motion would be transformed into heat, which if intense enough would convert all the matter of the stars into a gaseous form again: in other words, such a collision might create a nebula.

Then we encounter once more the question of the 'ether': this is

'the greatest and most urgent of the problems which the astronomy of the future has to solve. The ether … is not ordinary matter, but very different, and is believed to be absolutely everywhere. The vast 'empty' spaces between the stars are all completely filled by it. It is the medium which conveys their light from one to another across billions of miles, just as it conveys the light a few inches from this page to our eyes… It is the medium through which universal gravitation exerts its power'. (p. 2866)

In a later article (Volume 7), the question of the ether arises once again in connection with heat. It is shown, correctly, that heat in a body arises from atoms in motion, and this motion is said to be transmitted, like light and heat, in the form

---

[4] As already pointed out (see footnote in Chapter 3), it is now reckoned that the earliest specimen of *Homo* emerged some three million years ago, *Homo sapiens* only about 150,000 years ago. Dr. Saleeby is within this wide bracket. At any rate, his estimate reflects a scientific approach, conscious of the vastness of time, although the author does not try to discuss how this can be reconciled with Bible-based calculations.

of waves. But how then does the heat of the sun reach us across space? The author admits that:

> 'as yet we know very little about the ether ... but all over the world astronomers, ... students of light and electricity and chemistry are working at the riddle of the ether... There is reason to hope that ... its solution will be the deepest scientific discovery of all time'. (p. 2866)

The next series of articles returns to Earth with items on geology and natural geography. There is further explanation of the Earth's crust, including the fossils which archaeologists can discover and which reveal successive stages of living creatures. It is pointed out that Earth's face has altered over time, in particular with changing sea levels. It is suggested that the Earth is becoming drier, with forests turning to desert – for example in Palestine even since Old Testament times. This is attributed to a loss of molecules of water thrown out of the Earth's atmosphere by the spinning of the Earth, and to loss of water through cracks in the Earth's surface into its interior – both questionable arguments. But there is also recognition of Man's role in deforestation.

It is pointed out in this connection that the growing demand for rubber (for car tyres – artificial rubber did not then exist) leads to exploitation, mentioning in particular the Congo forest, with disastrous effects on 'the lower races of men'. There is a revealing sentence:

> 'Even if we admit that they are lower than we are – and that is true in some ways – yet they are deeply interesting, and have many lessons to teach us.' (p. 3136)

Animals such as the chimpanzee and the gorilla, recently 'rediscovered', are also disappearing. In fact, 'our blind and wasteful ways are working havoc on almost every part of the earth'.

The Crust of a Fiery Furnace (pp. 3227–32) repeats the suggestion already made that mountains result from the crumpling of the earth's crust as it cooled and shrank, but it also discusses the role of glaciers during the Ice Age. There are dramatic drawings of volcanoes and earthquakes (reproduced): these, it is said, are phenomena not yet well understood.

The Soil and its Uses (pp. 3339–44) explains in particular the nutrients required by plants. It observes that cultivation to feed a growing population will eventually exhaust the soil, unless these nutrients are replenished: there is brief mention of the use of chemicals such as nitrates, carbonates and salts of ammonia, but it suggested that hope for the future lies in feeding the soil with living microbes. However, we would be wrong to think that when rich soils are exhausted, or coal is exhausted, science will supply something else. 'Science can do wonderful things, but it cannot make something out of nothing.' We are in fact using up the sunlight of the past, and 'we cannot borrow the sunlight of the future.' (p. 3344)

How Movement changes Matter (pp. 3465–70) is a particularly important piece, and one that seems remarkably advanced for a *Children's Encyclopædia*. It explains that physics means the study of motion, heat, light, sound and electricity. 'Motion' is not a 'thing', but it is real:

THE SPLITTING OF THE EARTH'S CRUST

The interior of the earth is like a huge furnace, and we all live and walk upon the crust that is stretched over it. As the molten matter inside the earth gets cooler, the crust shrinks and crumples up, just as the peel of an orange shrivels when the orange gets dry. By this wrinkling the mountain ranges are formed, as shown here.

We usually think of the ground as being the one solid and firm thing that we know, until some terrible earthquake, like that at San Francisco or Messina, reminds us that even the ground is not stable. When the earth's crust at any point wrinkles so much that it is unable to bear the strain longer, the rocks split, as shown here, and the shock sends a shiver through the earth for hundreds of miles, causing buildings to shatter and fall.

3230

'We are beginning to believe that it is more real than matter, and that matter is really a state of motion of something that we call the ether.' (p. 3465)

Light and radiant heat are states of motion of the ether (we have already discussed the problem of what is meant by the 'ether', but this does not fundamentally undermine the argument here.) An object in motion acquires new properties: a candle can be fired through a wooden panel without itself being damaged; a smoke ring resists attempts to destroy it, and is an example of a 'vortex ring'.

Further, it is pointed out that we only know the motion of a thing by comparing it with something else: the only motion we can understand is *relative* motion.

All this is difficult enough, but the text goes further.

'When we study the universe as a whole, and find things in motion about us, the first question we are bound to ask is: Where does this power come from? The only answer to this question is that it comes from the great Cause and Author of all things. He is the first and ultimate cause of all motion.' (p. 3469)

The following article continues the study of motion. We hear about Kepler's laws of planetary motion. Newton's laws of inertia have already been mentioned: now the author goes into some detail about his law of gravitation; but it is pointed out that we still know no more of the causes of gravitation than he did. Galileo's pendulum is also explained, and this leads to the point that perpetual motion is impossible.

How Things are Measured (pp. 3670–74) provides a relief from theory (probably welcome to young readers). As the length of the day and night is constant, it can be divided into hours, minutes and seconds, and fortunately those measures are accepted all over the world. However, it is pointed out that the unit of time is about the only thing that everyone does agree on: the author observes that English measures of weight and distance are needlessly complicated and points out – well ahead of his time – the advantages of the metric system. He suggests, slightly optimistically, that 'Most of the children who read this will probably live to see this change made'. (p. 3670)

There follow explanations of the concept of equilibrium, which may be stable or unstable; of specific gravity; and of the centre of gravity of an object (hence the need for ballast in a ship's bottom).

However, we soon return to metaphysical speculation.

'If gravity tends to pull every particle of matter in the universe towards every other particle, why does not all the matter in the universe get collected into one great ball?' (p. 3840)

Two reasons are suggested (it has already been pointed out that the theory of the expanding universe had not yet been advanced):

– either that the time has not yet come – but that implies a beginning and an end, and a universe that is running down;

– or that other forces are at work, and here the author refers to the discovery of 'radiation pressure'. [5]

The latter:

> 'helps to give us right ideas of the universe itself. It is the true notion, for which there is now the support of science as well as of pure reason: that the universe has neither beginning nor ending, but is an eternal thing, the eternal revelation of the Eternal God, who sustains it "from everlasting to everlasting".'

Once again, Dr. Saleeby – faced with phenomena to which science has no answers, departs from his own principles of scientific method and resorts – literally – to a *deus ex machina*. One senses that the general optimism of the time cannot bear the thought of an end to the universe, however remote, and seizes upon a theory which both avoids this conclusion and is consistent with the belief in a benevolent God.

With **The Pressure of the Air** (pp. 3941–8) we return to more practical matters, as the working of a barometer is explained. Low pressure in a particular area means that winds will rush in, possibly bearing rain. We also hear how pumps work, with a piston to 'suck up' the liquid: in fact, it is atmospheric pressure which is pushing into the pump from outside. This is the scientific basis for the expression 'Nature abhors a vacuum'.

We next learn about **Hot Things and Cold Things** (pp. 4047–52), which raises the question: what is heat? As already mentioned, the explanation is that heat arises from atoms in motion. There is discussion of 'absolute cold', at minus 273°C. The difference between convection of heat in liquids and gases and conduction along an object such as a poker is pointed out.

How Heat works for Us (pp. 4365–71) refers to machines such as steam engines. This leads into a discussion of thermodynamics; it is pointed out that there is always some apparent loss of energy between the energy supplied to a machine and that obtained from it, so men are constantly working to improve the efficiency of engines.

This dissipation of energy, it is suggested, might mean that

> 'the solar system and the whole universe must, at last, reach a stage in which all the other forms of energy have been degraded and dissipated into heat, and that heat will be spread equally through all the matter of the universe. That would be the end of history.' (p. 4368)

But once again the optimistic view takes over, with a reference to Herbert Spencer:

---

[5] Electromagnetic radiation does indeed exert pressure on any surface exposed to it. Dr. Saleeby is probably referring to experiments made by Lebedev in 1900 and Nichols and Hull in 1901 – cf. *Wikipedia* article on the subject. But it is a feeble force, quite inadequate as a counter to gravity, though it has been proposed as a means of propulsion for spacecraft.

'who stood alone among the great thinkers of the nineteenth century in declining to accept the doctrine of the dissipation of energy...; he declared that there must be other processes going on...[6] Steadily, during the last ten years... we are beginning to discover the processes which act in the other direction, and which will lead us to the belief... that the universe is from everlasting to everlasting.' (p. 4370)

This time, no *Deus ex machina* is invoked.

We move on to **The Waves of Sound** (pp. 4581–4). Unlike light and radiant heat, sound is a wave motion in a material medium, e.g. air, water or solids: it is not conveyed by the 'ether', for where there is no matter – as in a vacuum – no sound passes. (This seems to raise a conceptual problem which is not tackled here.) It is observed that music is pleasant to hear because the sound waves are regular (this is of course before the age of atonal music...). The loudness of sound depends on the amplitude of the waves, and on the pitch – the higher the note, the more easily it is perceived by the human ear.

In **Wonderful, Wonderful Music** (pp. 4859–64) the difference between melody and harmony is pointed out. Here and in the following article, there is remarkably clear exposition of the relations between notes in the scale, of chords, of overtones, of the difference in sound produced by bowing or plucking the strings of a violin. [7]

What Light is made of (pp. 5039–44) explains that the light we see is not all the light, but just one form of what is better called 'radiant energy', and this is made of waves in the 'ether': the laws of radiant heat and of light are therefore the same. Spectrum analysis can divide up the waves, and can show the materials in the source of light. Light passing through crystals can be polarised: i.e. most of the light is kept back and only rays moving in a certain direction are allowed to move on. Different wave-lengths correspond to different colours in the spectrum. There is mention of X-rays – a recent discovery – and of their use to doctors: the risks of overuse were apparently not yet known.

Finally we come to electricity and magnetism – developments 'within the last two generations' and still one of 'Nature's great mysteries', but discoveries which have led to such uses as the electric bell, electric light, the telegraph and the telephone; also, 'with or without wires, the machines which combine the properties of electricity and magnetism, turning motion into electricity or electricity into motion'. (p. 5253)

How these machines work is not explained here. Instead, after a brief explanation of magnets and their use in compasses, the author recalls the discovery

---

[6] Herbert Spencer (1820-1903) – already cited above – was mainly a philosopher and sociologist, and one of the principal proponents of evolutionary theory (he invented the phrase 'survival of the fittest', which was taken up by Darwin). However, he was not primarily a scientist, so is hardly an authority in the present context.

[7] I have personally been a keen amateur musician for most of my life, but I still learnt useful points from these articles.

of electrons within the atom and speculates, rather vaguely, on some of the implications: should we think of the atom rather as we think of the solar system, with the positive energy compared to the sun and the negative electricity compared to the planets? – and is gravitation perhaps also some form of electrical or magnetic attraction?

His final thought – which we might feel belongs rather to the domain of science-fiction, is that mankind might one day learn to control and use the force of gravitation...

Oddly perhaps to our minds, this **STORY OF THE EARTH** concludes with a poem by Wordsworth. It is a good poem, in line with the spirit of philosophical inquiry which permeates these articles, hence well worth reproducing:

> *'...For I have learned*
> *To look on Nature; not as in the hour*
> *Of thoughtless youth; but hearing oftentimes*
> *The still, sad music of humanity,*
> *Not harsh nor grating, though of ample power*
> *To chasten and subdue. And I have felt*
> *A presence that disturbs me with the joy*
> *Of elevated thoughts; a sense sublime*
> *Of something far more deeply interfused,*
> *Whose dwelling is the light of setting suns,*
> *And the round ocean, and the living air,*
> *And the blue sky, and in the mind of man :*
> *A motion and a spirit, that impels*
> *All thinking things, all objects of all thought,*
> *And rolls through all things.'*

Throughout this series of articles by Dr. Saleeby, the explanations are admirably clear, even when quite difficult topics are dealt with. It is in fact difficult to imagine that these articles – especially the later ones – were aimed at the 'little children' who seem to have been Arthur Mee's target: they correspond rather to secondary-school level, perhaps to a 15–16 year age-group. Indeed, and unlike some of the other contents of the *Encyclopædia*, Dr. Saleeby does not 'talk down' to his readers but treats them as intelligent and attentive students.

Taken as a whole, this section amounts to a comprehensive account of scientific knowledge at the time of writing. Some parts refer to recent discoveries and on-going research. With some exceptions, which have been pointed out where possible, the information remains mostly valid today.

A major exception relates to the theory of the 'ether'. Some explanation was needed as to how light and heat can pass through apparently empty space, not to mention gravity which raises still more complex issues. Perhaps the author should not have been quite so affirmative about the nature of this mysterious substance: in so doing, he departs from the principles of scientific study which he himself has cited. His certainty reflects what was still the mainstream view: in a universe governed by mechanical laws, the transmission of 'waves' (e.g. heat and light) required some kind of medium.

But in scientific circles, this concept had already been put in question in the late nineteenth century by experiments into the speed of light, and especially by Einstein's first theory of relativity in 1906. Einstein is nowhere mentioned in the *Children's Encyclopædia* – perhaps justifiably since his theory was still very recent and far from gaining general acceptance; moreover, this is very advanced stuff even for adults. This concept of the ether is one issue where the science taught in the *Children's Encyclopædia* differs from present-day thinking. [8]

Another issue concerns the nature and origins of the universe. Not that the explanations here are wrong: but the progress of astronomy has pushed our knowledge so much further out into space and back in time. The Edwardians could not have developed the theory of the 'Big Bang' and the expanding universe.

At such points where science reaches its limits, we find a *deus ex machina* explanation, though couched in vague terms. It is clear from other writings by Dr. Saleeby that he was not a religious man in the conventional sense, but here he is not prepared to challenge church dogma. The conflict between science and religion certainly existed at the time of the *Encyclopædia*; but the young reader could not guess it from this text (nor from any other section of the work). It is however fair to point out that science today, despite having got as far as the 'Big Bang', is still searching for an ultimate cause, though most scientists would not express this in terms of a personal deity.

It is interesting to note the prediction of atomic power. This has been fulfilled much sooner than the author expected; he did not foresee the destructive powers that this would unleash, which we now know only too well. [9]

Since Dr. Saleeby was also responsible for the articles on **LIFE**, he was a particularly important contributor to the *Encyclopædia*. As he trained and practiced as a doctor of medicine, the subject-matter of this series on **THE EARTH** – including in particular geology, astronomy, etc. – seems somewhat outside his field of competence, and it was not one which he appears to have tackled elsewhere. Nevertheless, he had a gift of clear exposition, and an energetic mind which he could apparently turn to whatever task was on hand. It is also a commentary on the time that one person could be regarded as an expert on many fields.

---

[8] Einstein always contested strongly the notion that 'ether' had any material content capable of transmitting motion. It has taken until nearly the twenty-first century to approach an explanation derived from 'quantum theory' – unfortunately so sophisticated that few of us can understand it, despite the efforts of Stephen Hawking in *A Brief History of Time* (1998).

[9] I remember clearly in 1945 hearing the radio announcement that an atomic bomb had been exploded over Hiroshima: my reaction, perhaps remembering the prediction in the *Children's Encyclopædia*, was 'They've done it!'. My father, who had seen enough destruction on the Western Front in the First World War, just looked gloomy…

COUNTRIES AND THEIR FLAGS

In the series on **FAMILIAR THINGS** there is an interesting article on **Flags of all Nations**, of which sixty-three were counted. As each flag was shown on top of a little map of the country, this is quite a comprehensive geography lesson, and the list of countries is also for us a lesson in history.

The illustrations occupied four pages (pp. 1639–44): here, only flags which are no longer to be seen or where the geography of the country has changed have been reproduced.

Only major colonies were included, which means that very few countries were shown in Africa, a continent then mostly divided up between the European states.

It is to be noted that:

British India included Burma (and of course what are now Pakistan and Bangladesh) and reached 'Siam' (Thailand).

No other country in Indo-China appeared, as this area belonged to France. Likewise, what is now Indonesia was mostly a Dutch colony.

South Africa consisted of the Cape Colony and 'British South Africa'.

Germany extended eastwards to meet Russia, and the German Imperial Standard was illustrated, with the Prussian eagle.

The flag of the **Russian Empire** was a blue cross of St. Andrew, as the country's patron saint. The Baltic countries and Finland were contained within the Russian Empire.

The **Austro-Hungarian Empire** covered what later became Czechoslovakia, and to the south Slovenia, Croatia and Bosnia-Herzegovina.

Poland did not appear: it had been divided between Russia, Germany and the Austro-Hungarian Empire.

Servia (*sic*) and **Montenegro** were separate countries, on the borders of the Austro-Hungarian Empire, as were **Romania** and **Bulgaria**.

Crete, the last Greek territory to throw off the Turkish yoke, was enjoying a brief period of independence.

Turkey had lost most of its Balkan possessions but retained Albania, Macedonia and Thrace, and of course Constantinople (Istanbul); its other possessions extended down the Red Sea and reached the Persian Gulf, including Mesopotamia; Iraq did not exist.

The **Chinese** flag was a dragon on a yellow background.

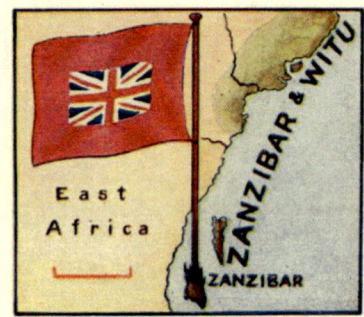

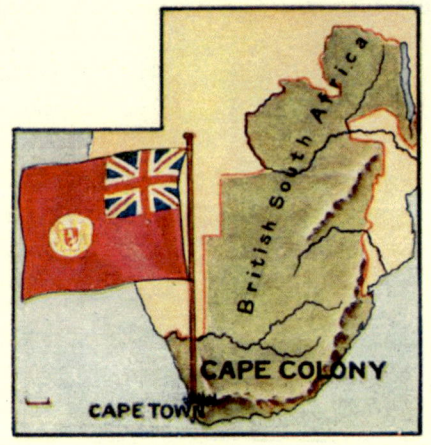

THE STORY OF THE WORLD

WHEN we are grown up and old enough to cross the sea, the greatest wonder that will come to us will be the great wonder of countries. Once upon a time men and women lived nowhere in particular, but spent their lives in wandering from place to place. So they wandered all over the world, some here, some there, till they settled down and made homes. Through all the years these homes have been growing into great countries, and nothing is so wonderful as to travel in ships and trains and see the places where other people live, with the glorious monuments that seem almost to speak to us of the way in which, through all the ages, men have lived and toiled and suffered and died to make the world a beautiful place. We shall read here the story of what the world is, and what the world has been, and we begin with a little island, the happiest little country in the world—the land in which we live.

THE LAND WE LIVE IN

By FRANCES EPPS

IF you ask a very little girl where she lives, the happy answer will come quite readily, "With father and mother," or, "In our home."

She feels satisfied that there is no more to say, because she does not yet know that the four walls which shut her in so safely with her loved ones stand in a beautiful and interesting homeland, which lies on the outside of a great, wonderful ball, rolling on always through space round and round the sun.

This knowledge must come to her as she grows older, and learns to notice, to think, to ask questions, and to enjoy pictures and stories. Little by little the veil which hid all but home from her baby eyes gradually becomes thinner, and at last fades away as she realises that there is space and life and stir all round her home. Later comes the keen longing to see clearly into the near and far distance, and to find out what is there and who is there. Day by day her thoughts widen, and her mind dwells upon what is beyond.

A journey to the seaside will show us that there are other fields and woods besides those near home which we know so well, other towns besides the town in which we live, and that everywhere there are yet more and more people living and working. When we find ourselves in the fresh, salt air of the seaside, we shall see that the land on which we walk about, with its trees, its fields and towns, does not stretch away and away for ever, but that the sea comes flowing up in little white waves to meet it. And then for some happy weeks we watch the sea and the curling waves, the golden sunbeams dancing on the water, the boats with their sails, and the smoke of the steamers, and we ask questions and try to answer them all day long. Why does the sea look green, or blue, or grey? Is it the paint off the boats? Why is there sometimes plenty of sand to play on, and sometimes no sand at all? How soon does it get deep, and how deep? What is there on the other side? How far could we walk on and on along the sand?

At last someone who knows the shapes by heart says: "Let us make a model in the sand, the shape of the country we live in—our homeland —and find out what we can from it." Stones and seaweed, and thick, damp sand, make a firm foundation, and then we cut out the shape of the island of Great Britain.

When the tide comes up we are delighted for the sea to surround it entirely, and with a stick we point out that there is shore and sea all round the edge of our island home. Day by day we make fresh and better models,

6. ALL COUNTRIES

The author of the articles under this heading was **Frances Epps**. There is little information about her: she does not appear in the *Dictionary of National Biography*, nor is she mentioned in Hammerton's biography of Arthur Mee. From bibliographical sources, it appears that she was a contributor to *Short Tales for Little Folk*, published in 1889 by the Society for Promoting Christian Knowledge; in 1906 she wrote for the *Parents Review* (a fortnightly aimed at teachers and parents, definitely not children) pieces entitled 'Songs for the Nursery' and 'Nursery Needlework'.

More substantially, and with greater relevance to the present work, she also wrote for this *Review* between 1906 and 1908 a series entitled 'The British Museum for Young People' (published in book form in 1914): this described what could be seen in the British Museum on Roman Britain, ancient Greece, Egypt, Babylonia and Assyria. It seems likely that this was the basis upon which Arthur Mee asked her to contribute to the *Encyclopædia*.

As the initial page explains, the articles in this section tell the story of 'what the world is, and what the world has been'. Many of these items are of great interest, as they reveal a world-view so significantly different from that which we have now, nearly a century later. Two world wars have changed the map of Europe and shifted the balance of power; and with the end of empires since the Second World War, many new independent nations have emerged. (See also the flags and maps reproduced on the previous pages.)

Great Britain

The first ten articles are about Great Britain itself, or more precisely, since Ireland is included, the 'British Isles'. The tone is set from the start: this is 'the happiest little country in the world – the land in which we live'.

In the first article (pp. 63–70), the geography is described as if seen by children travelling in a balloon over the length and breadth of the Isles. The travellers pass over London, with its thousands of chimneys, its busy docks and its big river ('What a pity it is so dirty'); over green country and farms; over the Midland cities and their factories with more chimneys pouring out black smoke; over the coal-mines; into Scotland, and over the River Clyde with the hammering of metal in the ship-building yards; then over the Highlands with their mountains and 'lakes' (no concession here to the Scottish 'loch').

The journey continues over the north of Ireland, with more ship-building at Belfast; then we see:

> 'the dark bogs and great lakes, bright green meadows, and low hills of the centre, to the grand and jagged mountain wall which lies round about it'. (p. 166)

Back over the 'beautiful, restful mountains of Wales' to the West Country, where all is 'peaceful and placid' and

> 'the pretty brown-sailed fishing boats move gently and slowly into the quiet harbours with their silvery loads... How blue is the sea, and how blue is the sky!' (p. 67)

Since it is unlikely that the author ever did travel in a balloon around the country, this is a vivid description – a far better introduction to geography than any I remember from my own school-days.

The next two articles (pp. 183–190 and 261–270) describe in greater detail the activities of the various regions: farming, fishing, the cotton factories of Liverpool and Manchester; the woollen industry of Yorkshire; linen manufacture in Belfast; the coal-mines and iron furnaces of the Black Country; the steel industry of Sheffield. A map shows many other, more localised industries: tin mining in Cornwall, glove-making in Yeovil; carpets in Kidderminster; lace in Nottingham; tweeds in Dumfries; paper in Edinburgh; and much more besides. The vital role of the extensive railway network in transporting goods around the country is underlined.

Again the author is eloquent:

> 'The labourer must till the earth to give us food; the miner must go down into the earth to fetch us coal, the fisherman must go to sea to bring us fish; the builder must put up houses for us to live in; the postman must carry our letters; the clerk must keep our books; the policeman must keep our streets in order. And so, day by day, the great work of the country is carried on, each man doing his share in helping to make his own life happy and the nation prosperous.' (p. 261)

This is a very utopian view of working life – confirmed by a large colour illustration showing robust workers – which many workers would certainly not have shared. There is a brief but suggestive mention of the 'pale-faced' girls in the cotton mills; otherwise there is no recognition of the arduous working conditions in many of the activities described, nor of squalid living conditions in the industrial cities. Clearly, neither the author nor the intended readers belonged to the working classes, and the author did not think it necessary to write about them.

IF WE COULD SEE IT ALL AT ONCE FROM A GREAT HEIGHT
very clearly what England is like, and what it would look like if we could see it all at once, from a balloon

F   69

THE DAILY ARMY OF WORKERS ALL OVER OUR LAND

Every morning, if some fairy's wand could give us power to see our country at a glance, we should see these workers setting out from their homes to do the work described in the CHILD'S BOOK OF COUNTRIES on page 25).

FACE PAGE 267

The next seven articles cover British history (in fact, primarily English history). They are written as a story, and are indeed far more readable than school textbooks would have been at the time (in my own school-days, three decades later, history textbooks were desperately dull!). Only the most important dates are mentioned: these articles are meant to be read, not learned. [1]

After brief mention of 'prehistoric' times, the four centuries of Roman occupation are seen as having had mainly a civilising influence: Julius Caesar and subsequent emperors are referred to as 'the great Roman soldiers who brought the light to England'.

> 'Sometime, perhaps in the third century, Romans, as well as Britons, began to give up worshipping the gods of their fathers, and listened to the preaching of Christians; so there presently arose British churches and bishops. The country improved in many ways – more corn was grown, trade increased, and it seemed that Roman law and order, and the liking for fine and comfortable lives, had all come to stay.' (p. 352)

However, as the Roman empire grew weaker, the 'wild Picts and Scots' and especially the 'sea-rovers' from across the North Sea gradually forced the Romans to withdraw. 'The light shed over Britain by the presence of the civilised Romans went out.'

We are told about King Alfred's resistance, and of course hear the legend about him 'burning the cakes'. Eventually, Canute, who already ruled Denmark and Norway, added England to his empire: but 'Canute was a good king in the end'. And these newcomers were the forefathers of our race:

> 'Many of us are as fair-haired and blue-eyed as they were; we love the sea and adventure... Half the words in our language – all the everyday words – come from their speech... Most of our laws and customs have grown from those they brought with them, together with the passionate love of freedom which we inherit from their old homes across the North Sea.' (p. 516)

Then comes the invasion by the Normans under William the Conqueror: it is recognised that they too left their mark on England and that their influence remains, especially in the language and in the abbeys and cathedrals. But as time went on, there was fighting for the crown and great insecurity. Eventually King John ('a bad king') was forced by the barons to sign 'Magna Carta' in which he 'promised certain rights to the people, so that they might live in safety under good government' (p. 576) – a somewhat generous interpretation since the charter was more obviously in the interests of the barons than that of the common people.

---

[1] The author would certainly have known *Our Island Story*, written by Henrietta Marshall and first published in 1905 (it has been republished in 2005). This, as its Preface indicated, was 'not a history lesson, but a story-book'. So its treatment of historical events was in some ways similar to that of the *Encyclopædia*. But its approach is much simpler, even simplistic; it no doubt helped to provoke the parody *1066 and All That* by Sellars and Yeatman in 1931.

It is unnecessary to recount here all the following articles, which cover England's history through successive dynasties. There is a tendency to concentrate on the doings of kings (and queens) and to classify them as 'good' or 'bad'. As regards most of the Plantagenets, 'their first care was not the welfare of the people'. Some of the Tudors were 'still tyrant kings'; Henry VIII swept away the old freedom of the country, abolished the monasteries which had been so useful for their scholarship and help to travellers, beheaded a considerable number of people and of course got through several wives, separating the Church of England from Rome in the process.

Elizabeth is noted particularly for her great speech at Tilbury encouraging her troops to repel the Spanish invaders, should they manage to land; but she also had Mary Queen of Scots beheaded. Among the Stuarts, Charles I in particular is reproached for believing, like his father James I, that 'kings can do no wrong' ('the divine right of kings'). Cromwell gets praise for his role in overthrowing the king; but on the whole the Puritans were 'overbearing and disagreeable'. Charles II had a 'bad reign' and James II was 'a bad and useless king'.

Those who have read *1066 and All That* by Sellars and Yeatman will inevitably be reminded of that parody of historical teaching – unfairly of course, since it was published in 1931.[2] The author of these *Encyclopædia* articles, in line with its characteristic moral approach, is determined to make clear the duties of monarchs. (Not, as we have seen in the Introduction, that there was anything to be feared from the amiable Edward VII – the main difficulty was in getting him to attend to his kingly duties).

The last article on English history is entitled **The End of a Long Struggle** (pp. 1007–14). After discussing the Napoleonic Wars, the story comes to the long reign of Queen Victoria: a reign 'full of great and stirring events for our country, and her reign was not only the longest, but the most prosperous reign in the history of our land.'

There were 'things we have grown ashamed of and swept away', including slavery, but also 'bad and unhealthy houses' and 'paying people too little for their work, making them work too long, and in other ways oppressing the poor and the weak' (this corrects to some extent the impression of indifference referred to above, but did the author imagine that this task had been completed?).

Further,

> 'We have seen all through our country's story the struggle it has been to prevent the kings trying to rule as they pleased, and the hard fight that Parliament has had to keep its rights… Step by step, more and more people have gained the right to share the government, and slowly great

---

[2] E.g.: 'Canute began by being a Bad King on the advice of his Courtiers, who informed him (owing to a misunderstanding of the *Rule Britannia*) that the King of England was entitled to sit on the sea without getting wet.' This particular fable (the king ordering the tide to turn back) is not mentioned in the *Encyclopædia*.

rights have been won, the right to think and worship as we please, to speak at public meetings, to write in newspapers'. (p. 1014)

And finally: 'The times in which we live are the happiest times that have been in England since the Romans brought civilisation to our shores, and it lies with us to make our country happier still for those who are to come.'

There is a religious moral too, with practical consequences:

'Nearly two thousand years ago the great Master and Teacher sent forth a message to all times and all countries. That message reached our islands some five centuries later... We call this message the Golden Rule: "Do unto others as you would that they should do unto you". It matters more than anything else in the world that people should understand and act upon this rule, for our country's story is not finished...

If our Great Britain is to rise and grow to still further heights of power, it will not be by adding more colonies, by getting more trade, more population, more riches, but by the keeping of the Golden Rule.'

It has already been pointed out that the writers of the *Encyclopædia* tend to say 'England' when they probably mean Great Britain. Here, in the articles on geography, there is brief but adequate treatment of Wales, Scotland and Ireland. In the items on history, after the mention of the 'wild Picts' on the far side of Hadrian's Wall, Scotland barely appears until we come to the Union of the Crowns under James VI of Scotland, James I of England.[3] After the eviction of the Stuarts, there is brief reference to the 'Old Pretender' (who would have been James III) and to the 'Young Pretender' – Bonnie Prince Charlie. But there is no mention of the latter's attempted rebellion in 1745 nor of the crushing defeat of the Highlanders at Culloden in 1745 – events which have shaped so much of Scottish folk-lore.

The union of the Parliaments (in 1707 – the date is not mentioned) does get a couple of paragraphs. This was 'to the great gain of both countries... The English gained much from the friendship and help of the Scotch, and the Scotch had better chances to enlarge their trade and get their country into good order.' (p. 899) [4]

---

[3] There is however an article on the kings and queens of Scotland in the section on **MEN AND WOMEN**. It is one of the few technical shortcomings of the *Children's Encyclopædia* that it does not have cross-references, which would of course have raised practical problems since the work initially appeared in instalments.

[4] At the time, the union was by no means so popular in Scotland. Writing later, Sir Walter Scott summed up the attitude of the Scottish 'man in the street' at the time in the words of one of his characters: *'I ken, when we had a king, and a chancellor, and parliament - men o' our ain, we could aye peeble them wi' stones when they werena gude bairns - But naebody's nails can reach the length o' Lunnon'.* This sounds much like later attitudes to regulations from 'Brussels', though the Scots seem to object less to this than to rule by Westminster. The Scottish Parliament was not 'reconvened' until 1999.

When these articles were being written, Scottish nationalism was not yet a significant issue. 'Home Rule' for Ireland certainly was, and one would expect the *Encyclopædia* to give its readers some understanding of the basic causes. It is pointed out in one of the articles on geography that:

> 'in many parts of Ireland, especially towards the west, there is much stony and poor ground, where it is very difficulty to grown anything, even enough potatoes and oats for the poor Irish peasants to live upon.' (p. 183)

As regards Ireland's history under British rule, Cromwell's persecution gets mentioned. It is also said – not mentioning Ireland specifically nor explaining the reasons – that at the time of George IV

> 'thousands of men were now thrown out of employment, and good openings were found for many to emigrate and make new homes in Australia and Cape Colony.' (p. 1004)

This is hardly how one would describe the forced mass emigration of Irish peasant families, mainly to America, during and after the Great Famine starting in 1745. The writer does say:

> 'The ill-feeling between Catholics and Protestants lived on in Ireland, and was the cause of much misery. By far the greater number of people in Ireland clung to the old faith, and they were bitterly persecuted by the Protestants, who made and enforced the laws. These laws were often most unjust.' (p. 1009)

There is no explicit mention of exploitation by English landlords, often absentees who left their estates to be run by unscrupulous managers.

At the beginning of the nineteenth century,

> 'There suddenly came a time when the Irish were listened to, and many demands were granted, especially that its parliament should be quite independent of that of England. Unhappily, the Irish now quarrelled among themselves, and a great English Minister, Pitt, carried an Act of Union, whereby the Irish Parliament ceased to exist, and Ireland sent over members to the British Parliament to represent this wishes of its people.' (p. 1010)

Coming to the contemporary period:

> 'Many Irish people are still anxious to have their own Parliament again, in Dublin, instead of sending men to sit at Westminster. These, and the English who agree with them, are called Home Rulers.' (p. 1010)

A few years later Ireland erupted in conflict which led to the creation of the Irish Free State, Ulster remaining within the United Kingdom.

The British Empire

The introduction to the next series of articles emphasises the vastness of the Empire, 'on which the sun never sets': a world map shows British flags on every continent. 'One-fifth of the earth and one-fifth of its peoples live under the British flag'.

The first article (pp. 1111–17) gives a brief account of the various ways in which the colonies were acquired. It deals especially with North America, explaining the early settlements by British, French and Dutchmen, and how war with France ended with Britain gaining possession of the whole of Canada.

The USA came into existence because of 'the stupidity of the rulers at home'. In South Africa, the Dutch were there before the British, but the Boer War (dismissed in a couple of lines) brought the Dutch states under the British flag.

In New Zealand, the Maoris 'agreed to obey our rule', and 'a great English governor, named Sir George Grey, insisted on seeing fair play' between the Maoris and the British settlers. In Australia the natives were 'a feeble kind of savages when the British first went there'.

India exerts a special fascination, for it is recognised that there were great states with rich cities and strong armies. Yet 'the British themselves and the native princes learnt that a few British soldiers, or native soldiers led by British officers, could defeat huge native armies'. And so

> 'our nation … has taken upon itself the task of giving justice and order and good government to all those millions of people, whose ways are so utterly unlike ours that the wisest men who go to India, and spend their lives trying to do what is best for the people under their charge, come back at the last saying that they still know hardly anything about them'. (p. 1115) [5]

The moral responsibility of empire is emphasised:

> 'Our race … has not only made itself rich and powerful – which is a small thing after all – but it has made itself the guardian of the welfare of millions and millions of people who had less knowledge, or skill, or courage; it has taken upon its own shoulders what a poet has called the White Man's Burden…
>
> 'There is a duty for the boys and girls of today: of giving to all those peoples a rule merciful and just, peaceful and free. That is what it means to be a citizen of the mightiest empire the world has ever seen – an empire which has done more than any other to teach the world what freedom means, an empire that will no longer live, or deserve to live, if ever its citizens forget its own greatest lesson.' (p. 1117)

This is an admirable sentiment and one hopes that the lesson was learned by the young readers of the *Encyclopædia*. But it glosses over the undeniable fact that becoming 'rich and powerful' was for many people the primary motive of imperial expansion, and neglects such important factors as the exploitation of raw materials,

---

[5] Whereas most of this quotation reflects traditional attitudes, the final phrase suggests that the author may have had some doubts. One thinks of the mutual incomprehension depicted in E.M. Forster's *Passage to India* (1924) or, more recently, Paul Scott's *Raj Quartet*. A much less favourable picture of British behaviour is given by William Dalrymple in *The Last Mughal – The Fall of a Dynasty*, Delhi, 1857 (2006).

the search for markets and – for Britain especially – the strategic need to secure access to distant possessions. [6]

Canada (pp. 1239–48)

The geography of this – 'The Empire's Wonderland' – is vividly described in the form of a journey across the continent from Montreal to Vancouver. The vastness, great variety and potential of the country are underlined.

> 'If we try to see before us a picture of the wealth of Canada, there is the blazing yellow of the corn, the glow of rosy apples and ripe fruit, the golden butter and cheese, the silvery salmon. These, with the grand woods of the forest trees, in shiny glossiness or in powdery pulp for paper, all stand out in splendid profusion from the land of the maple leaf and the beaver.' (p. 1246)

The history of the conquest of the country is also told, mentioning the conflicts and final victory over the French. Somewhat optimistically in view of the later separatist movement, the author declares that

> 'The French Canadians, living contentedly under their ancient religion, laws and customs, have proved themselves to be among the most loyal sons of the Empire'. (p. 1247)

In discussing the plight of the Red Indians, the author is mindful of her principles of good governance quoted above:

> 'One feels very sorry for the Indians, who have changed greatly since the white men first set foot on the banks of the St. Lawrence River, about 500 years ago. Now the "Pale Faces" have come in their thousands, brought by the great iron horse. Setting up their homesteads, they plough, sow, reap and carry the precious food for the millions in the Mother Country... The bisons and buffaloes are gone, and the poor Red Indians who lived on them have almost gone too. Here and there are the Reserve Lands where they put up their tents and live with their fast little ponies... They must learn to live as white men do, or suffer great want and wretchedness.' (p. 1242)

Australia (pp. 1355–64)

The discovery and exploration of Australia, by Captain Cook in particular, is recounted with enthusiasm; but the subsequent convict settlement was 'a very sad chapter in Australian history'.

---

[6] Cf. in particular Hobsbawm, *op. cit.*. The poet responsible for the expression 'White Man's Burden' was of course Rudyard Kipling: this was in fact the subject of a poem he had addressed to the USA on its responsibilities in the Philippines. Kipling's equally famous *Recessional* – written for Queen Victoria's Diamond Jubilee in 1897, stresses the impermanence of Empires and expresses a sentiment similar to that of the *Encyclopædia*: 'Lo, all our pomp of yesterday / Is one with Nineveh and Tyre! / Judge of the Nations, spare us yet, / Lest we forget, lest we forget.' The hymn based on this poem was a favourite at my own public school in the late 1940s, though I doubt whether we grasped its full meaning.

The author describes the gradual occupation of the more fertile areas: the introduction of sheep (and, less usefully, rabbits), the cultivation of wheat and fruit, the discovery of gold and silver, the creation of Sydney and other cities, the arrival of the telegraph enabling Australia to be connected with the rest of the world.

> 'In the short space of time since the white nation came to settle in the island-continent, nearly every known plant that is good for food has been introduced... Think of the work of the pioneers in getting the land ready, in choosing crops, in bringing to perfection all the produce of this wonderland... Every year sees some fresh outlet for the energies of Australians.' (p. 1364)

But the aboriginals are dismissed with contempt:

> 'These first dwellers in Australia, owing to very poor food, were stunted and stupid... the ugliest and most uncivilised of all the native races... They have never been numerous nor of much account.' (p. 1355)

New Zealand (pp. 1453–60)

The beauty of these islands and their pleasant climate is vividly described. 'In this far-away blue ocean, under the golden sunshine, in the clear balmy air, it is like fairyland.' It is recognised that the first settlers came from Polynesia, and when Captain Cook arrived the Maoris were

> 'very fierce and warlike; but since his day many missionaries have gone out to teach them to be more gentle, and to give up their old wild ways and their cruel religion'. (p. 1453)

White settlers, including many from Scotland, have established 'splendid farms for dairy produce, and thousands and thousands of sheep flourish, giving great quantities of valuable wool'. Gold and other minerals have been found.

In elections for the parliament in Wellington, women as well as men, Maoris as well as others, have a vote. There is an old-age pension scheme. 'In these and many other ways young New Zealand is ahead of the old Mother Country' – an interesting remark since the *Encyclopædia* avoids the very contentious issue of votes for women in Britain itself.

India (pp. 1545–52 & 1695–72)

The size and strangeness of this 'Pearl of the East' are emphasised: everything is on a huge scale, there are high mountains, great rivers, vast forests; elephants, tigers and other exotic wild animals. A population of over 300 million is ruled over by a few thousand British – one European for every thousand natives. The climate is very hot; British children have to be sent home for their schooling, leaving wives with the difficult choice of being parted from their children or from their husbands.

The ancient history of India is recounted in some detail. It is explained that its inhabitants are Mohammedans – who like Christians worship the 'true God' – or Hindus who worship many gods and have strange and sometimes shocking practices: for example, the British have had to forbid the burning of widows at the funeral of their husbands. The Hindu caste system is also described.

The author explains how the British – like the Portuguese, French and others – initially set up trading stations, and formed a trading company. Victories over the French and alliances with native rulers caused the British, 'although they had not planned any such thing', to become rulers of one province after another, till they came to govern the whole country. [7]

> 'The princes who had not forced us to war were allowed to remain the lords of their own realms, on condition that they did not rule as tyrants, or try to stir up wars.'

Finally:

> 'The British nation said that it was time to end the ruling of India by a company of merchants; so the Queen of England ruled India. Finally, a little more than thirty years ago, Queen Victoria was given the title of Empress, because the Moguls had been called Emperors'. (p. 1702)

Surprisingly, although two articles are devoted to India, nothing is said about the motives of those merchants. Even if Britain did acquire India in 'a fit of absent-mindedness', as was said of the British Empire in general,[8] the reader should have been told why the British took so much trouble, and what benefit was expected. The enormous economic value of India, both as a source of raw materials (cotton, jute, wheat, tea, etc.) and as a market for Britain's manufactures (by 1900 India took a fifth of British exports), is passed over.

Africa (pp. 1765–70 & 4251–62)

Of all the continents, it is in the case of Africa that the vision from Edwardian England differs most markedly from that of today. The *Encyclopædia* allows one short chapter to cover the areas within the British Empire; another for those outside the Empire.

The first of these articles describes, briefly, the work of explorers (these are discussed more fully elsewhere) and of missionaries. The map of the continent, it is pointed out, contains a number of 'red patches' where the British flag flies.

The author observes that the negroes are 'hardly civilised' – among other things, they wear 'hardly any clothes'! Many of them have been taught Christianity, but most are still heathen; some are still cannibals where there are no Europeans to stop them. The evils of the slave trade are mentioned:

> 'We do not like to think now that most of this was done by English people, but we do like to remember that it was the English who first woke up to the wickedness of it, and not only stopped the trade themselves, but persuaded other countries to stop it too.' (p. 1766)

---

[7] This is of course a very bland account. For a critical present-day view, see Dalrymple, *op. cit.*

[8] The phrase originated with the historian Sir John Seeley; it corresponded to what the Victorians wanted to believe, playing down the more commercial and aggressive reality – cf. David Gilmour's 2007 'Roy Jenkins lecture' on changing attitudes to Imperial history.

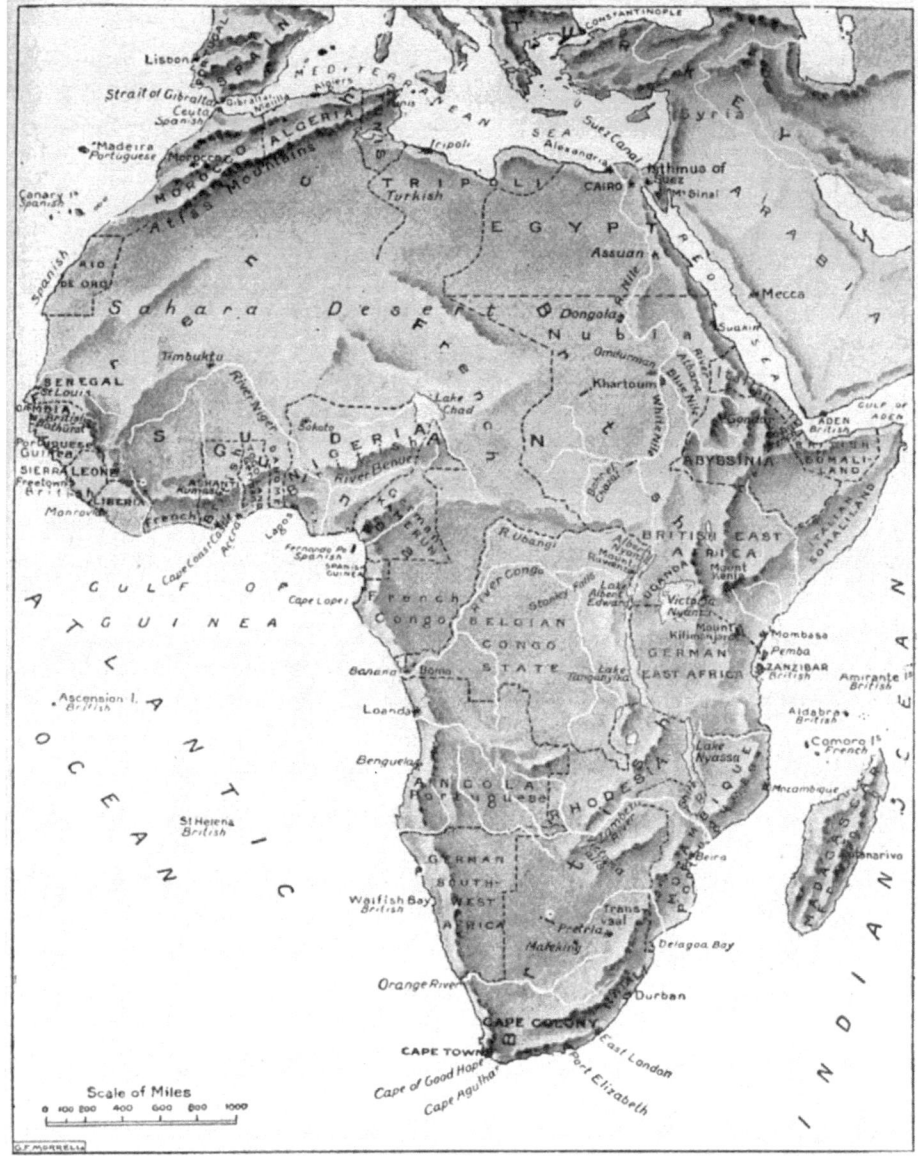

AFRICA, WITH THE NAMES OF THE EUROPEAN POWERS PRINTED ON THE LANDS THEY CONTROL

Three areas are described. The first of these is the 'Guinea coast' – including, presumably, Sierra Leone, Gambia, the Gold Coast (now Ghana) and perhaps Nigeria. Little is said about this, except that there were few white people; there were French and German territories too along that coast, which are 'much like ours'.

The tropical centre of the continent includes lands which are 'in the British sphere of influence', but where there are as yet not many white people: there are diseases which are more fatal to Europeans than to native races. This appears to include 'British East Africa' (which covered what is now Kenya, Uganda and the Sudan). Egypt is 'not really a part of our empire, although we are looking after the government there at present and are likely to go on doing so for some time to come' (p. 1766). (Ancient Egypt is covered in a much later article).

Most of the attention is given to **South Africa**. Having a temperate climate, this contains many Europeans. The complex history of white settlement is recounted, in particular the conflicts between British settlers and the Boer farmers; the Boer War gets a very brief mention, indicating mainly its outcome: the inclusion in the British Empire of the two Boer states, Transvaal and Orange Free State, the Boers themselves being given equal status to British citizens. Britain already had the Cape Colony and Natal; also Rhodesia. Gold and diamond mining are mentioned as major industries.

The article on Africa outside the British Empire comes later in the *Encyclopædia* (pp. 4251–62) but can be briefly considered here. It gives further description of the geography of the continent (see map) and of the races which inhabit it. Only a few countries are (nominally at least) independent, notably Egypt and Morocco, also Liberia. The main interest of this article lies in its account of the 'scramble for Africa' by the various European powers. 'Except in a few cases, the uncivilised black races and tribes have been unable to hold their country either against Arabs or white men.' (p. 4262)

So France has Tunis and Algeria, 'enormous possessions' in West Africa, and the southern flank of the Congo river; the Congo State is under the rule of the Belgians; Germany holds parts of eastern and south-eastern Africa; Italy has the 'horn of Africa'; Angola is Portuguese. And the map 'is still filling up'.

There is a small hint of the abuses of colonial exploitation in a sentence saying that 'serious attention is being called to the cruelties practised on the natives forced to collect rubber'. This sounds like a reference particularly to the atrocities perpetrated in the Congo under Leopold II of Belgium: as this had recently been the object of a reform campaign in Britain, more could have been said. [9]

But as usual, the author prefers to take a positive stance. She returns to the role of the British in opening up the continent. Cecil Rhodes dreamed of a railway from the Cape to Cairo. Part of this dream had come true: the line from the south had crossed the Victoria Falls on the Zambesi river, while from Cairo the railway had reached Khartoum.

---

[9] Leopold II had used the explorer Stanley to gain possession from native chiefs of a huge area of Central Africa, and at the Berlin Conference of 1865 had gained recognition for his Congo Free State, which he exploited as his personal fiefdom. The boom in demand for rubber led to the use of forced labour in its extraction, often at the point of a gun, by his agents and soldiers; many natives were killed or tortured. On the other hand, Leopold invested little in developing the country. There were protests by Belgian missionaries and parliamentarians, but the establishment in England in 1904 of a Congo Reform Movement, together with protests in other European countries and in America, were also factors causing the Belgian State to take over possession from the monarch in 1908. These contemporary developments would have been well known to the *Encyclopædia* author.

'Enterprise like this strikes at the very root of the slave trade and the cruelties connected with the gathering of ivory and rubber; for rapid travel opens up dark places and draws together the great and varies interests of the huge continent. And it is this lighting up and linking up that will make it possible for Europeans to carry out the obligations they take upon themselves when they hoist their flags over vast numbers of uncivilised natives in Africa.' (p. 4262)

'Outposts of the British Empire' (pp. 1875–80)

The list is lengthy. The author points out that

'some of these places are real colonies, where our own people have made themselves homes, or live in order to carry on trade; and others we keep because the Queen of the Seas must have fortified harbours all over the world for her fleets to repair to, and ports from which they can get the stores they need when they want to remain a long time at sea.'

This seems a much truer account of the motives for imperial expansion than those previously advanced.

There are a couple of large territories: Burma, incorporated into India because its rulers had proved 'troublesome', and Ceylon, like India a major source of tea. At the other end of the scale, there are tiny islands such as Ascension Island, which have little significance other than as staging-posts (and, in the case of St. Helena, as a safe place to put Napoleon).

The Falkland Islands – claimed by Britain since 1833 – are not mentioned here.

The author places emphasis on the importance of naval bases in the Mediterranean, particularly since the opening of the Suez Canal: hence the possession of Gibraltar and Malta, and an agreement with Turkey over Malta. Aden is similarly an important base, and also a trading post for coffee, feathers, hides and skins). Hong Kong, acquired from China, provides a vital harbour and a channel for trade with the Chinese mainland. The Caribbean islands provide sugar, bananas, pineapples, etc.

These 'Crown Colonies' do not have parliaments or governments chosen by the people. The author makes an important statement:

'For self-government is only possible where there is a large enough population to make sure that the natives would not get the upper hand in the Parliaments and use their power to destroy the British rule. But the great thing we have to remember is that the aim of British rule has always been to maintain justice and order, and to help the peoples over whom we rule to be prosperous. And so long as this continues the British Empire will be something to be proud of. But if ever we forget this, and turn to oppressing the subject peoples for our own advantage, the British Empire will vanish away like the great empires of the ancient world.' (p. 1880)

The United States

After the proud imperialism of the foregoing items, one approaches the articles on the USA with trepidation. What will the author think of Britain's greatest colony which broke away so dramatically from the Mother Country? In fact, the attitude is highly positive: this is a 'free and great nation'. The accomplishments of the young nation are described with admiration. Blame for the rebellion which led to independence is laid squarely at the door of the British monarchy and government.

There are two articles on the US. The sub-title to the first – **The Birth of a New English Nation** (pp. 2015–24) – sets the tone: the US is not seen as a foreign country, but as an offshoot of Britain itself, and Americans as kinsmen, even though the large numbers of immigrants from other European countries are recognised. [10]

This article deals with US history, describing the successive waves of settlers, with emphasis on the Pilgrim Fathers and the Quakers. The struggles for territory between British and French are recounted. Also, there were 'many sore conflicts with the Indians, during which 'cruel revenges were taken on both sides'. The caption to the illustration below says that 'they have now almost all passed away'. Nevertheless, the condemnation of their treatment made in the case of Canada is not repeated here.

SCENES IN THE MAKING OF THE NEW AMERICA

In this picture, by G. H. Boughton, R.A., we see the new and the old inhabitants of North America. In front is one of the Red Indians, so named by Columbus when he mistook America for India. They have now almost passed away, and their place has been taken by the descendants of the group of Puritans marching behind in this picture.

As to the issues leading to the Declaration of Independence, the author writes:
'Causes of annoyance with the Mother Country became deeper and more frequent... There was continual quarrel between the governors of the colonies sent out from England and the chosen representatives of the

---

[10] As the *Children's Encyclopædia* was published in America in 1911-12, under the title *The Book of Knowledge*, it is highly likely that the authors already had this in mind when writing, and would not want to offend American readers.

people. Although many of these governors were tyrannical and dishonest, yet without their assent no law could be passed.' (p. 2020)

The author stresses the harshness of customs duties and taxation, and of course refers to the 'Boston Tea Party'.

After the successful revolution, the expansion westwards went on with greater energy. (The author does not point out that this meant forcibly taking Indian land, which led to the decline of the Indian tribes.)[11] By degrees new States were added to the Union. Napoleon sold Louisiana to the US. Texas and California were gained from Mexico. But:

'A miserable war with Great Britain set back progress for some time, but the Americans got the best of it, and made themselves respected in Europe; and emigrants now began to flock to America, chiefly to the backwoods, beyond the mountains.' (p. 2022)

The issue of slavery divided North and South. Abraham Lincoln:

'did wonders in guiding the ship of state. He was one of the great men of the earth: strong in brain, strong in will, strong in high aims and uprightness of purpose'. The Civil War put an end to slavery, but 'the sadness and grief of that terrible time have brought a lasting wish for peace.' (p. 2024)

The second article (pp. 2063–72) describes the geography of the country. It is illustrated by several photographs. These include the Statue of Liberty; the skyline of New York (the tallest building was then the Singer, forty storeys high[12]); the cattle-yards of Chicago; reclamation of desert land (Arizona?) demonstrating 'the wonderful results of the energy of the people of the United States'.

There are also photographs of the President Theodore Roosevelt, and of Booker Washington, to illustrate 'the two types of the people of the United States: the white people of the north and the coloured people of the south.'

The author seems torn between the *Encyclopædia*'s general belief in the supremacy of the white race and the desire to speak only good of the US:

'The colour question in the United States is still, perhaps, the most terrible question that confronts any nation. Though belonging to the same nation, the two races are wide apart and do not mix in their daily life, the coloured people being admitted to the homes of whites only as servants. Mr. Washington, the leader of the coloured people, is educating his people to be worthy of a high place in the world, and *Mr. Roosevelt, when he was President, invited Mr. Washington to lunch.*' [my italics] (p. 2072)

---

[11] Neither 'Native Americans' nor the black slave population derived much benefit from America's independence – see *The Unknown American Revolution* by Gary B. Nash (2006).

[12] The Singer was built in 1906-08 and was 204 metres high. The Empire State Building was not built till 1930-31 and is 381 metres without its radio mast.

LOOKING DOWN A NEW YORK STREET

New York, the commercial capital and chief port of the United States, is built on a narrow island. This means that as the city grew there was not as much room as people needed for building. So, instead of spreading buildings over the ground, the Americans built them high in the air, until New York is now largely a city of "skyscrapers," as the Americans call them. Broadway, shown in this picture, is the principal street in New York, and is like no other street in the world. A great part of it is like a deep ravine, lined on each side with buildings from ten to more than thirty storeys high, and at some points the sun seldom reaches down to the level of the street.

France

The first of three articles (pp. 2193–2202) tells the history of France from the beginnings, touching on the Gauls, the Roman conquest, the arrival of the Franks and the rule of Charlemagne; wars with England and the 'shameful' burning of Joan of Arc; persecution of the Huguenots; the development of absolute monarchy culminating in the reign of Louis XIV, with his splendid court at Versailles while the lot of the peasants grew worse and worse. Louis XV 'cared for nothing but his own wicked pleasures... The state of the people was piteous indeed. Money was dragged from them by the king to spend in disgraceful luxury'. (p. 2202)

The second article (pp. 2267–77) carries the story on into the Revolution, the causes of which are clearly and extensively described.

> 'It is difficult for us who live in happier days to understand the greatness of that misery. There were thousands of poor creatures, not only untaught and uncared for, but worse housed and worse fed than the very pigs. They were forced to work for their lords of the manor without pay... if they dared to complain of all the injustice and hardship, they were silenced by the hunting-whip and the dungeon, even the gallows'. (p. 2267)

At the beginning of his reign, Louis XVI had

> 'wise ministers, who tried to get the money affairs of the kingdom into order ... but the queen did not like economy, and the nobles hated that their old 'rights' should be interfered with; and timid Louis gave up his good intentions.' (p. 2268)

The Revolution, however, led to the 'terrible madness of killing' under the Reign of Terror, until more moderate influences prevailed.

Continuing unrest brought Napoleon to the fore. The writer describes his successive victories, until the failure of his Russian campaign and his final defeat at Waterloo. There is also mention of his 'many good works at home – roads and bridges were made, trade was encouraged, education was improved...'

The next sixty years were 'difficult and troubled times', with many changes of government, until 'little over thirty years ago' (i.e. 1870), Napoleon III

> 'was persuaded to rush into war with Germany without due reason or preparation... Terrible battles spread ruin and sorrow over the beautiful borderlands of the two countries.' (p. 2277)

Paris was occupied, and the King of Prussia was proclaimed German Emperor in the Great Hall of Mirrors at Versailles. Alsace and Lorraine were lost to Germany.

As in the articles on England, this history is told in vivid, narrative form, with very few dates: it is clearly intended to be much more readable than a school history lesson.

The third article is entitled **France as it is to-day** (pp. 2389–99). It describes the variety of the country and its people (see illustration): its mountains, plains and rivers, the richness of its agriculture (there were still mulberry trees producing silk in the Rhone valley). The main cities and their activities are described, especially the 'gay and beautiful city of Paris' with the 'splendid treasures in the museums and galleries' and the shops selling china from Sèvres and Limoges, brocades and velvets from Lyons, cloths from Amiens, clocks and jewellery made in Paris itself, costly lace made in various parts of the country – and of course the fashion clothing for which Paris was famous.

In our present time of virtually free movement across frontiers in Europe, it is useful to be reminded that France, at its land frontiers with its neighbours, maintained 'forts and strong towns, and thousands of soldiers are massed in silent watchfulness, and baggage is carefully examined to see that no smuggling goes on.' (p. 2390) Still, trains passed uninterruptedly across the frontiers carrying passengers and goods.

As for empire: under the incompetent reign of Louis XV, France had lost most of its possessions in the New World and in India. France now held just

> 'two small islands off Canada, two in the West Indies, and a strip of land on the continent of South America. In India proper there remain to France but a few isolated towns. In the peninsula to the east of India the French hold a territory larger than France – Indo-China – whence come all sorts of things grown in hot climates, especially rice.' (p. 2399)

But the future of France lay in Africa. Algiers had been conquered in 1830, and France held parts of West Africa, the Sudan, and the French Congo. France also owned Madagascar and some other small colonies and islands. The total area of the French colonies was as large as all Europe (only one-third of the British possessions); but the number of Frenchmen living in them was comparatively small.

In fact, though France was almost twice as large as the United Kingdom, it had a population of only 39 million compared with 42 million in the UK.

> 'And the number of people in France does not increase year by year as in other countries. France possesses a great deal to make it a flourishing country: its people are clever, and a good education is within reach of all. The country is rich, because it has a good government, and the people are thrifty, they work hard, and save. France is powerful because her people are both brave and polite. But what France needs more than anything else is more of these people... to join in the growing work of the motherland and her colonies. There are not enough people in France to do all this work, or to make the most of the beautiful country, with its advantages of sea-washed shores, mountain masses holding hidden treasures, navigable rivers spreading over fertile plains.' (p. 2399)

It is an eloquent plea, and a generous one in view of traditional Franco-British rivalry (the author is of course writing after the *Entente Cordiale*). Nevertheless, with the *Encyclopædia* tendency to avoid unpleasant topics, it omits the main motive for French natalist policy: the desire for military reasons to catch up with the larger population of Germany. [13]

---

[13] An *Alliance nationale contre la dépopulation* was established in 1896. Especially after the tragic losses of so many young men in the First World War, France took measures to encourage larger families.

PICTURESQUE PEOPLE OF FAIR FRANCE

A fisher-girl of Picardy

A girl of Provence

A Normandy fisher-woman

Peasants of the country round Paris ; from a painting called " The Gleaners," by the French artist, J. F. Millet.

A Bernardine nun digging

A northern prawn-fisher

A woman of Brittany

The people of different parts of France are very unlike one another. We can see, for instance, from the pictures of women of Provence and Normandy, that not only the costumes, but the types of faces in the north and south are quite distinct. In Brittany the people speak a different language from the rest of France, more like our Welsh, and in fact a Welshman can partly understand a Breton when he is talking.

The photographs on these pages are by Messrs. Mansell, Valentine, and the E. N. A.

2395

113

Germany

Since the main aim of this review of the *Children's Encyclopædia* is to find out what people were thinking shortly before the outbreak of war in 1914, the articles on Germany are likely to be of particular interest. Indeed they are; and to a later generation they contain some surprises.

In the first two of three articles (pp. 2521–30 and 2635–42), the author does her best to make sense of the complicated history of the Germanic tribes, describing in particular the emergence of the 'Holy Roman Empire' under Charlemagne, the internal and external wars over religion, territory and monarchic succession.

For our purposes, it is sufficient to pick up the story after the fall of Napoleon, at the Congress of Vienna in 1815. The author has provided a convenient map: the caption points out that Austria was the supreme power among the German-speaking nations, the rest of the area consisting of several separate states, of which Prussia was the most significant.

The second map shows the situation after Prussia's victory over France in 1871. The caption here observes how Prussia's influence had extended over all the other independent German countries, except of course Austria. This was initially a confederation, but in subsequent years Prussia had taken the lead in creating a customs union (the *Zollverein*). War with Denmark had brought in Schleswig-Holstein; and war with Austria had settled Prussia's pre-eminence. In January 1871, while the German army was besieging Paris, William I, King of Prussia, had been proclaimed German Emperor, head of the confederation. The *Reichstag* was established in Berlin, capital of Prussia.

The third article deals with **Germany as it is today** (pp. 2747–56). It first describes Berlin, an 'immense and magnificent city', though there was little that was more than two hundred years old. It had fine streets and square, splendid palaces and museums, public buildings of all kinds; there were many statues, including those of world-famed writers such as Goethe and Schiller, 'whose beautiful thoughts are a bond of union not only for all Germans, but for all human beings who can read and understand them.'

Other great cities are described. There are photographs of Hamburg, Dresden, Cologne and Coblentz, while Munich is praised for its art treasures; others of the 'lovely, lovely Rhine' and the Black Forest. It is pointed out that formerly Germany was an agricultural country, but now its chief wealth lay in manufacturing. In the north-west of the country, the Ruhr valley contained enormous iron and steel works: the Krupp factory alone employed thirty thousand people.

Three photographs (reproduced) illustrate the 'open-air life of German children', and the author stresses the quality of education:

THE GROWTH OF THE GERMAN EMPIRE

If we compare together this map and the one below we can see how much the power and influence of Prussia have grown in Europe since the fall of Napoleon Bonaparte. At the Congress of Vienna, in 1815, which settled the map of Europe for a few years, Austria was the supreme power among the German-speaking nations ; and, although Prussia was given nearly all the territory she had lost in Napoleon's wars, and much more besides, her influence did not extend beyond her own land. From this time there was great jealousy between Prussia and Austria

With the coming of Bismarck, Prussia's power and influence grew until it reached out far beyond her own territory. This map shows Central Europe at the close of the Franco-German War, in 1871, and we see in the dark shaded part how Prussia's influence had extended over all the other independent German countries except Austria. These countries do not belong to Prussia, but, as parts of the new German Empire, they all acknowledge the power and follow the lead of Prussia. Austria has ceased to influence other German nations.

THE OPEN-AIR LIFE OF GERMAN CHILDREN

The Germans pay much attention to the health and education of children, and they are always thinking out new ideas for schools. Kindergartens and open-air classes like this one studying botany were first started by them.

All German children are taught that it is important to live as much as possible in the open air, and here we see a German mother with her children and their nurse taking their midday meal together in the garden of their house.

This is a familiar street scene in many German towns, and we can see how the children look as they go to, or come from, their schools. The tradesmen' carts are drawn about many of the cities by big dogs.

2753

'Germany has always been in the forefront in matters of education, and to-day – except in the districts where so many poor Polish Jews live, on the borders of Russia – there are very few people unable to read and write. It was from Germany that we first learnt how to make first lessons interesting to little children in kindergartens, and great pains are taken not only in elementary schools, but in higher grades, to make learning useful and attractive. The fees in the higher schools are so low that even poor people can send their children, and as it is much cheaper to attend the universities than it is with us, and there are so many of them, almost any student can take advantage of the highest education to be had.' (p. 2755)

DROPPING THE PILOT

This, the most famous of all Sir John Tenniel's " Punch " cartoons, shows Prince Bismarck, the old pilot who had guided the German ship of state into the harbour of prosperity, passing from the direction of affairs, while the new captain, the young Emperor William, who dismissed him, looks down from the deck.

The role of Bismarck, the 'Iron Chancellor' under Emperor William I, is emphasised, both in the unification of Germany under Prussia and in many of the achievements which followed. Yet:

'he could not see his way to new plans of work, nor had he any sympathy with the many-sided activities and the living personal touch with affairs displayed by the grandson [i.e. William II].'

The famous Punch cartoon of the 'dropping of the pilot' is reproduced here.

The author goes on to speak admiringly of William II (who reigned from 1888 to 1918):

'The Kaiser has never rested till he has made Germany powerful, with armies ready and perfect, able to put out the flames of war, if unhappily any should burst out on her borders. Nothing is too small for him to attend to when the well-being of the Army is in question – the boots they wear, the bicycles they use, as well as the guns and powder.'

She points out that every German must do military service at the age of twenty: 'so the whole nation are soldiers, ready and trained to defend their fatherland'. (p. 2748) [14]

---

[14] Even for the time, this was a strangely favourable picture of the Kaiser. Perhaps the author was influenced by his relationship to the British royal family (he was a grandson of Queen Victoria and was present at her deathbed. But it disregards, among other things, a series of slights which he had inflicted on Edward VII (cf. Hattersley).

It is recognised that it costs a great deal to keep up the Army, and there is implicit recognition of the arms race in which Britain too was involved.

> 'It is sad, indeed, to think of the vast sums spent on guns and battleships and armies, not only in Germany, but in the countries that feel obliged to keep pace with her. So long as men keep to the old barbarous idea of settling disputes about boundaries, or trade, or insults, by sending thousands of men to kill thousands of their fellows, every country is afraid to have fewer thousands ready to send to kill and be killed than its neighbour.' (p. 2750)

Germany's colonial ambitions are mentioned with approval:

> 'Before the Kaiser came to the throne, Germany had been very slow in extending her borders beyond the seas and finding new markets for the goods she manufactured. At first travellers visited foreign parts, and traders from the old free cities followed them, setting up factories on the west and east coasts of Africa in places yet empty and ungoverned. A telegram from Bismarck, directing the German flag to be hoisted in certain of these places, thus taking the merchants under the empire's protection, was the beginning of German colonies. Later, large territories in various parts of Africa have fallen to Germany. She has fought the cruel slave trade of the Arabs, and is spreading railways and civilisation over inland districts whose snow-topped mountains, magnificent lakes and waterfalls, are among the wonders of the world.' (p. 2756)

The article ends by quoting *'Was ist das Deutsche Vaterland?'* – 'the song, full of inspiration and patriotism, that is sung to-day over all the great German Empire.'

Was the author exceedingly unworldly, or did she really fail to see that those military preparations, those colonial ambitions which she has just described were bound at some point to bring the British and German Empires into conflict? Did she really believe that those troops massed at the frontiers were purely for defensive purposes? Did she not notice any connection with what she had written in the previous article about the French army positioned on its side of the frontier? Did it not occur to her that Germany's annexation of Alsace-Lorraine in 1871 might remain a highly sensitive issue?

And if she did not realise these things, was she exceptionally naïve – and likewise Arthur Mee in his role as editor – or did they perhaps want to spare their young readers from worry about the risks of war? (In fact, the young readers, if they were old enough and bright enough to follow these articles, might well have drawn their own conclusions.) Or does this attitude reflect a more widespread unwillingness to face realities, not unlike the widespread refusal in England in the 1930s to recognise the danger from Hitler? Was there perhaps even a misguided notion that the Kaiser, in view of the royal family links, would never provoke war with Britain?

One must guard against the wisdom of hindsight. Nevertheless, as has been pointed out in the Introduction, Britain had by 1906 been forced to start building more battleships to keep ahead of growing German naval power, and this expensive programme was a controversial issue by the time the *Encyclopædia* was being written. The brief mention of the arms race quoted above shows that the writer was indeed aware of this: so either she underestimated its significance or thought it an unsuitable subject for children.

Whatever the reason, and while one can share in her enthusiasm for German achievements, particularly in culture and education, the author certainly did not prepare her readers for what was to come. [15]

Austria-Hungary (pp. 2851–59)

This article begins by describing the successive invasions, by tribes from further east, of the Danube basin. It goes on to recount the long reign of the Hapsburgs, who acquired Charlemagne's title of 'Holy Roman Emperor', and by the time of Charles V included Spain and the Netherlands (including present-day Belgium) in their empire. As defenders of the Catholic faith, they had 'nourished a very bitter spirit with regard to the Reformation, and during the terrible Thirty Years War the Hapsburgs were chiefly to blame for the prolonged ruin and misery spread over Germany'. (p. 2852)

The boundaries of **Austria** had moved backwards and forwards over time. The outcome, as it stood at the time of writing, is well summed up:

'There is no united Austrian nation, no common Austrian tongue; the empire consists of a leading German State, broken off from the rest of the German-speaking peoples when Prussia rose to be their head; of various states that are fragments of other nationalities, some still speaking their own languages, some more or less absorbed by their German rulers. Besides these, there is the whole independent nationality of the Hungarians, of quite different origin from the Germans, with its own speech, manners, customs and constitution.' (p. 2856)

Indeed, the map of this part of Europe at the beginning of the twentieth century looked very different from later situations. The second of the two maps shown above for Germany illustrates this in broad terms. (It should be remembered that in the late eighteenth century and at the Congress of Vienna, Poland had been carved up between Prussia, Austria and Russia: its southern province of Galicia had gone to Austria, who later took over Cracow, Poland's ancient capital, as well. Austria's territory also included Bohemia and Moravia, and most of what became Yugoslavia after the First World War.)

---

[15] Of course, the spark which set off the First World War came from Sarajevo, not from any of the issues just mentioned. But by the time the *Encyclopædia* was being written, a scenario had been set up – the *Triple Entente* of Britain, France and Russia facing the alliance of Germany and Austria-Hungary – which virtually ensured that any local incident would draw all the great powers into conflict. See Hobsbawm; also *inter alia* David Fromkin, *Europe's Last Summer: Why the World went to War in 1914* (2004).

The current Emperor was still Francis Joseph, who had reigned since 1848: a 'dignified, grey-haired old man', noted for 'his kindness to little children and to the poor' and for 'his tact and good feeling in carrying out his share of the government of an empire of such varied nationalities'.

Hungary had a constitution 'perhaps older than our own', dating back to St. Stephen, Hungary's first Christian king; 'and the story of its relations with Austria is one of incessant struggle to preserve its ancient and free manner of government'. The author remarks that if you travel by train from Vienna to Budapest, at the frontier the Austrian guards take down the German notices and Hungarian guards put up Hungarian ones; the engine-drivers are changed too!

> 'Hungary has long been called "the bulwark and shield of Christendom",
> so often has it withstood the attacks of the Mohammedan Turks. The
> terror of these invaders along the old Danube highway hung over Europe
> for centuries.' (p. 2854)

(In the sixteenth century Ottoman forces had reached the gates of Vienna and conquered Budapest).

On its south-east boundary, Austria-Hungary still faced the much weakened Ottoman Empire. As the author notes, Vienna had recently (in 1908) annexed Bosnia-Herzegovina. She does not point out here (but see article on the Balkans below) that this act had already nearly provoked a European war by provoking Russia, Serbia's ally (Bosnia-Herzegovina contained about a million Serbs), but Russia was not then ready for war.

In fact, the author here follows her usual tendency to play down disagreeable facts. She is over-generous to Emperor Franz Joseph, who was a conscientious ruler in the traditional Habsburg mode. He could hardly be blamed for the brutal repression of the Hungarian rebellion in 1848–49, the first years of his reign, and he did implement in 1867 the agreement with Hungarian leaders creating the double monarchy (though his wife Sisy is generally given most of the credit for this). But in the early part of his reign he had embroiled his country in disastrous wars with Italy and Prussia, whereby in particular the empire lost northern Italy.

It is true that subsequently Franz Joseph held together a huge empire consisting of very disparate parts. But when in 1914, following the assassination in Sarajevo of Franz Ferdinand, heir to the Austro-Hungarian throne, by a Serbian nationalist, Franz Joseph signed the declaration of war against Serbia, he started the chain reaction of opposing alliances which brought all the great powers into the conflagration. [16]

The *Encyclopædia* writer could not have foreseen these precise events; but as in her treatment of Germany, she left her readers totally unprepared for the impending disaster. Such lack of awareness of the significance of events as far

---

[16] Franz Joseph had asserted that he wanted peace, and he had previously restrained ministers and generals who wanted a 'preventive' war. Yet he seems to have failed to realise the consequences of this act. (Cf. Richard Rickett, *Österreich, Sein Weg durch die Geschichte*, Wien 1991). He still belonged to an age in which war seemed the way to resolve problems between nations.

away as the Balkans was no doubt characteristic of the time (and more understandable than Neville Chamberlain's infamous description in September 1938 of Hitler's aggression of Czechoslovakia as 'a quarrel in a far-away country between people of whom we know nothing…').

In fact, as we shall soon see, the writer was well aware of the precarious situation in the Balkans, and it is odd that this should not have been reflected here.

Switzerland (pp. 2958–68)

One turns with relief to a country which for a considerable time has lived peacefully within stable borders and has never interfered in the affairs of others.

Nevertheless, the *Encyclopædia* article makes clear that Switzerland's peace and unity were not easily won. It describes the early conflicts between the French- and German-speaking cantons, and the oppression of the Hapsburg Empire. The famous oath sworn at Ruetli by leaders of three cantons and the legend of William Tell's defiance of the Austrian governor are of course recounted, with pictures. Eventually, after further unrest during and after the Napoleonic wars, the Federal State emerged (this was in 1848).

The natural beauties of the country give the author another opportunity for vivid description. She speaks of the grandeur of the Alps, and continues:

'Valleys separate the ranges and groups of mountains; some wider, and green with grass and gorgeous with wild flowers in spring and summer; others again are filled with deep, dark forests. In nearly all the valleys are leaping and dancing streams. Very high up the rivers only slide and crawl a few feet in a year, for they are frozen hard… At sunrise and sunset in clear weather both sky and snow are bathed in glorious colour – rosy red and gold.' (p. 2960)

There is praise for the educational system, and for Switzerland's democracy:

'Arrangements for teaching are such that they reach to the poorest child in the most remote valley, thus fitting all to take part in the universal voting by which the country is governed'. (p. 2968)

Credit is given also to Switzerland for promoting in Geneva 'a great meeting to try and arrange matters between the nations so as to lessen the horrors of war' [17]; and the Swiss flag (with colours inversed) became the emblem of the Red Cross, with its headquarters in Geneva.

Italy (pp. 3011–3024)

In this comparatively lengthy article, the author describes with enthusiasm the natural beauties of the land. After crossing the Alps:

'travellers pass into a soft, warm air and a smiling, sunny country, where bright flowers make gay with colour the little white villages and fine villas,

---

[17] Presumably a reference to the first Geneva convention, 1864.

and fruitful vines grow twined round mulberry trees, and luxuriant orange
and lemon groves give out their sweet, faint scent.' (p. 3011)

There are several illustrations in this article, one of which is reproduced here; all
these photographs are, of course, in black-and-white, which in this case especially
must seem to us a severe limitation.

The historical development is described from Roman times, with emphasis on
the emergence from the tenth century onwards of the great cities. Milan is praised
for its splendid cathedral:

'One can well believe that the snowy pinnacles of the frozen Alps
inspired the architect with the idea of this wonder of the world in white
marble, with its slender shafts and sharp spires gleaming in the rich
sunshine.' (p. 3016)

Venice is 'the fairy city of the sea'. Florence is 'one of the most wonderful places
for art in the whole world'. Genoa, Bologna, Pisa and other cities are mentioned.
And of course Rome, where St. Peter's and the Vatican Palace with its treasures are
described (there is much more about ancient Rome in other sections).

Particular emphasis is placed on the gradual unification of Italy. Formerly, the
country had been split among many badly-governed states. The Congress of Vienna,
after the fall of Napoleon, set many of the Italian princes back in their states, and
Austria was the chief gainer. The Kingdom of Sardinia, which included Savoy and
Piedmont, took the lead in driving out the Austrians; by 1866 Austria had lost
Lombardy and Venetia. Mazzini and Garibaldi are among the 'great names in this
wonderful struggle for freedom'. In 1870 Italy became one country under 'the honest
king' Victor Emmanuel, with Rome as its capital. When the king entered Rome in
state in 1871, he received an enthusiastic welcome;

'but the pope shut himself up in the Vatican quarter and refused to
acknowledge the kingdom of Italy. Ever since that time the pope has shut
himself up and refused to leave his palace'. (p. 3024) [18]

There is little doubt on which side the *Encyclopædia* stands:

'Italy has steadily made great progress since the union. There are now in
it over thirty-three millions of people, who have an increasing share in
the government; education is improving; also trade and industries, as
roads have been developed, and railways and telegraphs connect the
most distant parts with each other and Europe beyond. Many parts of the
country have been drained, and so made both profitable and healthy. In
the great cities there are new streets and squares, and a new sense of
order, and quiet, and responsibility, which is only possible when a
country is free.' (p. 3024)

---

[18] It was not until 1929 that relations between the Vatican and the Italian state were formally
settled under the Lateran treaties.

EVERYDAY SCENES IN SUNNY ITALY

For centuries Carrara has been world-famed for its wonderful marble, tons of which are here awaiting despatch.

Cattle drag the marble from the great quarries to the railway. The world's finest statues are of Carrara marble.

Sicily, the great island that lies at the toe of Italy, has had a famous history. But its people now are poor and uneducated. They have quaint customs, one of which is to decorate their carts with paintings, as shown here.

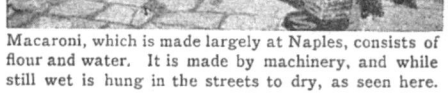

Macaroni, which is made largely at Naples, consists of flour and water. It is made by machinery, and while still wet is hung in the streets to dry, as seen here.

In Naples the poor people live together in a part of the city called the Lazzaroni, after Lazarus, the poor man in the Gospel This is a typical scene in the district.

The Balkans and Turkey

Working through these articles in **THE CHILD'S BOOK OF COUNTRIES**, one begins to admire the skill and breadth of knowledge displayed by the writer, Frances Epps. The following two articles (pp. 3148–58 & 3219–26) not only give vivid descriptions of the various countries in this region but also contrive to make some sense of its notoriously complex politics.

The first article begins with a general description of the geography of the Balkan peninsula, pointing out how rugged highlands separate fertile plains, thus contributing to the diversity of races, nations and religions. (An illustration, reproduced here, shows twelve different national costumes, with useful brief captions.) Among these peoples,

> 'an unconquerable desire for independence has led to grim and tragic warfare all through the years… Every mile of the wavy border lines … has been fought for, lost and regained, often amid scenes of incredible cruelty.' (p. 3149)

And the writer adds: 'It is felt some of those lines are even to-day not permanent' – a notable understatement, but which might have been taken into account in the foregoing discussion of Austria-Hungary.

After a reminder of Greece's 'brilliant past' (dealt with more fully in other sections), the article explains how the ancient Greek city of Byzantium was taken over in the fourth century by the Roman emperor Constantine – hence its new name – and became the centre of the Eastern or Byzantine Empire. As the Roman Empire weakened, the Churches of the East and West split up, with the patriarch of Constantinople becoming the head of the Eastern Church. Then:

> 'in the picturesque mountain country between the Black Sea and the Adriatic, a perfect ferment of peoples settled and fought and struggled with each other and with their neighbours… The kingdoms of the Bulgarians and Servians were particularly large and important, and towns and monasteries rose up among the mountains in the sunny valleys. Bosnia, too, managed to keep itself distinct, and to develop into a kingdom.' (p. 3150)

Under Justinian, in the sixth century, St. Sophia in Constantinople was rebuilt into 'the magnificent place of worship that we see today'.

Later, the followers of Mohammed

> 'set forth to conquer the world to their faith by the sword… Jerusalem, and province after province in Asia, fell to them. The magnificent walls of Constantinople saved it for another three centuries, but nearly all the time the emperors of the East were engaged in fighting the followers of the prophet.' (p. 3152)

The Ottoman Turks, carving their way through the Asiatic provinces, eventually crossed the Dardanelles and spread throughout the Balkans. Constantinople became more a city-state instead of the heart of a great empire. In 1453 it fell to the Turks; St. Sophia was turned into a mosque. During the years that followed:

'the crescent on the Ottoman banner shone triumphantly over an immense and powerful empire from the Danube to the Euphrates, from the Caspian Sea to the Straits of Gibraltar. The discipline and unity of purpose of the Mohammedans prevailed against the jealousies and quarrels of the Christian kingdoms.' (p. 3156)

In 1683 Vienna was saved only when King Sobieski of Poland came to the rescue. Since that time,

'the tide of Turkish power in Europe has steadily ebbed: they were driven out of Hungary; many towns and islands in the Mediterranean were taken from them; Greece passed for a time to the Venetians before entering on its long final struggle for freedom against the Turks'. (p. 3158)

Russia, now growing into a power in Europe, began to interfere in the provinces north of the Danube. This also restored the influence of the Eastern or Greek Church, after years of depression while it was the religion only of the oppressed and ever-rebelling subjects of the sultan. Now, 'as the Church of a chief Power in Europe, it bound that Power in sympathy with its poorer brethren of the smaller and despised nationalities, and gave many chances of encouraging their revolts'. In consequence:

'All through the eighteenth century, when Western Europe was dreaming of wider life and greater liberties, and a feeling of growth was spreading to its remotest parts, a heavy dead weight of oppression of almost hopeless sorrow, and fierce hatred between Mohammedans and Christians, between widely differing races, hung over the mountains and valleys of the Balkan Peninsula, and the weight was held down by the jealousies of surrounding nations.' (p. 3219)

The second article turns to the more recent developments in the individual countries. (It has to be remembered that the political map of the Balkans looked very different at the beginning of the nineteenth century to that which emerged after 1914–18, in particular with the creation of 'Yugoslavia'.)

In **Greece**, 'desolate and ruined by the long mismanagement of both Venetians and Turks', the people finally determined to fight a final struggle for freedom. The article describes their heroic efforts and the contribution of volunteers from western countries (notably Lord Byron).

After the English, French and Russians had joined together to destroy the Turkish fleet at the battle of Navarino, Turkish rule in Greece came to an end. Then:

'The difficult work of restoring and building up has gone steadily on. The present king is the brother of Queen Alexandra, and there is a fine constitution by which the people have a voice in the government. By degrees better ways of farming are being introduced, and much care and money expended in bringing water to parts which are very dry... There are not many railways yet. Education is becoming more general, and there is a very fine university at Athens.' (p. 3220)

MEN & WOMEN OF THE BALKAN COUNTRIES

This is a young Servian woman of the Greek Orthodox Church, the religion that most Servians profess.

The picturesque national costume of Montenegro is shown in this picture of one of the prince's bodyguard.

The people of Albania were formerly all Christians, but many of them, like this man, are now Mohammedans.

This is a Servian woman belonging to the Roman Catholic Church, as indicated by the way she dresses.

The sailors of the Greek seas are very unlike our ideas of what a sailor should be. This is a mariner of Cos.

This is another type of Albanian warrior, and shows the curious kilted costume worn in the south.

There are many Albanians who still remain Christians, and here we see a Roman Catholic lady of Albania.

The people of Bulgaria, as shown in this picture, are a fine type. Elementary education is compulsory.

This is a typical peasant woman of European Turkey in the quaint costume she wears on gala occasions.

The Macedonians have often revolted against their Turkish rulers. Here we see a Macedonian shepherd.

The Bosnians, of whom this is a type, have much in common with Servia, but they are now Austrian subjects.

The Bosnian women wear a picturesque costume, an important part of which is the many-coloured sash.

3225

Roumania, after 'long and sore trials and sufferings', had gained its independence from the Turks and become a kingdom.

> 'A good constitution was arranged to give the people rights in their government… It is a flourishing country now. The Danube and other rivers make splendid waterways by which to convey the stores of golden grain from the fields, and the minerals, metals, oil, salt and coal from the mountains. Railways are progressing, and Bucharest is a busy trade centre, as are also the ports on the Danube and the Black Sea.' (p. 3220)

In **Bulgaria**, 'the ruins of the palaces of its old rulers show what was their magnificence a thousand years ago'. Russia had supported the war for independence from Turkey, the Bulgarians being of the same (Orthodox) religion and largely the same race. After a period during which the country was a principality still under the Sultan, in 1908 Prince Ferdinand declared himself king.

> 'A great deal of corn is grown in the wide fields…; agriculture is improving…; there is plenty of convenient water power, and coal and ores in the mountains.' (p. 3222)

The author mentions the rose-gardens of Shipka and the scent made there known as 'attar of roses'. The description suggests personal knowledge:

> 'A bright cheerful scene it is in Sofia, with the gay uniforms of the soldiers and the picturesque dresses of the peasants. These are best seen at the early morning market, when they bring their fresh produce in for sale.' (p. 3222)

'**Servia**' (or Serbia) had once been a much larger country. Its capital, Belgrade, had been hotly fought over many times in history, being one of the most important 'gates' of central Europe. Its independence from the Ottomans had come by degrees. A peasant leader called 'Black George' had organised a constitution and schools. Agriculture was prospering; there were no large estates, but every peasant cultivated his own land 'and there is no need for workhouses'. A great deal of Servia's trade was with Austria-Hungary, by way of the Danube and its tributaries.

There is a significant hint of trouble to come:

> 'Servia much desires certain lands and ports for its development, which Austria is unwilling to grant, and great forbearance is needed to soothe ruffled feelings and keep the countries of the storm-centre of Europe at peace'. (p. 3221)

Bosnia and Herzegovina had been part of the Turkish Empire for four hundred years, 'during which time they seem almost to have disappeared from civilisation… at last their exasperated people rose against their oppressors in 1875', and later (under the Treaty of Berlin of 1878 which concluded the Russo-Turkish war) were handed over to Austro-Hungary to be managed by her for Turkey.

> 'Austria had promised not to do anything to alter the footing on which Bosnia and Herzegovina were governed, but Europe was surprised in October 1908 by Austria suddenly adding the two provinces to her own dominions without asking the permission of the Turks'. (p. 3224)

In **Montenegro**, 'a little, mountainous country':

> 'the inhabitants ... have always been famed for their bold spirit and energy and for the amount of freedom they have managed to retain. Tilling the fields in the valleys and tending flocks on the mountain sides are the chief occupations of these brave, handsome, kindly people'. (p. 3224)

The prince held his court in the tiny inland capital, Cettinje. Austria still possessed the port of Cattaro. [19]

Albania, with the old provinces of 'Kossovo', 'Macedon' and Thrace, made up the remaining Turkish dominions in Europe.

Finally, we come to **Turkey** itself. This,

> 'having for so long been a badly governed country, is in many ways behind the times. Education is backward, farming is scarcely understood, though three-quarters of the people spend their lives cultivating the soil'. (p. 3224)

The Sultan lived in a closely-guarded palace in Constantinople (the *Encyclopædia* does not use the Turkish name of Istanbul).

> 'It is difficult to realise how much power could be centred in the grasp of one man. It included absolute power of life and death over all subjects, absolute control of the finances of the country, and absolute tyranny in preventing freedom of the Press or of speech.' However:
>
> 'Many of the best Turks were ashamed of the state of things in their country, and formed themselves into a society to try to devise a plan to better them.' (p. 3226)

In 1908 – this was a very recent development when the *Encyclopædia* was being written – the Young Turks had staged their revolt, led by Enver Bey (i.e. 'Ataturk', as he came to be known). The Sultan gave way: a constitution was granted, a parliament was created and opened by the Sultan himself. And four hundred members of the British House of Commons sent a message:

> 'Your House has entered the ranks of the great Parliamentary Assemblies of the world, as the child of a peaceful revolution, and we confidently believe that its exertions will lead to the contentment and welfare of all races within the Ottoman dominions'.

---

[19] The Prince declared himself King in 1910. Cettinje is the former capital (now Podgorica – once Titograd – is the capital). Cattaro is the present Kotor, a UNESCO-protected site; the main harbour is now Bar, which has a railway to the interior. A reference in the text to the 'wonderful zigzag carriage road from the roomy and beautiful harbour of Cattaro to the tiny capital, Cettinje' is a further indication of personal knowledge on the part of the writer: I have also travelled this road, which remains frighteningly narrow and tortuous.

The historical background contained in these two articles – briefly and inadequately summarised here – could no doubt be contested on some points by present-day historians. Nevertheless, at the time of the *Encyclopædia*, it would have given readers a very helpful guide towards understanding the 'Balkan problem'. (Given the complexity of the subject-matter, one assumes that the readers in question were certainly not the 'little children' frequently addressed elsewhere in the work.)

Indeed, it remains highly relevant to more recent issues, especially the conflicts leading to the break-up of Yugoslavia in the 1990s; it is noteworthy that Serbia and Montenegro have re-emerged (with approximately the same flags as those which introduce this chapter), as well as the former parts of the Austro-Hungarian Empire, Slovenia, Croatia and Bosnia-Herzegovina. And the historical legacy of Ottoman dominion underlies some current attitudes towards Turkish membership of the European Union (such as Greek, Austrian and Hungarian reluctance in this matter).

Spain and Portugal (pp. 3353–64)

We are here following the order of the *Encyclopædia*: one might have expected these countries to be considered after Italy.

Once again, the treatment is thorough and readable. There is a brief survey of the main geographical features: the high central plateau ('bare and bleak'), more like Africa than Europe, contrasting with fertile coastlands and the wet Atlantic seaboard. Then we hear of the Roman occupation, bringing the foundation of great cities. Merida, 'the Rome of Spain', gets special mention, with its amphitheatre, circus and magnificent long bridge over the Tagus.

After the invasions of Goths and Vandals came the Moorish conquest and long reign. The Moors are described as 'warlike and fearless', but also 'industrious and clever', and credit is given to their feats of irrigation and their building of wonderful mosques, palaces and castles; the Alhambra at Granada is 'a fairy palace'.

With the Reconquest, and under the joint reign of Ferdinand of Aragon and Catherine of Castile, Spain became a united country, Portugal remaining as a separate kingdom. We are told of the great voyages of discovery by the Portuguese and Spanish explorers.

Under Charles V, Spain became the centre of a great empire. But Philip II was an 'incompetent bigot', under whom the Inquisition wrought its cruel work, while the Netherlands revolted successfully. (The Armada is only briefly mentioned here: it gets full treatment elsewhere in the *Encyclopædia*.)

Napoleon's attempt to subdue the peninsula is recounted, also Wellington's successful campaign.

This leads into the troubled nineteenth century, with disputes and civil wars, and the loss of the colonies. 'But now things are more settled'. The young king,

Alfonso XIII, had married an English princess; prosperity was increasing, railways were being built, agriculture was improving.

Here the author displays her usual tendency to gloss over problems. It would certainly have been too soon to judge Alfonso, who had only come of age in 1906. But after revolution in 1868 and a short-lived republic, the restored monarchy remained contested and precarious, especially after the disastrous year 1898 when the colonies were lost to America. As a modern historian has put it: 'A Catholic monarchy, sustained by a narrow conservative oligarchy, had been challenged by the assumptions of democracy and free thought'.[20] It would take most of the twentieth century for Spain to become a democratic country.

The people of the Iberian peninsula, the author says, come of 'a very noble and dignified stock. Foreigners often consider them proud, but a great deal of their grand manner, especially among the peasants, is prompted by self-respect.' Bull-fighting, of course, is described as 'a horrible and cruel thing'; but 'we in England cannot say too much about the barbarity of it so long as we ourselves hunt tame stages and shoot tame pheasants, and set dogs on to timid hares, and call it "sport".' (Curiously, nothing is said about fox-hunting.)

The author sums up the chapter with her usual eloquence:

> 'While studying or drawing the map of the peninsula of contrasts, or modelling its rugged surface, there is much to think over and 'see' with the inward eye. We know where to look for green valleys and ashy mountains, some tipped with snow; for the bright gardens of vines, olives, oranges, nuts, and the trackless wastes. And as we glance again round the long coast, what a pageant rises before us: of the Roman galleys, bringing soldiers and colonists; of the Moors pouring in near Gibraltar; of the little ships of Columbus sailing to the golden West, pilots of the rich treasure fleets – the "galleons of Spain" which Drake and others used to intercept. And then we see the gathering and sailing of the mighty Armada in all its glory, and from time to time through the centuries the bridal trains of princesses of the peninsula on their way to become Queens of England.' (p. 3364)

Holland and Belgium (pp. 3455–64)

The author does a good job of disentangling the history of this region. To mention here only the major points: after forming part of Charlemagne's empire, the 'Netherlands' (including the territory of present-day Belgium as well as the Netherlands) broke up into a number of feudal states. From belonging to the Dukes of Burgundy, it passed into the hands of Charles V along with the other Hapsburg possessions, Austria and Spain. The reign of his son Philip II brought

---

[20] Cf. Raymond Carr, chapter on 'Liberalism and Reaction' in *Spain: A History* (Oxford: OUP, 2000). Giles Tremlett, in *Ghosts of Spain* (London: Faber, 2006), concentrates on the Civil War and its aftermath, underlining the instability of Spanish politics until recent times.

cruel repression, against which the Protestant North revolted, gained independence in 1581 after heroic struggles.

After the French Revolution, Napoleon annexed the Low Countries. The Congress of Vienna joined the whole area into a single kingdom under the House of Orange, until in 1830 the Catholic South revolted to form the kingdom of Belgium (under a German prince).

In describing 'Holland', the author stresses its particularities as a flat land of dykes, polders and windmills; the constant battle with the sea has developed a 'wise and determined' national character. The quality of its farm produce, especially butter and cheese, gets special mention. With Amsterdam and Rotterdam it also had its great ports.

A SNAPSHOT IN A STREET OF HOLLAND
Although the people of Holland are industrious, no matter where we go, we can see the men standing about, dressed in their big, balloon-like breeches, smoking or talking.

Belgium too had a major harbour with Antwerp, and fine old cities with Brussels, Ghent and Bruges. It had rich coalfields, as well as mines of iron and zinc; a dense railway network; and in Liège a great engineering centre. Great quantities of sugar were made from beet. Belgium is also famous for its lace.

The Belgian Ardennes had become a favourite trip for visitors from England: the sea passage from Dover to Ostend could be made in three-and-a-half hours (about the same as the ferries took until this service was suspended in the mid-1990s).

One important point is missing from this description: i.e. the Flemish-Francophone division of Belgium, which has subsequently caused so much trouble. But the omission is understandable: this was not seen as a significant issue in the early twentieth century.

Norway, Denmark and Sweden (pp. 3591–3602)

This article describes the warlike tendencies of the early Scandinavians, as their chiefs fought each other for possession of desirable tracts of land that gradually grew into small kingdoms. Towards the end of the eighth century,

> 'the Norsemen burst like a destructive tempest over lands, by this time somewhat civilised and Christianised, on the coasts of Ireland and Scotland ... and on the coasts of England and France. For a time they were content to leave with their booty, returning year by year for more; and then they began to settle in the attacked countries ... In Normandy the Northmen became French; in England we know how the Danes mingled with the English.' (p. 3592)

In the meantime the three kingdoms gradually settled down, and from about the tenth to the fourteenth century kept fairly distinct and independent of each other. For a time all three countries were united under the rule of Denmark, till Sweden broke away. Under a succession of 'hero-kings', Sweden won victories against Denmark, Poland and Russia, and became a major European power.

After the Napoleonic wars, Norway had to accept union with Sweden, while keeping its own free constitution; it separated from Sweden only in 1905. Denmark remained an absolute monarchy till the great revolutionary year 1848, when King Frederick VII gave his people a constitution. 'And now all three Scandinavian kingdoms are independent of each other as they were at the beginning of their history.'

Education was 'very advanced' in Sweden. The author omits to mention the important developments in Denmark, where already in 1814 schooling had been made compulsory between the ages of six and fourteen, and where 'Folk High Schools' had been instituted in the 1840s.

The article describes the varied scenery of Scandinavia, from the farmlands of Denmark and southern Sweden to the fiords of Norway and to the land of the midnight sun beyond the Arctic Circle; the Laps and the Finns get a mention in this context.

Denmark's dairy farming gets special praise, and there is a surprising statement that 'many Danes go to Siberia, where vast farms are gradually rising up over the country, giving us butter to spread on the bread grown on the wheat farms of Canada'.

Russia (pp. 3623–32 & 3745–54)

If there was any sense that this long series on 'Countries' might be running out of steam after dealing with the smaller (and less problematic) European states, the two articles on Russia revive the impetus.

The first of these shows 'how this vast Eurasian empire has grown through the centuries from some small inland states about the Dnieper and Volga rivers, till it reached the White Sea, the Baltic Sea, and the Black Sea, and across thousands of miles to the Pacific'.

Some reigns stand out. In the fifteenth century, Ivan III increased his power through conquests and alliances, and is considered to be 'the founder of the state of modern Russia'. In the following century, Ivan IV – 'The Terrible' – further extended his dominions and was the first to take formally the title of 'Czar'; in his reign, trade with England was opened up by way of the White Sea, and 'a Russian ambassador and his suite, in gorgeous coats of velvet, with fringes of silk and chains of gold, made a splendid entry into London'. Ivan even proposed to marry Queen Elizabeth, without success.

Towards the end of the seventeenth century, Peter II – 'The Great' – sought to modernise his country. The *Encyclopædia* tells us of his journey to Holland and England to study various handicrafts, especially shipbuilding, which he put to use in creating a Russian navy. He was a reformer:

> 'He made new regulations for the government of the Church, altered the customs of society, forbade all Eastern habits brought in by the Tartars, insisted on people shaving, and did all in his power to make Russia like Western Europe... He built canals, had books translated, founded libraries and museums, and travelled with unflagging energy all over his dominions... He took a most important step when he seized Baku, on the Caspian Sea, for here are the wonderful oil-wells that today bring much wealth into Russia.' (p. 3630)

And of course, he created St. Petersburg on the swampy islands of the Neva.

Catherine II – also termed 'The Great' – had a long and eventful reign. She made many enemies by taking away the lands and peasants belonging to the Church to be the property of the State. She extended her possessions in Poland and to the Black Sea, and won Crimea from the Turks.

By this time, Russia already held most of Finland. Alexander I got the rest from Sweden. His greatest trial was the duel with Napoleon: 'Thousands of Russians had to march hither and thither over the face of Europe, to try to cope with the conqueror. Twenty-one thousand Russians lay dead at Austerlitz.' He reached agreement with Napoleon to divide Europe between them, but this truce broke down and the Grand Army forced its way to Moscow; but 'the Russians determined to sacrifice their splendid and ancient city, and to let the French enter without striking a blow.' With most of the city destroyed by fire, the French had to retire, 'beaten by the terrible foes of cold and starvation'.

Under Alexander II, the serfs were set free in 1861, and 'many other reforms were set in hand: railways were begun, trade and industries were encouraged.' But a constitution was still delayed.

When the *Encyclopædia* was being written, Nicholas II was Czar. The second of these two articles describes the vastness and variety of his empire: the frozen tundras of the north, the endless forests, the near-desert plains of the Asiatic regions. Most of the population lived in the areas where the soil is rich and watered by many rivers. 'The peasants, for the most part, lead dull, sad lives and are terribly poor.'

THE PEOPLE OF EUROPEAN RUSSIA

Here is a Russian gipsy girl. There are fewer gipsies in Russia than in England.

These are peasant girls of Little Russia, that part of the Russian Empire in Europe that includes the important town and province of Kiev.

This moujik, or peasant, girl belongs to the province of Tver, to the north of Moscow.

The great mass of the people of Russia are very poor, their despotic and selfish Government grinding enormous sums from them in the way of taxes, a great proportion of which is wasted or embezzled. The poverty of the people can be seen from this picture of Russian road-menders at their work, the men having to use rags instead of shoes.

The people of the Baltic provinces are more intelligent than other Russians, owing to their contact with the rest of Europe. Their character and dress may be seen from this picture of an Esthonian girl.

Peasant girls of Lithuania, the country that was formerly included in the ancient kingdom of Poland, but is now known as Western Russia. The girls are shown in the picturesque costume in which they usually work.

3747

Russia had great mineral wealth – iron, copper, gold and silver – but this was not yet half worked, 'neither does it go to enrich the country nor to help pay for the costly reforms which are so urgently needed'.

One may be surprised to hear that 'it is an easy journey from England to Russia, either by land or sea' – perceptions of distance were different before the age of air travel! The article describes the places to visit. These include, of course, St. Petersburg, with the treasures of the Hermitage (this reference is puzzling since the museum was not opened to the public till after the Revolution); and Moscow, with the Kremlin, seen not (as we might feel after the days of Stalinist dictatorship) as a sinister seat of government but as a 'sacred spot, for here are the Synod buildings, where the Council of the Russian Church meets in solemn state'. Kiev and Novgorod are also singled out as fine, ancient towns. At Nijni Novgorod on the Volga, a great fair is held every summer, with wares from every part of the empire and beyond.

The Siberian railway was now running all the way to Vladivostok, and many towns were growing up along the line. But 'the last part of the line is full of reminders of the dreadful war between the Russians and Japanese in 1905, when Russian soldiers were brought across Asia by thousands on the Siberian railway, to perish miserably in the struggle'.

The text does not cover the **Baltic countries**, contained at this time within the empire, but the caption to one of the pictures (reproduced) mentions them, and declares that 'the people of the Baltic provinces are more intelligent than other countries, owing to their contact with the rest of Europe'.

Finland is easily reached from St. Petersburg. Here too, though also part of the empire, conditions seem much better.

> 'The Finlanders are highly educated, and are deeply interested in reforms
> and good government, and in finding out the best ways of living.'

Moreover, in view of the controversy in Britain at the time over votes for women, the following comment is significant:

> 'Finland is one of the countries where women are counted as citizens, and
> are allowed to help to choose the representatives who settle public
> matters, as well as men. They can even be elected as representatives
> themselves.' (p. 3753)

The author does not hide her distaste of the czarist regime. 'The reins of the government of the vast empire are held in St. Petersburg. Here the Czar lives, the autocrat, the holder of supreme power, whose will is law.' The machinery of government was out-of-date; there was an enormous number of officials; many police and spies; also

> 'thousands of soldiers spread over the great provinces, not only to defend
> or extend the borders of the empire, but to repress the risings of those
> who live within it... It is generally but a stifled whisper of the struggle
> going on in Russia that reaches the ears of Europe. Millions in the vast
> empire still live on in blind obedience and submission... But,
> occasionally, it is more than a murmur of this seething discontent that we
> hear. Sometimes the people burst out into open revolt. From time to time

Europe is horrified by the news of assassinations of the leaders of the government, by men banded together to destroy the existing state of things in the swiftest way they can devise.' (p. 3753)

The text does not specifically mention the failed revolution of 1905 (suppressed by the army which remained loyal to the Czar, who unfortunately failed to learn the necessary lessons); nor does it cite the Bolsheviks among the potential revolutionaries (neither Marxism nor Lenin are anywhere mentioned in the *Encyclopædia*, but it is perhaps only with hindsight that we can recognise their significance).

Nevertheless, the frankness of the passage above is unusual in the *Encyclopædia*, given its tendency to gloss over unpleasant facts; it would not have been difficult to conclude that an even more violent revolution had to come. Still, the author strives for an optimistic conclusion:

'Mercifully, all reformers in Russia do not believe in using bombs to gain their righteous demands. Many go on in patience, teaching and preparing the ground for the final struggle and the success that must come sooner or later'. (p. 3754)

Interestingly, Tolstoy (still alive – he died in 1910) is held up as

'the greatest leader of thought in Russia, as well as the greatest influence for gaining freedom by peaceful methods… Perhaps he is the only man in Russia who is not afraid of the Czar… His voice rings loud and clear as he denounces the wrongs of the peasants, the evils of luxury, the hollowness of the state religion, the wickedness and waste of drawing men from their home to train them to kill their fellow men. And no one dares to touch Tolstoy as he utters his brave and inspiring words, standing out boldly against the background of Russian misery.' (p. 3754)

Persia and Asiatic Turkey (pp. 3873–82)

This article provides a good survey of the history of the Middle East, covering in particular the origins and spread of Islam, the arrival of the Seljouk Turks, the Mongol invasions and the rise of Ottoman power. It also describes the general topography of the region. Mesopotamia was

'chiefly a dry and dreary country, with very few people living in it, and its fields beyond the river banks are little cultivated … Arabia, apart from a fringe of fertile lowlands on parts of the coast, consists mainly of deserts where neither vegetation nor animal life can exist.' (pp. 3874-5)

There is no mention here of oil: the first discoveries in the region were made a few years later.

When the *Encyclopædia* was being written, the Turkish possessions extended through Mesopotamia to the Persian Gulf (see map with flag in colour section). Iraq was created only after the defeat of Turkey in the First World War.

Particular interest is shown in **Persia**. This country had emerged from Mongol rule in the sixteenth century: the Shahs had then rebuilt the beautiful city of Ispahan, encouraged the silk industry and generally promoted prosperity.

The article describes a journey across the country – initially by motor-car, for there were only two short railway lines. This is worth quoting at some length, for it provides an image of travel so different from that which we know today:

'We must pass over the pleasures of running round the south of Russia, the tossing on the Black Sea, the run by train from Batum to Baku, the smell of oil on the puddles, the difficulties on the Caspian, especially in landing the car on Persian soil. Round the south of the Caspian, the Garden of Persia, we pass through a paradise of green vegetation of every kind, from rice-fields, shimmering in water, to stretches of daisies, lilies, irises, so high that one can easily be lost in them; and everywhere are lovely lilacs and other flowering trees, in which the nightingales sing.

'But this is only one aspect of Persia, as we soon discover when we push on through the mountain barrier that guards the great plateau of Iran; and we shall be lucky indeed if the car does not break down with bounding from rock to rock or sinking into the stiff mud of the almost neglected roads. If it does break down, the only alternative is to hire a native carriage, without springs, and change horses at the post-houses; and a long and weary journey it is, for hotels and inns, as we understand them, are unknown.

'Day after day we plod along over the stony desert, occasionally relieved by dark forests and spots of cultivation… And the sun pours down in intense heat, so that the caravans with the camels which we meet only travel by night.

'It is a relief to see the white-pointed peak of Demavend, and at last to enter Teheran. Under its sky of fixed blue, the roses flower for which Persia is so famous, and the fresh dry air makes us ready to enjoy anything. The palaces and gardens are very fine, also the beautiful lustre pots, and glorious old stuffs, brocades, and carpets that we are invited to buy… There are women with long, thick white veils and full black cloaks covering them up completely, and men of different nationalities, besides the Persians in their high black hats and flowing robes…

'But our object is to push on to Ispahan, over many more miles of burning desert, with the sand too hot to touch, though at night the air is crisp and dry, and the deep sky is simply blazing with stars. Every now and then there is the joy of an oasis, with its limpid streams and little villages surrounded by fields of corn and rye and cheering wild flowers…

'At last we see the domes of the mosques of Ispahan between the trees… The avenues of trees, the fields of roses and white poppies, the gardens, the pale green streams and canals, the buildings of the great Shah Abbas, which date from the end of the sixteenth century – everything is wonderful and interesting. The enamelled tiles and plaques, the blue cupolas and minarets of the mosque, the fine square, all fill us with admiration.' (p. 3881)

Did Frances Epps herself make this journey? – the detail and vividness of the description suggest so; or if not, either she must have talked with someone who did or is quoting some travel writer. It would be good to know.

Persia, she remarks, is 'one of the countries now struggling for a constitution': one was granted by the Shah in 1906, but 'it was of little use to the bulk of the people; and fresh attempts to win freedom have plunged Persia into civil war and great difficulties which are not yet settled.' (Note the demonstration shown in the illustration.)

The Heart of Asia (pp. 3931–40)

Only about 21 million people were living in the part of Asia lying between Siberia and India on the north and south, and Persia and China on the north and west. Most of these made their homes in tents, and wandered about in search of fresh pasture for their flocks; others tilled the soil of the fertile valleys and oases.

The 'Roof of the World' contains the mighty heights of the Himalayas.

> 'Most of the mountains are far above the line of perpetual snow,
> surrounded by glaciers and ice-folds, all of immense size. In contrast are
> the dark, bare pinnacles of rock, the fearsome precipices and cliffs,
> girdled lower down by dark forests and rushing streams.' (p. 3932)

Between these mountain walls lie the countries that make up Central Asia. The article describes the grassy uplands of **Mongolia**, where most people were shepherds, tending their flocks as their ancestors had always done; we are reminded that from this region the Mongol warriors had come to conquer all the world within their reach. Camel trains also had plodded along the trade routes, bringing silk from China, jade from south Turkestan, carpets and other treasures from the East.

The journeys of the Swedish explorer Sven Hedin in **Turkestan** get particular attention: he travelled along the river Tarim, which is as long as the Danube, though it dwindles away into shallow lakes and sand far from the sea in Chinese Turkestan (this expedition was in 1899–1902, just one of Hedin's journeys).

Afghanistan, after suffering invasions from Arabs, Turks and Mongols, had become independent again in the mid-eighteenth century. 'The British have bitter memories connected with many of the towns and passes': we are reminded of the annihilation in 1842 of a British army on its retreat from Kabul.

Tibet is 'one of the most extraordinary countries in the world – a citadel strongly guarded by glittering, icy ramparts in the clouds'. Till recently it was barely known to the West. There is a photograph of Lhasa, which a British force, 'sent to settle some trade arrangements', had succeeded in entering only in 1901.

The Dalai Lama lived at Lhasa in a 'mysterious and huge palace on the crest of a hill, the centre part a blaze of crimson, the roofs of glittering gold'. Many pilgrims came here to worship. There were many monks in Tibet, as each family dedicated at least one son to the priesthood. The Buddhist religion had deeply influenced the Tibetan people; religious inscriptions and prayer-wheels were everywhere to be seen. At the end of each day, people gathered in the squares and open places, prostrating themselves on the earth, to chant the evening prayers.

THE PEOPLE OF PERSIA AND ARABIA

An excited and infuriated crowd of Persians rushing through the streets of Tabriz clamouring for a parliament and a constitution. This was granted by the Shah, but was afterwards withdrawn, an action that led to civil war.

A wealthy Persian merchant of to-day. An armed caravan guide of Arabia. A group of Bedouins from the district round Petra in Arabia. A poor peasant woman of Persia. A wealthy Persian lady of high rank.

The Bedouin of the Arabian desert is always seen either riding on his dromedary or resting in his portable tent. The Arab carries everything belonging to him upon his camel—his wife and family, his clothes and his house.

3879

FAMOUS CITIES IN THE HEART OF ASIA

A few years ago no such photograph as this existed; for Lhasa, which is shown in the picture, was the unknown, mysterious city of Tibet that no European was allowed to approach. Its name means the Home of the Gods, and it is at Lhasa that the Dalai Lama, or high priest of Buddhism, lives. A British expedition entered Lhasa in 1904.

Here, the author describes Buddhist practices objectively and respectfully: this contrasts with the contemptuous and largely ignorant treatment meted out elsewhere in the *Encyclopædia* (under **MEN AND WOMEN**, dealing with the Buddha).

The Chinese Empire (pp. 4035–46)

This is described as the 'oldest nation in the world'. Its written history goes back for four thousand years: 'so that when Europe was just beginning to make for civilised ways and thoughts, the Chinese nation was as old as we are now.'

> 'But she lost the advantage of her start by standing still, going to sleep, and keeping herself to herself for centuries while the young Western nations were forging ahead.'

There were many reasons for this:

> 'One is that the Chinese have always greatly revered their parents and ancestors, going so far as to make it a first duty to carry on the work of life in exactly the same way that their forefathers had handed down. Another reason is that, with few exceptions, the Chinese have stayed at home within the limits of their own country... As they seldom encouraged foreigners to visit them, no new ideas of progress and reform, no new knowledge of outside discoveries and inventions, could penetrate the well of reserve.' (p. 4038)

We are told of the teachings of Confucius and of the spread of Buddhism. About the time of King Alfred in England, Chinese records mentioned the printing of books by wooden blocks; an immense Encyclopædia was written. The Ming dynasty lasted nearly three hundred years; very beautiful porcelain was made, and another Encyclopædia was brought out, said to be the largest in the world as it ran to many thousands of volumes.

MEN, WOMEN, AND CHILDREN OF CHINA

A woman and child of Macao, a Portuguese settlement in China.

Chinese girls of various ages engaged at embroidery work in a mission school at Canton.

A young lady of Canton dressed in her best walking costume.

A choir of Chinese boys at a mission school. The study of expressions on the faces in this picture is very interesting, as only two of the boys in the group knew that they were being photographed.

A Chinese woman with tiny feet. The cruel custom of crushing the feet of girls has been in fashion for 900 years.

A group of Manchu gentlemen. The Manchus conquered China in 1644 and founded the present line of emperors. They introduced the wearing of pigtails into China.

A typical Manchu lady. The Manchus are still the ruling class in China, most Government officials belonging to that race.

The photographs on these pages are by Messrs. Underwood and Underwood, and others.

4030

141

A CHINESE EMPRESS ON HER THRONE

This picture of the late Empress Tze-hsi, the slave girl who rose to rule an empire, is typical of China, the land of all that is picturesque. The gorgeous costume of dazzling colour is a true emblem of Eastern pomp, which is well represented by this able woman, who was once described as "the only man in China."

In the previous seventy years, the Western Powers had sought to gain footholds in China. But foreign merchants had brought opium into the country, and that had 'quite as bad an effect as taking too much strong drink'. With remarkable frankness, the author writes:

'The chief object was to force the Christian religion and Western ideas upon a country which detested them, and to open up trade with people who had so much to sell, and whose great numbers mean great buying power.' (p. 4042)

The 'Boxer' rising took place against missionaries and other foreigners. Indeed:

'The efforts of Christian missionaries in China have been sadly hampered by the actions of traders of their own faith, by their want of principle, and by the bad example that many of them have set.' (p. 4044)

The population at that time was around 300 million. The main regions of this vast country are briefly described, including major tourist sights such as the Great Wall and the gorges of the Yang-tse.

The writer is incensed by the practice – fortunately then dying out – of tying up the feet of little girls to keep their feet tiny (there is a photograph – reproduced – to show the result).

There is brief mention of the emperor's court and the Forbidden Palace in Peking, and of the grand pageants when the Emperor visits the Temple of Heaven; there is a picture (gaudily coloured – reproduced here) of the late Empress, 'a slave girl who rose to rule an empire' (she had died very recently, in 1908).

Unusually, nothing more is said about the political regime, which was of course highly autocratic. It was also extremely unstable: the Empress had named a three-year boy as her successor, and he was forced to renounce the throne in 1912 (the 'last Emperor'). Appropriately, the article concludes by speculating:

'Who can say what may be the future of a country with such a great seaboard on provinces, and millions upon millions of thrifty workers?'(p. 4046)

Japan and Korea (pp. 4147–58)

The author describes the beauties of the Japanese countryside, again in terms which could suggest personal knowledge. She writes of the mysterious wonder of Fuji-Yama, the sacred mountain so deeply beloved by the Japanese and reproduced by hundreds of their artists:

'What a view from the top! over fertile plains and glinting water, to mountains beyond… The lovely scenery is set off with a garment of most gorgeous and wonderful colouring, made of blossoms of every hue… The purple wisteria hangs in profusion over great trellises, the camelia-trees grow as high as a house, and the masses of roses, convolvulus, and azaleas form dazzling banks of colour… We can take the train along the lovely shores between Nippon and the two smaller southern islands; or, better still, pass on our way from Nagasaki in a steamer through the deep, clear, blue water, passing countless islands and hills clothed in vivid green; and there is ever the living interest of the numerous fishing boats, and curious-looking junks, and the tiny villages hidden in unexpected nooks.' (pp. 4152-56)

Japan was an ancient civilisation, ruled for many centuries by the same dynasty, and under a system similar to feudalism in Europe. There had been many quarrels between the noble families, leading to battles between private armies of samurai. Shintoism was the prevailing religion, complemented rather than replaced by the arrival of Buddhism. Ancestors were revered; the emperor was held sacred, and was inaccessible to most of his people; powerful Shoguns controlled the government.

For most of its history Japan had remained closed to the rest of the world: but a big change had taken place in the mid-nineteenth century after the arrival of Captain Perry with an American fleet. Treaties were signed, Yokohama was opened to foreign trade, the last Shogun had to retire, feudal ways were swept away. Roads and railways were built; the telegraph and the telephone arrived; banks, warehouses, factories sprang up. Law courts were established; and in 1889 a constitution was granted, establishing a House of Commons elected by the people. Education on modern Western lines started everywhere. And a 'splendidly efficient navy and army have been created within a few years'.

War with China in 1884–85 had added Formosa to the Mikado's empire. Then in 1904–05 Japan defeated Russia, gaining the southern half of the island of Sakhalin, and obtaining Korea as a protectorate. The *Encyclopædia*'s account here is unduly bland; as these events were quite recent, one might have expected fuller treatment.[21] Indeed, it is curious, given the generally pacifist tendency of the *Encyclopædia*, that Japanese militancy is described approvingly.

'Every Japanese boy is brought up to believe that the greatest honour that can befall him is to die for his emperor and country if need be... So it is no wonder that the flag of the Rising Sun was carried triumphantly from start to finish in such strong hands.' (p. 4152)

Perhaps there is a (misguided) sense of fellowship with the British: Japan, it is pointed out from the start of this article, is an island like Britain, and the Japanese are 'sailors and traders', like the British. With more justification, there is also admiration for Japanese family life:

'Perhaps Japanese children have the happiest time of any children in the world. Their father and mothers are devoted to them, and train them from babyhood to be self-controlled and polite to everyone; to be gentle in their ways, and to be fond of work.' (p. 4158)

---

[21] Both these wars arose out of Japan's desire to control Korea and Manchuria. They caused great loss of life. The US-imposed Treaty of Portsmouth which concluded the Russo-Japanese war, though it gave Japan half of Sakhalin and a protectorate over Korea, required both parties to restore Manchuria to China. The settlement was judged unfair by the Japanese, who felt they had not got enough benefit from winning the war: historians consider this resentment played its part in subsequent events up to Pearl Harbour... (Cf. *Wikipedia*, Russo-Japanese War.)

JAPANESE WOMEN AND CHILDREN

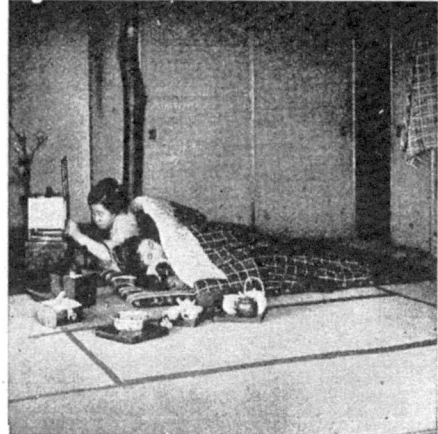

This is a Japanese bedroom, and the inmates are just retiring for the night. The bed is a mattress spread on the floor, and the wooden pillow fits the neck.

Japanese ladies are fond of playing upon a stringed instrument something like our banjo. The music that they produce sounds very crude to Western ears.

Japan is called the Paradise of Children, and some babies are so happy that they never cry, and the people say that in Japan every other shop is a toy-shop.

These boys seem to have heads like blacking-brushes. As soon as boys can go out they are taken to have their heads shaved so that their hair will grow stiff.

In Japan the gardens seem like fairyland, and the Japanese gardener always tries to arrange his shrubs so that one at least shall be in bloom all the year round.

The poorer women of Japan work hard, and in the summer they go into the fields with their children and all work together. Here we see them taking a midday rest.

4153

Indeed, these two quotations pinpoint the duality of the Japanese character, which Westerners have found so difficult to understand; the first characteristic leading them into their aggression on China and South-East Asia from 1936 onwards, the second helping to explain their submission to McArthur's rule after defeat in 1945.

The Koreans, on the other hand, are described as 'poor and spiritless'. The valleys are very fertile, and metals are believed to be abundant; 'but there is still much to do in developing the resources of the country'.

Mexico and Central America (pp. 4381–92)

After the usual – excellent – description of the geography of the region, this article deals mainly with the Spanish conquest and its aftermath. It tells how, after Columbus' discoveries, Cortes, with just four hundred soldiers, contrived to defeat the Aztecs. Subsequently, viceroys were sent out from Spain: 'Some were good and kind: some terribly the reverse': some levied oppressive taxes, while great riches were sent to Spain.

Missionary priests 'tried to influence the natives towards a spirit of quiet obedience... Many beautiful towns were founded after Spanish models, with Spanish names and fine cathedrals'. But many natives who refused conversion to Christianity were burnt at the stake. The writer – usually forthright in her opinions – here seems uncertain whether to condemn the Spanish occupation for its cruelties or to approve the bringing of European civilisation and religion.

Eventually, some hundred years before the writing of the *Encyclopædia*, Mexico and other countries of the region gained their independence. Still, 'both earthquakes and revolutions are common occurrences in Central America'.

The pre-Columbian history of the region was still being, literally, unearthed. The ruins of temples were being discovered; a great palace testified to the high civilisation of the Mayas.

The Panama Canal was still under construction as the *Encyclopædia* was being written – 'the biggest engineering enterprise ever known' (see picture; it was opened in 1914.)

CUTTING THE NEW WORLD IN TWO

This picture shows how the Panama Canal will look when finished. De Lesseps, the famous builder of the Suez Canal, began the work in 1881, but it had to be abandoned after nearly £70,000,000 had been wasted. The United States took over the work in 1903. There is now a vast army of men engaged in the stupendous task of cutting the New World in half, and it is estimated that this marvellous canal will cost £40,000,000 to finish.

4389

South America (pp. 4497–4506 & 4571–80)

Two articles cover South America. The first, after describing its geography, with several illustrations, deals with the history of the continent. It tells in particular the story of Pizarro's conquest of Peru, including the treachery by which he captured the Inca ruler, Montezuma, and recounts how the attraction of gold and jewels brought adventurers from all over Europe.

This article contains its own summary:

> 'As we look in imagination over the long past of South America, we see it first in possession of the old tribes... For long centuries their descendants wandered over the wide country, leading their primitive lives. Then, out of the mists of time, we distinguish the dazzling Incas with their high civilisation... And we see this civilisation all brought to a sudden and tragic end as the white men from an unknown western world swarmed over the sea to seize the lands and treasures of the unfortunate Incas...
>
> 'We see Spain and Portugal in possession of the continent for nearly 300 years; explorers seeking gold up the wide rivers, through the great forests, over the dangerous passes of the Andes; and the black-frocked priests in their wake, many of whom were ready to lay down their lives in their efforts to teach the Indians, whom their countrymen were ever ready to enslave.' (p. 4506)

The second article deals with the contemporary situation. Ten independent Republics then covered almost all the continent (only the three Guianas – British, French and Dutch – were still European colonies); there are more illustrations showing all the major cities. The total population of South America is said to be less than that of the British Isles, though Brazil, much the biggest country, had 20 million people.

There is some reference to the instability of the new republics. But, always in search of a positive conclusion, the author stresses how the continent is being opened up by railways and bridges, making available the hidden treasures of mines, plains and forests.

> 'Man has fought and conquered Nature. Science has swept away the barrier; and the day will soon dawn when the dreams of many men of many nations will be realised.' (p. 4580)

The World around the Poles (pp. 4719–30)

This article describes these worlds of snow and ice: in the Arctic, the lives of the Eskimos, the polar bears, seals and whales; in the Antarctic, a vast, desolate waste. Above all, the author recounts the various voyages of discovery, hazardous and sometimes fatal: journeys seeking a north-west route round North America and a north-east passage round Scandinavia and Siberia.

One senses in particular the excitement stimulated by very recent attempts to reach the Poles:

> 'As this is being written, two American explorers, Captain Peary and Dr. Cook, report that they have reached the North Pole, a goal for which men have striven so long, and the whole world eagerly waits for their proofs.'
> (p. 4726)

In fact, this claim was not authenticated.

In 1902, Captain Scott had got to within 540 miles of the South Pole, and in 1909 – presumably just before this issue of the *Encyclopædia* – Lieutenant Shackleton had come to within just 111 miles.

> 'Every one of the polar explorations makes enthralling reading for those who feel the intense charm of the mighty icefields and mountains, the mysterious midnight sun, the long light and long darkness, the glittering stars, the gorgeous effects of the northern and southern lights… and the call in the blood to be up and doing… The blinding blizzards, knife-like ridges of ice, unspeakably bitter cold, constant anxiety lest hardships prove too severe and lest food should fail, are nothing new – they have been the portion of polar explorers from the first'. (p. 4730)

Numerous illustrations accompany this article, and one feels grateful that the art of photography had so far advanced as to make these records possible. Two of these photos – showing Shackleton and Peary on their journeys – are reproduced here. Another very recent photograph, of poor quality but nevertheless remarkable, was taken from Shackleton's published account of his expedition: it showed his party standing on the edge of the crater of the Mount Erebus volcano.

FARTHEST NORTH AND FARTHEST SOUTH

Lieutenant Shackleton and his fellow-explorers suffered many hardships during their great dash to the South Pole. Food fell short, and the ponies of the expedition had to be killed until only three remained, as shown in this picture.

As Lieutenant Shackleton is the hero of the Antarctic, so Captain Peary is the hero of the Arctic. Both men have surpassed all previous efforts to reach the Poles. Here we see Captain Peary with some of his Eskimo dogs.

4728

Egypt, Babylonia and Assyria, Persia, Greece, Rome
(pp. 4779–92, 4971–84, 5057–66, 5121–30, 5259–68)

The series of articles on **COUNTRIES** concludes with a survey of each of these 'Dead Empires'. These do not tell us so much about the Edwardian outlook, so it is not necessary to review them in any detail.

It should however be noted that these articles are written with the author's usual clarity and thoroughness. They provide a comprehensive introduction to the history of each civilisation, often told in story form. The text is supported by illustrations, which in this case, of course, are mostly reproductions of paintings or drawings, though there are photographs of the Acropolis in Athens (the temples stand on their hill above a relatively empty landscape) and of the Coliseum in Rome.

The glory of ancient Athens, once the finest city in the world, is represented to-day by a pile of noble ruins, and in this view we see the famous Acropolis, the hill on which many temples stood.

A youngster who had read these articles attentively would have emerged with an extensive cultural knowledge. Though travel to the distant lands in question would have been more of an adventure than it is today, there are frequent references to artefacts in the British Museum which might have stimulated interest in a visit there. In the hundred years since the time of the *Encyclopædia*, archaeological studies have of course extended our knowledge, but without significantly altering the basic facts set out here (the most obvious gap is the tomb of Tutankhamen, discovered in 1922). Also, there is no mention of the 'Elgin marbles' from the Acropolis, kept in the British Museum; but Greece, having only recently emerged from Ottoman rule, had not yet made an issue of this.

From our present point of view, the introduction to these articles is significant. It quotes St. Paul – 'The things which are seen are temporal; but the things which are not seen are eternal' – and continues:

'Even empires pass away, and nothing remains of them but the unseen things which made them great. Many great empires have existed in the world of which not as much as a shadow remains today. Thousands of years ago they rose, and grew, and flourished, and then decayed, because not all their power and wealth could save them when cruelty and selfishness and bad government crept into them ... No story in our book brings home to us more deeply the truth that the greatest power in the world lies in things which we cannot see – in love, and truth, and hope, and faith, which have never once passed out of the world, but without which even empires perish.' (p. 4779)

Reaching the end of this long series on **COUNTRIES**, some general remarks are called for. To cover 'all countries of the world' was an ambitious enterprise, and the result is impressive. The overall scheme must have been planned in advance, to correspond to the fifty fortnightly issues of the *Encyclopædia* (with some telescoping, the number of countries – then much fewer than today – could fit quite neatly within this schema).

No doubt some of the writing was also done in advance, but references to current events (such as the near-discoveries of the Poles) show that the work continued over the two years of publication.

Unity of style confirms that the same author, Frances Epps, was responsible throughout. Though little is known about her, and her previous writings (see footnote at the beginning of this chapter) were modest by comparison with her contribution to the *Encyclopædia*, she must have been a very talented woman.

Her treatment is always thorough, reflecting knowledge that is both extensive and deep. Yet she also makes her subject-matter interesting: history, in particular, is told as much as possible as a story, with much human interest. Discussing geography, she has a gift of description which often makes it sound as if she has been there herself. This was not humanly possible, though some details (which have been pointed out) do suggest personal knowledge; but she must have been very good at making use of descriptions, written or verbal, from other travellers – and, no doubt, material from the British Museum as regards ancient civilisations.

Unlike some of the passages written by the Editor, Arthur Mee, she never 'talks down' to her readers. What was her target audience? – one imagines, intelligent teenagers. And if they did read these articles over the two-year period, or later, they would have been far better informed than most present-day school-leavers.

The world she describes was a very different one from that which we know today. Fewer countries: yes, because much of the world was contained within empires, the British Empire in particular. In Africa there were very few independent countries. The word 'imperialism' has become pejorative: not so for Frances Epps or others of her time. She is proud of the Empire. At the same time, she constantly stresses the duty of the parent nation to improve the lot of its subjects. This involved material progress – the construction of railways was seen as a basic need. It also meant education, and bringing Christianity, though on this point she seems less doctrinaire than some other contributors to the *Encyclopædia*: she writes with respect of the Oriental religions. That she was naïve in this approval of imperialism is obvious with hindsight; even for her time, she seriously glosses over the abuses and the commercial exploitation arising from imperialism.

Dealing with foreign countries, her world-view reflects a context which was soon to be drastically altered by the First World War. France, she said, had a good government and clever, hard-working people, but needed a bigger population to make the most of the country and its empire. She did not point out that the main motive for increasing population – with the recent memory of defeat in the 1870 Franco-German war – was to have more soldiers to defend the country in case of another German attack.

One is struck by her positive attitude to Germany: she admires its progress in science, industrialisation and education. There is no suggestion here that Germany was posing a military threat: the editor, Arthur Mee was certainly aware of this (see the Hammerton biography in the Appendix), and the fact that he did not do so suggests either that he did not interfere with his contributors or that both felt that their young readers should not be troubled with unpleasant thoughts.

Likewise, and still more surprisingly, Japan is viewed favourably despite its aggressions against its neighbours, because here too the people had admirable qualities and there was progress in many fields, including education.

A weakness in her assessments is a reluctance to convey disagreeable facts – was she anxious not to upset her young readers? and was this perhaps editorial policy? This is particularly obvious in her failure to recognise the implications of the conflicting aims of Germany, Austria-Hungary, France and Russia.

Nevertheless, the Czarist regime in Russia incurs her strong disapproval: the duty of rulers is to look after their people, not to leave them in dire poverty. The current situation in China – very unstable – is treated inadequately. The United States was not yet a world power, but she recognises its great potential.

As for the series on Britain itself: the historical exposition may seem superficial, too concerned with the doings of successive kings. Still, this serves to underline the point about the duties of monarchs; good government is a recurring theme throughout these articles.

The writer's determined optimism appears in her assessment of Britain in her time. Current problems are avoided – e.g. the Irish problem, and votes for women (though in dealing with New Zealand and Finland she mentions approvingly that women participate in political life). Above all, she takes a very Utopian view of the lot of the working class.

This, along with many indications in other sections, suggests that the *Encyclopædia* was destined essentially for the prosperous classes. For these, but perhaps not for others, it may have been true that Britain seemed 'the happiest little country in the world'.

THE STORY OF GREAT LIVES

HAVE you ever thought, when looking through the window, that once upon a time there was not a pane of glass in the world? Then a man dug things out of the earth, mixed them, and made something hard, smooth, and clear, so that he could see through it; and it was called glass. Who was he? We do not know. But let us think of the great debt we owe him as we stand at the window and look out upon the world. And all through our lives let us remember that we owe more than we can ever pay to those who lived before us—to those who wrote books and painted pictures, who found steam and made railways, who found gas and lighted our houses, who made our roads, who gave us tools to work with; to the doctors who found out the secret of health, to the travellers who found new lands, to those who laid down their lives that we might live and know more and more. We shall read here of some of the greatest of these.

MEN WHO MADE THE WORLD KNOWN

By MANY WRITERS

ALTHOUGH millions of people live in Great Britain, nobody in this country is so stupid as to think that these are all the people there are, or that ours is the only country in the world.

We know that England, Scotland, and Wales are three countries joined together, with the sea all round them, but we know that away over the sea to the west there is Ireland, and right away still farther to the west, thousands of miles away, there is America, with twice as many people as Britain has. We know that crossing the sea to the East from England we reach Europe, and going forward, first over the land, then over the sea, we may get to Egypt and China and India, and the great lands of the East. Far down to the south, right under our feet, as it were, we come to Australia and New Zealand, with all their people.

It does not seem a clever thing to know all this now, but once upon a time people in Britain thought that there was no other land but theirs, and no other people but themselves. Other people in different parts of the world used to think the same thing about their countries and themselves. They did not travel from country to country as we do now, so they could not get to know of far-off places and different peoples. When they did begin to learn that the world had many different countries, and many different peoples, they were as surprised as we should be if we suddenly discovered the air above to be full of islands and peoples.

People living where the weather is always warm never dreamed that there were such things as snow and ice. Those who lived where the weather is always cold did not imagine that there were parts of the world where it is always summer, where oranges and grapes grow wild in the sunshine, where birds of paradise fly like living rainbows amidst the trees and fireflys dance like winged rubies in the glowing air.

The story is told in the CHILD'S STORY OF THE EARTH, on page 5, of how people used to think that the earth was flat. The people of those early times did not find it easy to make their way about the world, and to discover other countries and people. Still, little by little, they did learn their way about. There were people living all round the Mediterranean Ocean, and they began to spread about, and to find that the world was larger than they thought. There were wonderful people living in the north of Palestine called the Phœnicians. Their country ran along by the sea for a distance as great as that between London and Preston, and they built tiny ships and began to explore this great sea. They made friends with King David and King

7. GREAT LIVES

The title given to this series in the *Encyclopædia* is 'Men and Women': however, the subtitle to the first article – 'Great Lives' – seems a more appropriate description. The series is attributed to 'many writers': we do not know if these included some others besides those named as responsible for other series.

In contrast to other parts of the *Encyclopædia*, this series follows no particular order. As a whole, it provides very comprehensive coverage of people who have played an important role in various fields. The treatment, moreover, is thorough: some of the greatest names get several pages. As elsewhere in the *Encyclopædia*, the articles are very readable; they are often enlivened by anecdotes which may or may not be true but which help to fix the character in one's mind.

The articles are abundantly illustrated; only a few of these pictures can be reproduced here. Except for some recent personages, where photographs were available, these are of course artists' impressions. Some are by famous artists; many are anonymous. There is a predilection for Victorian-style romanticism, often sentimental.

Rather than try to summarise all these articles in their original order, we shall gather them under some main headings and pick out points of general interest.

Science and engineering. Among the great astronomers we hear especially of Copernicus, Kepler, Galileo and Newton. (There is no mention of Einstein: his 'Special Theory of Relativity' had appeared in 1905, but had presumably not yet gained sufficient acceptance).

The work of several great inventors is described: these include Newcomen and James Watt who developed the steam engine and George Stephenson who built the first railways; Brunel also gets a mention, especially for his Thames Tunnel. (At the time of the *Encyclopædia*, the London Underground was in the process of replacing its steam engines by electric traction, which must have been a boon to travellers.) There is also coverage of Edison, Faraday and Bell for their work on electricity and telegraphy.

Medicine. The first of the 'Great Doctors' was Hippocrates. We are also told of comparatively recent discoveries: William Harvey (circulation of the blood), James Simpson (chloroform), Pasteur (vaccines), Lister (antiseptics). But there was still no cure for cancer, and consumption (tuberculosis) was much too prevalent, despite better understanding of the risk of catching it in the milk from diseased cows.

Painting. One article covers 'Twelve Great Painters': Leonardo da Vinci, Raphael, Titian, Van Dyck, Rubens, Corregio, Velasquez, Rembrandt, Hogarth, Reynolds, Gainsborough, Turner.

This is a fair choice in terms of paintings that could be seen in galleries in Britain at the time, though one might quibble about the inclusion of Corregio among the Italians, while noting an anglo-centric bias in the inclusion of four English artists among the twelve and the absence of any Germans or French; 'Impressionism' had not yet taken hold in Britain. More Italian painters are covered in other articles, particularly the Venetians (though Venice itself is 'slowly decaying').

Music. The list of great composers starts with Handel: there is no mention of Purcell (the revival of early music came later in the twentieth century). Bach gets less attention and is seen mainly as an organist. 'We may not hear much' of his compositions: this is surprising, since it is generally considered that Bach had been rediscovered by Mendelssohn, but may be due to the comparative difficulty of his choral works, and indeed of most of his compositions for the keyboard. (Before the availability of radio and records, knowledge of music was largely dependent on what could be sung in the local choral society or played on the family piano.)

Mozart, Haydn, Beethoven, Schubert get their fair share of attention.[1] The works of Chopin, Wagner and other nineteenth-century composers are described.

Among the English composers of that period, it is noteworthy that Sullivan gets the most attention; Elgar is barely mentioned, though several of his greatest works had been composed around the turn of the century.

Literature. The choice of writers is eclectic. It starts with Homer, Virgil, Horace, Dante; it includes several great French authors (Molière, Voltaire, Victor Hugo, Dumas) and Germans (Goethe, Schiller, Heine). It covers the writers of fairy-tales: Perrault, the brothers Grimm, Hans Andersen; also Lewis Carroll and J.M. Barrie (for *Peter Pan*). Under the heading 'story-tellers' it has Bunyan, Defoe, Swift, Goldsmith, Walter Scott, Thackeray, Dickens, Trollope, Stevenson.

---

[1] I have included the reproduction of a painting (unattributed) of Haydn and Beethoven during the French attack on Vienna: it is one of the illustrations which has remained in my mind since my childhood. It is over-dramatised, but it is correct that in 1809, when Napoleon occupied Vienna, Haydn had himself carried to the piano and played his 'Emperor's Hymn', which had become the Austrian national anthem; he died a few days later. It is also correct that Beethoven, then aged 39, was already suffering from deafness.

HOW HAYDN PLAYED WHILE VIENNA BURNED

A hundred years ago, when the French army was firing upon Vienna, two men sat listening to the guns that thundered through the streets. In a cellar sat Beethoven, vainly trying to shut out the sound of the guns from his ears, lest they should ruin his hearing and make him deaf to music ; in another room Haydn struggled up in his bed, and with his dying fingers played the Austrian national anthem to try to drown the noise of the enemy's fire. It is a wonderful picture that this tale brings to our minds—the picture of two of the world's great *musicians, whose music will live for ever, sitting, while life and power* were ebbing from them—for Beethoven *did* become deaf, and Haydn died—helpless in the face of the great destroyer of mankind, the cruel curse of war.

The *Encyclopædia* makes a point of listing women authors: the success of the Brontë sisters, of Jane Austen, George Eliot, Mrs Gaskell, demonstrates a 'very great change in regard to the position of women in our country' (p. 2591). There is also an article on American writers, citing Washington Irving, Fenimore Cooper, Longfellow, Poe, Whitman, Mark Twain and others. Among English poets, Chaucer comes first, and the description of him is interesting:

> 'a very hearty, good-natured, laughter-loving sort of man, who did not take life too seriously or yet too lightly... Indeed, Chaucer was in every sense a typical Englishman.' (p. 3327)

A painting of Chaucer by Maddox Brown, in 'pre-Raphaelite' style, is reproduced. Shakespeare naturally gets full attention, as does Milton.

There are special articles on American writers, with descriptions of the lives and works of Washington Irving, Fenimore Cooper, Longfellow, Edgar Allen Poe, Walt Whitman, Mark Twain and others.

Architecture. We hear of the great builders of Florence; also of Christopher Wren's rebuilding of Westminster Abbey and other London churches after the Great Fire.

Philosophers. To begin with, the lives and main ideas of the Greek philosophers are explained.

Later on, an article on 'Famous modern thinkers' includes Rousseau (who 'sowed the seeds of the French Revolution'), Bentham (whose 'utilitarian' philosophy 'sought the happiness of the greatest number'), and the 'classical' economists, Adam Smith and John Stuart Mill. Reflecting the priorities of the time, this list includes Ruskin, whose life 'was loyally spent in bringing home to the business and bosoms of men the thought of beauty – beauty in paintings, in vesture, in manners, in conduct.' (p. 4850)

Herbert Spencer has already been mentioned in other chapters. Here, he is described as 'a great teacher'. He was an evolutionist before Darwin, whom he influenced; he also wrote a whole scheme of philosophy in ten great volumes. We are told that his fame was world-wide, and – rather improbably – that 'those brave Russian peasants, of whose valiant struggles for liberty and enlightenment we so often read nowadays, all know their Spencer', as the books were translated into Russian and taken around the villages. (p. 5155)

THE FATHER OF ENGLISH POETRY

GEOFFREY CHAUCER READING POEMS FROM HIS CANTERBURY TALES AT THE COURT OF EDWARD III.

Chaucer, the first great English poet, lived in the 14th century, before the days of printing. The poet was a favourite at the court of King Edward III., and at times he would read his poems before the king and his courtiers, in the way which Ford Madox Brown, the celebrated painter, has illustrated so happily in this picture.

Rulers, leaders and heroes. Some of this overlaps with other parts of the *Encyclopædia*, particularly the history items. An early article speaks of the great Roman emperors, many of whom, however, were cruel rulers.

> 'It is strange that when Christianity was slowly making its way among the people, the world was under the sway of the wickedest rulers who have ever lived; but it is fine to think that the beautiful influence of Christianity spread through the earth until it became stronger than the empire of the Caesars, which fell to nothing, while Christianity took possession of the world [i.e. with the conversion of Constantine].' (p. 523)

There are articles on several British monarchs (including Scottish ones, pre-Union). Victoria's long reign is described with admiration: in this period, Britain grew 'great and prosperous'.

There is an interesting article on Joan of Arc: 'she lives for all time as a great example of stainless heroism' and 'we have to write with shame to-day that they burned her alive in the market-place at Rouen'. (p. 904)

Napoleon's career is recounted at some length, with emphasis on his military campaigns; but he also did 'many good things' (presumably his civic and legal reforms, though these are not described). The same article also relates the achievements of his opponents: Nelson at the Battle of the Nile and at Trafalgar, and Wellington in Spain and at Waterloo.

For the defence of Scotland against the English, William Wallace and Robert the Bruce get special mention. The legend of William Tell is retold. A more recent patriot fighting for his people's freedom was Garibaldi.

A long article on the French Revolution contrives to make some sense of this confused and tortured period. It speaks with sympathy of the hapless King Louis XVI and especially of Marie-Antoinette: but it also describes the brutality of Robespierre, Danton and others.

'Famous reformers' are discussed in an article which throws interesting light on the writers' views on recent and current issues (pp. 3697–3706). Not all the characters mentioned are well-known today. Samuel Romilly, a barrister who became Solicitor-General, opposed the death penalty for a wide range of relatively minor offences, and spoke effectively against the slave trade. William Wilberforce also 'broke the chains of slavery and released thousands of slaves to become men in the world of men'.

Lord Shaftesbury created the 'Ragged Schools' to give some education to street children in London. Robert Owen, who owned a cotton-mill, improved conditions of work for his employees, established schools for their children, improved their housing and introduced habits of thrift and cleanliness. Other

This is the kind of scene that moved the great social reformers to change the conditions of child-life. Little boys were bought from their parents by sweeps, and made to climb up inside chimneys to clean them.

reformers stopped the practice of using small boys to sweep chimneys by climbing up inside them. [2]

William Morris was a less practical reformer: he 'struck a blow at the vulgarity and tawdriness that grew up in the Victorian Era', but 'the mass of men to this day remain dead to beauty'. Similarly, John Ruskin (already mentioned among the philosophers) had tried unsuccessfully to set up model factories according to his aesthetic ideas. The Encyclopædia comments that:

> 'Although the co-operative and socialistic attempt at a model industry came to an end, the idea lived, lives now, gathers in force, and is destined one day to rule the world.' (p. 4850)

This may be a foretaste of the idealism which would later cause some English intellectuals to look favourably at Soviet Russia, overlooking its excesses and abuses.

Richard Cobden and John Bright are praised for their successful campaign to abolish the 'Corn Laws' (in 1845 – these were import duties which significantly raised the price of wheat, hence of bread, penalising the urban working class in the interests of farmers). John Bright had joined Cobden in the campaign although he was in mourning for his wife, who had died of consumption. The *Encyclopædia* comments:

> 'He was a noble old Quaker ... nothing in his soul but devotion to God and love towards his fellow-men... His life stands out in the annals of England, telling us that it is good men – the men who think of others before self – who save the world.' (p. 3704)

---

[2] As has already been observed, the *Encyclopædia* rarely gives dates, presumably to avoid discouraging its young readers. Here, it may be helpful to supply them: Romilly 1757-1818, Wilberforce 1759-1833, Shaftesbury 1801-85, Owen 1771-1858, Morris 1834-96, Ruskin 1819-1900.

Explorers. The first articles in this series – as already said, the *Encyclopædia* does not follow any particular order – dealt with the 'men who made the world known'. These included Marco Polo (China), Vasco da Gama (India), Columbus (America), Magellan (the Pacific); also Livingstone and Stanley (Africa – 'we are getting to know more of the Dark Continent') (p. 146). There is a striking picture of James Cook (reproduced) setting foot in Tasmania: it leaves no doubt as to the superiority of the white man!

Missionaries. A later article (pp. 3483–99) describes the work of 'Some great Protestant missionaries:'

> 'The missionary, who fulfils the command of Jesus to his disciples, "Go ye into all the world and preach the Gospel to every creature", cheerfully leaves his native land, his home and his friends, to spend his life where there is no civilisation, no comfort or safety, to dwell with dark-skinned men who worship ugly idols and are given to superstitious and cruel practices.' (p. 3483)

This message is reinforced by pictures, one showing a missionary in full European dress struggling with a 'savage'.

Founders of religions. This is a particularly significant article (pp. 2995–3079). It deals first with Gautama, the Buddha, who created 'the most curious religion in the world':

Over and over again, Dr. Paton, the missionary to the New Hebrides, had to rush into the arms of some fierce savage who was about to kill him with his club, and cling round the man until his wrath abated.

> 'All solid and material things are useless and will pass away; the great object of life should be to destroy all desire... 'Nirvana' is a concept which no European can understand... At one moment you feel how beautiful it is; at the next you are inclined to laugh at its foolishness and uselessness.
>
> 'The whole teaching of Buddhism is the opposite of Christianity: it declares that nothing is worth while, while Christianity shouts "Everything is worth while".' (p. 2996)

The Buddhist is careless of life and indifferent to suffering, while the Christian nurses the sick beggar:

> 'Buddha did not tell people to be good, did not bid them repent, issued no rules of conduct... It is a purely Eastern religion, lacking altogether a universal note – it could never convert the world.' (p. 2996)

THE REAL DISCOVERER OF AUSTRALIA

This picture shows Captain Cook landing in Tasmania. He was a farm labourer's son, who ran away to sea and became a good sailor. None of the men who had been to Australia before him had realised the fruitfulness of the country, but Captain Cook found that there were in it fair and beautiful lands, and he called the land he saw New South Wales, and claimed it all for England. The little pictures at the bottom show the kind of men and women Captain Cook found in Tasmania when he landed there.

292

The writer thinks than Jainism is better than Buddhism, because it makes for action instead of despair and resignation, though the goal appears to be the same – an escape from life.

Today, as Buddhism spreads in the West, we have a fuller understanding of its teaching; the *Encyclopædia* writers, despite an effort at objectivity, reflect the prejudices and ignorance of their time.

The same article deals with Confucianism and Taoism; with Zoroastrianism; and with Islam.

Mohammed was the most recent of religious founders, and had become the prophet to millions of the human race. Much of his teaching, the *Encyclopædia* says, was borrowed from the law of Moses and his ideas were probably influenced by the primitive teachings of Christianity.

The Koran, says the writer, is a wonderful book, but he has reservations:

> 'In it, there are fables the most monstrous and horrible; but in it, too, there are occasional aspirations towards immortality, and expressions of repentance, which are beautiful…
>
> 'But his ideas altogether lack the exquisite clearness and the transparent purity of the Light of the World. With all its faults, the Koran rules millions of the human race; but it prevents progress… Mohammedanism, youngest of all religions, is perhaps the one most distasteful to European knowledge.' (p. 3002)

The conclusion is predictable:

> 'All religions are a struggle from ignorance to knowledge, an effort of man to understand his Creator; but the more one compares religions, the more brightly shines the pure and increasing light of Christianity… It is Christianity alone which seems to breathe the air of heaven itself'. (p. 3002)

The fifty articles which make up this series constitute almost an encyclopedia in their own right. A youngster who had digested them all would have known about the great philosophers from ancient Greece onwards, about scientists, astronomers and engineers; about writers, composers, artists and architects; about rulers, heroes and patriots; about recent political and social reformers; and about the founders of the great religions.

As always in the *Encyclopædia*, the articles with their illustrations are interesting and memorable. They would have contributed significantly to a young person's education: once again, it seems wrong to use the world 'children', for the readers are likely to have been in their 'teens unless they were remarkably precocious.

Moreover, the *Encyclopædia* – as usual – does not just convey information: many of these 'great lives' are held up as examples to inspire the young generation. This is particularly the case with the social reformers; and issues such as slavery, abuse of the death penalty, the absence of schooling for street children and the exploitation of children as chimney-sweeps were not then as remote as they might seem now.

The affirmation of Christianity's superiority over other religions (and, implicitly, that of Protestantism over other denominations) is not a surprise in view of other contents of the *Encyclopædia*.

THE QUIET HEROES OF THE WORLD

THERE are many kinds of heroes. The soldier who comes home in triumph, to the sound of trumpets and the waving of flags, leaves behind him on the battlefield the hero who has fallen in the fight. It is a fine and thrilling thing to see the conquering hero come, but not less thrilling is it to think of the hero who will never come again. And let us remember, always, the heroes of every day—the boys and girls who do noble things that are not written about in books. Let us remember the great heroism of simple lives, the golden deeds of quiet, simple people. We read in other parts of our book of great things done by great men and women, and many heroes will come into that story of famous people. But we shall read here of great things done by simple people whose names, perhaps, are not known at all. This is the great book of simple heroes and of the golden deeds that light up the pathway of the brave.

A VILLAGE OF HEROES

By MANY WRITERS

IF you have been to Derbyshire and have travelled among the beautiful hills which we call the Peak Country, you have passed, perhaps, through the little village of Eyam. It is only a hamlet, but the sight of this little group of houses and the little village church is one of the things that ought to thrill every boy and girl who loves a golden deed.

Perched snugly in a green hollow of the rocky uplands, Eyam must have been as pleasant a village to live in as could be found in the days when William Mompesson became rector at the village church and William Stanley preached at the village chapel. That was in the time when the Great Plague of London was raging, more than 240 years ago. Eyam was 150 miles away from London, and no place could have seemed safer from the plague than this.

But the little invisible microbes that carry disease about the world come in many ways. They may come on the wind, they may come in the train. They came to Eyam in a packet of patterns posted from London to the village tailor. The Great Plague of London was in that little packet, and in a few days the tailor and his family were in their graves.

There was terror in the village, and one by one the people fled. But the plague remained, and for a year it spread. All through this time the rector and his wife, with the minister at the little chapel, nursed the people through their sickness and sustained them in their grief. In their deep sorrow the people of Eyam were like one family.

Then the brave heart of the rector's wife, Catherine Mompesson, began to fail. People were dying on every hand; there was no hope for her husband and her children, and she urged the rector to fly. In that terrible hour the rector was true to himself. He urged his wife to take away the children and save herself and them. But Catherine Mompesson was not such a woman as that. She sent her children away to friends and stayed with her husband.

The crisis had come. The plague held Eyam fast, and it was clear that any further flight of people from the village would spread the plague in the villages around, perhaps through all Derbyshire, perhaps right up through the North of England, which was yet free from it.

When this time came the people of Eyam, led by William Mompesson and William Stanley, made a great decision, which ought to be written down in our history in letters of gold. They shut themselves off from the world. The church was closed, and every day the people met to comfort one another in a cave. Trade was given up, every man left his work, the schools were shut, and the houses became hospitals for the sick. Nobody came into the village and nobody went out, and all the work

8. GOLDEN DEEDS

This series is attributed to 'many writers'. Each fortnightly issue of the *Encyclopædia* had an article under this heading, with two or three short stories of heroism and self-sacrifice. The purpose is set out in the first page (reproduced opposite):

> 'Such stories help to make us brave, and to understand the goodness that is in the world'.

Many of these stories are about simple people. The one about Grace Darling contained in the front page is a good example – see too the picture of her brave deed, also reproduced.[1] There are many similar stories about ordinary people who risked their lives to save others; often these heroes are children, held out as models for *Encyclopædia* readers to follow. Several stories concern servants or apprentices who displayed loyalty to their masters.

Some of the heroes are historic figures and obvious choices, such as Florence Nightingale, 'The Lady with the Lamp' (picture reproduced), who nursed British soldiers during the Crimean War and established a new tradition in nursing care. (p. 628) [2]

Another well-known heroine is Elizabeth Fry, who a hundred years previously had initiated prison reform. She was a Quaker, and the *Encyclopædia* emphasises her faith:

> 'She cared for the vilest: she sought the most hopeless. So we find her praying on the deck of convict ships, reading the Bible in gaol, sitting all night in the condemned cell of a poor woman to be hanged on the morrow... Even in prisons, the spirit of Christ can enter, and the most degraded criminal can learn to forget his sufferings in the love and mercy of a Saviour who understands all his difficulties.' (p. 1298)

---

[1] This is a well-known picture, which has captured the imagination of many people. Hugh Cunningham, in *Grace Darling, Victorian Heroine* (2007), describes how her legend developed. The *Encyclopædia's* picture shows her alone in the boat: she was in fact with her father, the lighthouse-keeper

[2] Florence Nightingale died in August 1910, so she was still alive when the *Encyclopædia* was being written. Though she brought comfort to the sick and injured soldiers at the Scutari hospital, her efforts did not in fact reduce the death rate because sanitary conditions in the hospital remained deplorable – as she subsequently recognised. Back in Britain, she became an influential public figure.

THE HEROINE OF LONGSTONE LIGHTHOUSE

THE LIGHTHOUSE ON FARNE ISLANDS FROM WHICH GRACE DARLING ROWED TO THE WRECK

Grace Darling was one of the bravest girls who ever lived. Her father kept the lighthouse on Farne Islands, where, in the stormy night of September 6th, 1838, the steamer Forfarshire was wrecked. Through that bitter night nine men and women clung to the wreckage as it tossed on the rocks, swept by the waves and buffeted by the storm. In the morning, as soon as it was light, Grace Darling mounted the lighthouse tower with the telescope. On the rocks in the raging sea she saw the wreck. She launched the lighthouse boat, and, with her father, rowed through the storm to where nine people were in peril of their lives. They reached the wreck and brought the sufferers back in safety to the lighthouse.

Grace Darling's story is told on page 191

193

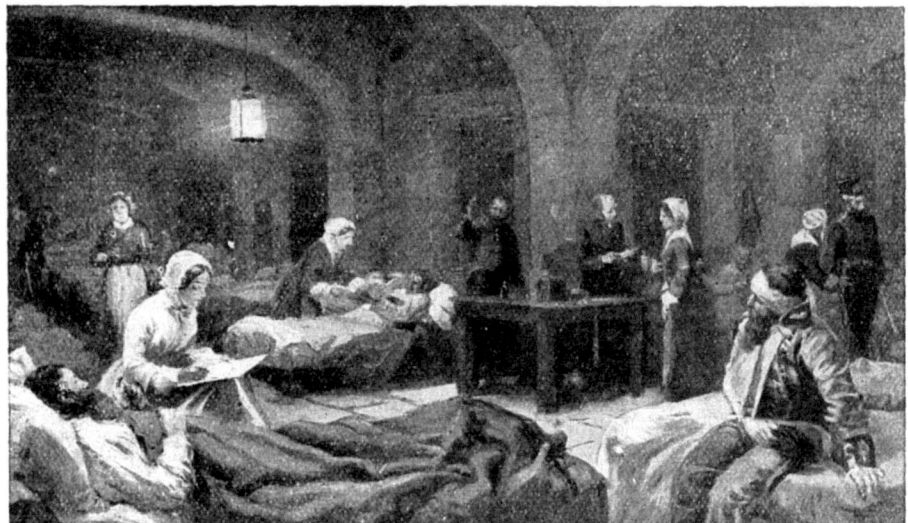

MISS FLORENCE NIGHTINGALE AND HER NURSES COMFORTING SICK SOLDIERS

Another story – rather an odd one – is said to demonstrate that 'Quakers are good people who believe that fighting is wicked'. This is about a Quaker on board an American trading vessel which was attacked by a French ship. The Quaker walked up and down the deck amidst the bullets, but did not take part in the fight. But when a Frenchman boarded the American ship, the Quaker took hold of him, saying 'very quietly and reprovingly, "Friend, thou hast no business here": upon which he lifted the Frenchman up and dropped him 'gently but surely' overboard.' (p. 1054)

There are also stories in favour of Catholics. We hear of Sainte Geneviève (p. 2317), who saved Paris from a Frankish invasion (and was made the patron saint of the city); of Saint Vincent de Paul, who among many other good deeds took the place of a galley slave; of Cardinal Borromeo of Milan (p. 1119), who in 1576 (a rare case where a date is mentioned) refused to leave the city when it was hit by plague and instead remained to care for the sick and dying; also of Father Damien (p. 519), who devoted his life to caring for lepers on one of the South Sea islands.

More surprising is an item on Isabella of Castile, who is described as a 'good queen' who cared for her soldiers and instituted the first camp hospital (p. 2413). She is better known to history for her role in creating the Inquisition and exiling or forcibly converting Jews and Moslems.

Equally odd is an item on Ferdinand III of Castile, 'The King who Loved the Poor' (p. 4717), of whom the *Encyclopædia* says that:

'his justice and love of truth caused him to be loved by all his people...
he would not allow violence of any kind to be shown to the poor.'

He attended in person to the needs of beggars, and

'he only fought the Moors because in the ignorant age in which he lived
this was thought to be a holy duty imposed on every Christian prince.'

Indeed, he recovered Cordoba and Seville from the Moors, but according to a modern historian, what he did there would today be called 'ethnic cleansing'.[3]

An article devoted to 'The Reformation Martyrs' begins with a plea for religious tolerance, which is eloquent though the reference to the 'true God' suggests that this open-mindedness has its limits:

'At the present day it has become the general belief of Englishmen that it is wise and just to suffer everyone to worship God in such fashion as his conscience bids him, and to say what he truly believes without fear; whether it be the thing that other people believe to be true or not. For we cannot force anyone to think that true which he is sure is untrue, though we may frighten him into saying that he thinks so.

'But in the old times, especially in the time of the Reformation ... people thought they could force other folk to think what they were told, as well as to do and say what they were told; and many times in history there have been great persecutions to deny what they really believed, or to worship false gods, or to worship the true God in a way which seemed to them to be wrong.' (p. 5067)

The ensuing text writes of Catholics who died for their faith, mentioning Thomas More and Bishop Fisher who refused to accept Henry VIII as head of the Church, and those such as Edmund Campion who were persecuted under Queen Elizabeth, when it was forbidden to teach Catholic doctrines. It also tells, at greater length, of Protestant martyrs in the reign of Queen Mary.

The previous chapter on **GREAT LIVES** has noted that the issue of slavery was still in people's minds. It is interesting to note that here too, many of the 'Golden Deeds' concern acts in favour of slaves. An article entitled 'The Friend of the Slaves' declares:

'It is the glory of Britain that she has done more than any other country to abolish the hateful slave trade, not only from her own possessions but from the face of the earth. Long after the slaves were freed in our colonies, as a result of the efforts of Wilberforce ... the slave trade flourished as much as ever in Africa, and though it has been greatly checked, it is still one of the evils of the Dark Continent.' (p. 4445)

This article speaks of Sir Samuel Baker, 'an intrepid English traveller, who, with his brave young wife, went to the stronghold of the traffic in Africa, and grappled with it there'. It tells of his efforts in the Sudan where, despite natural hazards and the opposition of local officials and slave-traders, he succeeded in freeing large numbers of slaves. The *Encyclopædia* says that 'his good work has now born fruit, for the slave trade has been suppressed in the parts which he visited'.

---

[3] See Raymond Carr: *Spain: A History* (2000). At the time of the *Encyclopædia* there was a lack of good history books on Spain. Ferdinand III (1217–52) was canonised, but more for his campaigns against the Moors than for any good works; and nobody thought that Isabella (1451–1504) deserved canonisation.

The *Encyclopædia* also recognises the efforts made in America. One story (p. 4957) concerns Frederick Douglass, who had died in 1895. He was the son of a wealthy white man in Maryland, but his mother was a black slave; his father did nothing for him, and he was brought up as a slave until he ran away at the age of twenty-one. A 'good, kind man' consented to give him work; he studied, and became an effective public speaker against slavery: his stirring appeals were among the strongest influences in bringing about the movement which gave the slaves their freedom.

The role of John Brown in the campaign against slavery gets special attention: this is, of course, the hero of the song which we all know in both America and Britain (without, perhaps, being quite sure why 'his soul goes marching on'). The *Encyclopædia* explains how he had, in his boyhood, seen something of the terrible cruelties of slavery. He became 'a true hero, prepared to make any sacrifice and to suffer anything for the sake of the negroes.' (p. 4957) He was eventually captured after taking up arms and trying to seize the arsenal at Harper's Ferry. The *Encyclopædia* has a picture of the moment when, being taken for execution, he took up and kissed the baby of a poor coloured woman.

JOHN BROWN KISSED THE LITTLE NEGRO CHILD

Many stories are related to the sea: a reminder that ocean travel was still not safe, and that Britain was still a sea-faring nation, where many people lived near enough to the coast to be aware of its perils.[4] We have already noted the first item about the lighthouse keeper's daughter. There is a similar story (p. 4069), set this time in Australia, about a woman who rescued the crew of a ship that had gone down on the rocks by riding on her horse into the waves. (This story too is accompanied by a dramatic if imaginative picture.)

Yet another story, vividly told, concerns the wreck off Africa of the steamer Birkenhead, 'not so many years ago'. There were women and children aboard, besides the crew and a company of soldiers. In a storm the ship hit a rock and began to sink. Lifeboats were launched, but there was room only for the women and children.

> 'So the soldiers stood in their lines, waiting for the ship to go down, as steady as if they were in the drill-yard. Then the hungry waves washed over the decks, and the brave soldiers were plunged into the sea… A very few managed to swim ashore… but the greater number perished, heroes no less than if they had fallen on the field of battle.' (p. 1804)

This article too is illustrated by a dramatic painting.

We can conclude this selection with another story of the Crimea. (It is noteworthy that events of the Boer War do not get any attention, although this was much nearer the time of the *Encyclopædia*: that war had divided the nation, and probably did not offer so much to be proud about.) This concerns a Captain William Peel, who with his men was defending a battery when a Russian shell dropped into it:

> 'Without a moment's hesitation, or a thought of his own safety, he rushed across, seized the shell, and ran with it to the side of the battery… Raising it high above his head, he hurled it over the earthworks that protected the guns. Scarcely had the shell left his hands when it burst with a terrific crash… Captain Peel's courage, energy and presence of mind saved the whole of the band of men. For this gallant deed Captain Peel was awarded the coveted Victoria Cross.' (p. 3789)

---

[4] At my 'public' school in Edinburgh in the late 1950s, one of our favourite hymns was: 'O hear us when we cry to thee / from all the perils of the sea' (text by W. Whiting, 1825-78).

THE MAN WHO CARRIED DEATH

These tales of **GOLDEN DEEDS** are easy to read, often exciting. If sometimes they appear too sentimental for modern tastes, that was probably not a problem in the Edwardian era. Like the previous series on **GREAT LIVES**, they hold up high ideals for the young readers: ideals of kindness, bravery and self-sacrifice.

Only a few years later, maybe some of those who had been brought up on this fare, certainly many of their fathers, uncles and elder brothers, were to be put to the test in the trenches and battlefields of Flanders and Gallipoli. There, they would meet many more dangers like that faced by Captain Peel.

WHAT THIS STORY TELLS US

THERE is no book in the world which contains so many interesting stories as the Old Testament. It is full of adventures, full of wonderful actions and strange occurrences, and as soon as we have finished one of these exciting stories we find ourselves at the beginning of another. The Old Testament, then, is a Book of Heroes. Eight names in this book stand out from all the rest, their stories being so wonderful that the world can never forget them. These names are Abraham, Joseph, Moses, David, Job, Isaiah, Solomon, and Daniel. Before we come to our Bible Stories, in which we shall meet these great figures again and again, we may read here something of the characters of the greatest heroes and heroines of the Bible, beginning with the eight great men whose names and lives stand out like gold among all others. All our first stories are from the Old Testament.

HEROES OF THE OLD TESTAMENT

ABRAHAM's story is a tale which takes us far back in the world's history, when men's riches consisted in the number of their flocks and herds. Abraham was a very rich man, for he had many oxen and sheep and camels, and a vast retinue of servants. He lived a happy life in the sunshine and the open air, and he liked to sit at his tent door of an evening and look across the plain at his many cattle going to the river to drink, and at the long line of his servants coming slowly back from the wells with water-pots upon their heads. He was happy, not so much because he was rich, but because he loved God, and trusted Him in all things. When his faith was put to a terrible test he did not shrink from it. He was so sure that God's way must be the right way that he could not refuse to go upon it.

So Abraham stands in the history of men as the great example of faith. When we hear of any man who trusts God with all his heart, we say of him: "That man has the faith of an Abraham." Abraham is the quiet, peaceful, God-fearing man who obeys God in all things, without any complaint and without even a question, however terrible and hard may be the work to which God calls him.

Joseph's story is the wonderful romance of a young genius, the favourite of his father and the envied of his brothers. Joseph used to dream

CONTINUED FROM PAGE 16

dreams, and these dreams made him more hated by his brothers than ever, for in these visions he saw that one day he would be raised high above his brothers. So the favourite son was taken by these brothers and sold as a slave. He passed out of his own land, and was carried to a foreign country, and presently he became a servant in the palace of the King. It seemed now that his life might become prosperous and happy, even though he was living in an alien land, for in the palace of a rich king men may rise to wealth and power. But the wife of Potiphar, one of the King's ministers, was not a good woman, and because Joseph was honourable she hated him, and said words against him, so that the King was angry and cast Joseph into prison. For many years Joseph lingered in the prison, but it came to pass, as we shall read when we hear the whole story, that the great King lifted him one day out of prison, and set him over his whole house to rule it for the happiness of the people. And Joseph prospered the land. He wore the King's ring upon his finger. He rode in the King's chariot. And when he drove forth the people cried: "Bow the knee!" And they bowed themselves before him.

Then came the day when Joseph's dreams proved true, for his brothers came into this land during a great famine to buy corn, and they bowed

9. BIBLE STORIES

These stories were written by **Harold Begbie**, 1871-1929. John Hammerton tells us that he was a close friend of Arthur Mee. Begbie too was a journalist, also an author, poet and playwright. His books, which were numerous, included political satire, comedy, fiction, science fiction, and studies of the Christian religion. Most of these, however, came after the publication of the *Encyclopædia*.

He had a strong religious bent: he was involved in the 'Oxford Group' (which later became 'Moral Re-armament') and with the Salvation Army. His concern with social reform appeared strongly in his book *The Little that is Good* (1917), where he wrote about charitable work among the poor of London.

There is a short article about him on Internet:

www.pnc.com.au/voyager/voyagerfiles/harold.htm

This biography makes it clear that the author was a committed Christian, of the evangelical tradition. It is therefore to be expected that his account of the Bible will be that of a convinced advocate. Indeed, his introduction on the first page (reproduced) makes this clear: it is 'a marvellous book ... the Wonder Book of the whole earth ... the Book of Life...'

He goes on to explain the content of the Bible, consisting of the Old and the New Testament. These correspond to the eras 'BC' and 'AD', with Jesus as 'the centre of history and time', and is illustrated by a dramatic picture (reproduced). This picture made such an impression on me as a child that for many years I remained convinced that the periods before and after the life of Christ were approximately equal in duration – which remains roughly the belief of 'creationists' today.

Begbie relates how the English Bible came into being, through the work of John Wyclif (pp. 1320–84), then William Tyndale (d. 1536) who probably made use of Martin Luther's German translation. Though the author does not mention it, Tyndale's work formed the basis of the 'Authorised Version' of 1611, which remains in use alongside modern translations.)

His attitudes to the two Testaments are significantly different, as will be seen.

THE CROSS STANDS IN THE MIDST OF TIME

Think of time and of all human history as a picture—the picture of a vast country stretching under the sun and the moon and the stars for ever and ever; and then, in the midst of this picture, very lonely and sad, you will see a cross rising out of the ground, with the figure of a Man hanging upon it, dying for love of His friends and enemies. Behind that lonely cross all the country is called B.C.—in front of it all the country is called A.D.

13

The Old Testament

The Old Testament, the author explains, tells the history of the Hebrews; his articles on it take up the first four volumes of the *Encyclopædia*. He recounts in his own words the story of Creation in Genesis; mindful perhaps of possible conflict with the scientific articles in the *Encyclopædia*, he is careful to use repeatedly the phrase 'The Bible tells us ...' rather than to assert the Genesis story as being factually correct.

Explaining God's creation of man and woman, he does not say that Eve was made from a rib of Adam's body. He deals lightly with Eve's transgression, saying she did argue with the Evil One over the apple before giving in to temptation (not quite what Genesis says). And God's punishment was not so cruel: they were expelled from Paradise to toil for their existence, but

> 'though work is hard, it is yet far better than idleness; and in setting man
> to till the earth, God has provided him with the opportunity of making
> himself better and kinder and purer.' (p. 356)

He retells – at some length (though much less than the Bible texts, since minor detail is omitted) – the experiences of the Israelites in Egypt, their flight to the 'promised land' and the subsequent history of Israel with its leaders and kings (Joseph, Moses, Solomon, etc.) and its prophets (Elijah, Jonah, Isaiah, Daniel, etc.). His rendering is lively, interesting and abundantly illustrated.

The Ten Commandments are dealt with rather briskly, considering their importance (probably the author wanted to avoid having to explain the meaning of 'adultery'):

> 'These laws commanded obedience to the worship of the One God, who
> made both heaven and earth; they forbade the making of images, and the
> taking of God's name in vain; they enjoined resting from work one day in
> the week, and honouring parents; they forbade murder, stealing,
> impurity, and lying; and they closed with a law which Jesus was to show
> in a more clear and beautiful light – the law which forbade men to wish
> *in the heart* for things which did not belong to them.' (p. 1025)

The Psalms 'of David' get particular attention: several are reproduced *in extenso*. In fact, David could only have been the author of some of the psalms. However, the author comments:

> 'It is the sublime fame of David that he put into words the deepest
> feelings of the human heart. He is the singer of humanity. He gave to the
> heart of the saddest sinner, and to the lips of the most unlettered beggar,
> language in which they may address the Creator of the world.' (p. 1593)

We need not describe these articles individually. The main interest for us today lies in the author's attitude to the Jewish nation. They were, he writes, 'a wonderful nation, because ... they worshipped One God', and he inquires:

> 'Do we ask ourselves why it was so important for Israel to believe in one
> God? It was chiefly important in those days because faith in one invisible
> God, who was stern and severe, and who would not suffer the least of his

laws to be disobeyed, meant the raising of a clean, healthy and moral human race... On every side of Israel there were nations who laughed at the idea of an invisible God...' (p. 1734)

'Israel was of the greatest value to humanity in its earliest stages, because it discovered Truth. Truth saves. Superstition kills. While other nations worshipped false gods and images made of stone and metal, Israel believed in one God, the invisible Creator, who demanded of men a struggle to be good, a hatred of evil. Israel stood for what we now describe as Evolution.' (p. 2305)

But often the Jews were too concerned with ceremony and with obeying rules, in fear of God's wrath. Writing of Isaiah, the author comments:

'This was the great work of Isaiah, to make Israel see that God had only one interest with His creatures, their happiness, and therefore their goodness... God cared neither for sacrifices nor for long prayers, nor for ceremonies; He cared for one thing, goodness. God was revealed not as the special and national God of Israel, but as the God of righteousness, a Being who only favoured Israel in the past because of its faith in him and its devotion to goodness.' (p. 2247)

And too often the Jews turned to false gods. Despite Isaiah's warnings:

'Altars were raised to heathen gods, Baal and Ashtaroth. Human beings were sacrificed to a god call Moloch. The streets of Jerusalem, it is said, ran with blood. The whole nation sank into the most horrible depths of superstition and evil.' (p. 2305)

Then with the invasion of the Babylonian army under Nebuchadnezzar, Jerusalem was destroyed, and the people were led into captivity:

'Israel as a nation was wiped off the face of the earth, to become only the Jewish race. The power of Israel was broken for ever. Its glory ceased to be. We have reached the destruction of this mighty nation.' (p. 2306)

Nevertheless:

'When they sinned, and sorrow came upon them, and their enemies conquered and ill-treated them, still they said that God would deliver them, because He had promised. So in the midst of their sorrows they began to watch for the coming of some mighty being whom they called Messiah, thinking that this Son of God would destroy their enemies, give them back their flocks and herds, and set them up as rulers of the whole earth.' (12)

Subsequently the Jews spread far and wide, still in expectation of the Messiah.

'But when the Messiah came, they found that He was not a mighty warrior but a beautiful young peasant, who sat in a weather-beaten ship with simple fishermen, and taught people that to forgive their enemies was better than to fight them. And then the Jews were angry, and refused to believe that He was the Messiah.' (p. 12)

The New Testament

While the author's treatment of the Old Testament has been eloquent, his rendering of the New is impassioned. Jesus, 'The Little Carpenter of Nazareth', is also 'the 'Good Shepherd' (both illustrations are reproduced here), and 'The Light of the World' as illustrated by Holman Hunt's famous painting.

> 'Through all ages of time, men have agreed always, everywhere, that the life of Jesus was the noblest and gentlest and purest life that men can dream of, the one sinless life that has been lived on the earth.' (p. 2711)

THE LITTLE CARPENTER OF NAZARETH

For his account, the author uses initially the gospel of St. Mark, explaining that this was the first and also the simplest of the four gospels. On this basis he retells – again mostly in his own words – the story of Jesus: baptism by John, the temptations he endured in the wilderness, his gathering of disciples, his teaching, his conflict with the Pharisees, his betrayal, trial and ultimate crucifixion, and his resurrection.

The other gospels provide more elements. Luke, he points out, filled in blanks in Mark's account and brought it into proper biographical order; Matthew, he says, was anxious to correct anything objectionable to the Jews.[1] John added an extra spiritual dimension.

---

[1] The author seems to have got this the wrong way round. It is Matthew who has the Jewish mob utter the words – fatal to Jews in subsequent ages – *'His blood be upon us and upon our children'*.

'Neither St. Matthew nor St. Luke would "make up" things; but where they found blanks or difficulties in St. Mark they would consult the Christians around them, and set down what they found agreeable to truth.' (p. 3812) [2]

From these sources, the author draws in particular his accounts of the Nativity (from Luke), Christ's doings (including the miracles), his sayings (including parables) and teaching.

John the Baptist, we are reminded, had taught that the Messiah was at hand. Jesus claimed to be the King for whom Israel was waiting; but he also said that his kingdom was 'not of this world', and that 'the kingdom of God is within you'. He changed the whole thoughts of his age. Instead of the Jewish tradition of 'an eye for an eye...' he said: 'Resist not evil; whosoever shall smite thee on thy right hand, turn to him the other also'. Thus he taught that the way to overcome evil is through goodness. This, the author says, is a fundamental part of the Christian teaching.

'It was one of the main objects of Jesus to teach men that to live they must become masters of their bodies. To hate an enemy might be natural, but it showed that a man's soul was carried away by animal passion... To forgive is sublime; to exact vengeance is merely animal law...' (p. 2957)

'Jesus gave to His friends the most simple and yet the most profoundly true way of securing peace. He bade them think of other people. His religion ... is the greatest force for unselfishness among the nations of the world.' (p. 3065)

Yet Jesus was charged by the high priests of Israel of blasphemy in asserting that he was 'Son of God' and 'King of the Jews', and brought before Pilate where the Jews demanded his crucifixion. The author recounts these events in vivid terms:

'We can scarcely bring ourselves to think about Jesus in the hands of the Roman soldiers... We shut our eyes and feel the appalling horror in our souls... It is not only that He was so innocent of the charge laid against Him, not only that He was so tragically misunderstood by the men who condemned Him; but because of all the beings who have ever lived, we can think of none more tender, more gentle, more loving.' (p. 3533)

For the Resurrection story, the author's narrative follows first Mark, up to the discovery of the empty tomb, but as he observes, it is probable that Mark's gospel originally ended at that point; the subsequent appearances of the risen Christ to his disciples are told more fully in Luke.

---

[2] There is of course much more to be said about the authorship of the gospels and the relationship between them. Begbie does at least introduce the notion that they were written at different times and in different contexts, though he glosses over inconsistencies between them.

JESUS THE GOOD SHEPHERD

In this beautiful picture we see Jesus represented as the Good Shepherd who cares for the sheep, and seeks the wandering lamb over hill and dale and thorny steeps until He finds it, and brings it safely back to the fold.

This picture is reproduced from the painting by Sybil C. Parker, by permission of the Berlin Photographic Company. The picture on page 3897 is from a painting by Henry Tidey, reproduced here by permission of Mrs. Fuller.

3900

The author, however, entertains no doubt as to the reality of Christ's resurrection. He sees proof of this in the transformation of the disciples from their initial despair into 'burning missionaries of Christ':

> 'Instead of fleeing in despair from Jerusalem ... we find them forming themselves into an assembly or brotherhood ... and sending men across the world with the message of the crucified Jesus... This birth of Christianity in the shadow of the Cross is the miracle of history. We can understand it only if we accept the written tradition that Jesus appeared to His disciples after death...
>
> 'That little band of humble, simple provincials created the Christian religion... They knew no fear... The boast of Rome, the power of the Jewish priests, the activity of commerce, the enthusiasm of art – these things were as dust to them. They had seen and spoken with a Man risen from the dead... The King had come.' (pp. 3683–6)

Later in the *Encyclopædia*, the writer points out that the disciples initially saw their faith as applying only to the Jews – they were described by their opponents, contemptuously, as 'Nazarenes' – and opposed the spread of Christianity to the Gentiles. He describes the roles in this expansion of Peter and of Paul after his conversion:

> 'Paul showed them [the Gentiles] no conquering emperor, no miracle-worker, no great and impressive scholar; he turned their gaze to the Cross of Shame, and showed them Love hanging there with bowed head and stricken side, Jesus dying in anguish to prove the truth of what He preached that God is Love.' (p. 4606)

And it was as a result of Paul's preaching that the term 'Christians' first came to be applied, in Antioch. The author sees here proof of the truth of Christ's claim:

> 'We are stating here historical facts... Eleven years since the Carpenter of Nazareth died a criminal death in a Jewish city, Greeks, Romans and Syrians in a city so splendid and cosmopolitan as Antioch are striving to make their characters like His character, are praying in His name to a God of Love, are ordering their lives not by strength, self-assertion, and pride, but by sweetness, gentleness, charity, and humility... This must be the base of our historical faith in Christ.' (p. 4607)

In the last article of the series (pp. 5231–8), after explaining the establishment and growth of the Christian Church, the author says that 'the Bishop of Rome was declared pope and ruled as a king'. However, Germany and England 'threw off this domination'. In discussing the Reformation he refers in particular to Wycliff, Luther, Calvin and Knox.

All over the world, Christianity has ever since flourished where it was free.' England became, 'on the whole', a Protestant country. This takes us beyond the Bible story. But we can note his closing words:

> 'It is for us to carry forward the influence of Jesus by the gentleness of our lives, to spread goodness and hopefulness throughout the earth, to keep

for ever shining in our lives, undimmed and unbroken, the beautiful Light of the World.' (p. 5238)

Harold Begbie is so sincere and so eloquent that it seems churlish to subject his work to the same kind of critical review as been applied to other chapters. His faith is simple and transparent: one could wish for similar commitment to love, gentleness and unselfishness from our leaders today (including many Christians).

Nevertheless, some comments have to be made. He believes firmly in the historical truth of the New Testament, but he is untroubled by the inconsistencies between them (notably in the trial of Jesus). Moreover, he does not allow for the facts that we do not possess original manuscripts and that alterations and additions may have been made before the earliest known texts appeared, some considerable time later. (He does admit that the end of Mark's gospel, making important claims about the reappearances of Christ to his disciples after his resurrection, was probably added later: but he does not draw any general inference from this.)

His interpretation has to be set against subsequent research, which has sought to place the life of Jesus and the subsequent expansion of the Christian church in the context of their times: in particular, the strained relations between Romans and Jews in Palestine and elsewhere in the Roman Empire. In the absence of clear corroboration from non-Christian sources of the Biblical events, it is not implausible to suggest that Jesus had some role in the Zealot uprisings, in which case his execution by the Roman authority makes more sense.

It has also been observed that, with the early Christian disciples seeking to extend their faith to Gentiles within the Roman Empire, the later Gospels may have had reason to accentuate the responsibility of the Jews for the condemnation of Jesus and to diminish that of the Roman authority. [3]

As to the resurrection of Jesus, an essential element in Christian faith, the fact that a number of disciples set out to convert others, including Gentiles, certainly demonstrates their own courage and conviction but does not necessarily prove that they were right.

This however is a debate which would take us far beyond the scope of this work (and one where personal views are bound to intervene). The significant point for present purposes is the effect which Begbie's teaching would have had upon his young readers. For them, as yet unconcerned with historical accuracy, Begbie's conviction and eloquence would have made a great impact.

---

[3] Note in particular the works by S.G.F. Brandon: *Jesus and the Zealots* (1967), *The Fall of Jerusalem and the Christian Church* (2nd edn. 1968), *The Trial of Jesus of Nazareth* (1968).

Begbie was an active Christian and an accomplished writer; he was not a theologian. Apart from the indispensable beliefs in the divinity of Christ and his resurrection, there is no dogma here. The Pauline concepts of 'original sin' and in consequence redemption of man through Christ's sacrifice on the Cross – awkward concepts even for an adult mind – do not appear in these articles. As he wrote:

> 'Thousands of men and women, who have never thought about creeds and dogmas, have done the work Jesus told them to do, simply because they felt it was the best kind of work in the world.' (p. 3066)

Begbie's assertion that England became, on the whole, a Protestant country reflects his own Bible-based faith. In the Anglican church, to which most of his readers in England belonged, some would not have regarded themselves as 'Protestants' of Begbie's school. He also ignores the Catholics (though all Ireland was still within the United Kingdom). For Begbie, no doubt, the true believer could do without priests and sacraments, and he certainly did not approve of the Pope.

His attitude towards the Jews is ambiguous. On the one hand, he admires their moral qualities, and sees the history of Israel as a long preparation for the coming of Christ. But the Jews failed to recognise the Messiah when he came. He follows the Gospels in attributing to the Jews the main responsibility for the condemnation of Jesus, though to his credit he does not quote Matthew's 'His blood be upon us and our children'.

At the time he was writing, the Jews were dispersed around the world. There is no suggestion that he was anti-Semitic. He would certainly have been horrified by the Holocaust; one can only wonder what he might have thought of the re-creation of the State of Israel.

One must regret his disregard for other religions. In fact, his only mention is a scornful reference to the ascetic practices of 'holy men' in India. If he had known more about Oriental religions he would have found teachings much closer to his own than he imagined. He may have helped his readers to be good Christians; he did not open their minds to understand and respect other traditions. But perhaps that could not be expected of any religious writer of his time: this was not an age for ecumenism.

It has been observed that Begbie's articles are abundantly illustrated, and this merits some attention. Throughout the *Encyclopædia* there are many pictures, mostly unsigned – possibly by illustrators hired for the purpose. On biblical themes, there was of course an abundance of paintings to choose from – albeit with reproduction in black-and-white. A somewhat disquieting feature is the tendency to describe such artistic works as if they were historically accurate representations; many are purely imaginative.

In many cases here, the names of the artists are given. Most are nineteenth-century artists, and most are English: exceptions are Millais, Munkacsy, Tissot. Most tend to romanticism and sentimentality, some excessively so – typical examples have been shown here – and the majority are little-known today. The pre-Raphaelite influence is evident; there is one picture by Burne-Jones.

More surprisingly, there was little recourse to the Italian Renaissance: there is one Fra Angelico, and a much-reduced copy of Da Vinci's 'Last Supper'. Painters of the early Flemish school are totally unrepresented; it is true that their delicate work would have made little impact in black-and-white and with fuzzy reproduction.

THE WORLD'S GREAT BOOKS

BOOKS are among the most precious things man has been able to invent. The world's great books are its greatest treasures. For the man who writes a book may tell us a story that will never be forgotten, or he may express some great thought that will set all other men thinking. It is through books that we know nearly everything. There are two kinds of writing—prose and poetry, about which you can read on page 41. Great books may be written either in prose or in poetry, but here we shall deal with the famous books just as if they were written in prose, as it is the long stories they tell which we are going to tell over again in the form of short stories. The dramas of William Shakespeare, which are chief among the great treasures of English literature, were all written in poetry, but we shall tell the stories of these famous works just like other stories. Though Shakespeare's plays were written for acting on the stage, they are also among the most beautiful books that we can read.

THE PLAYS OF SHAKESPEARE
A MIDSUMMER NIGHT'S DREAM

By J. A. HAMMERTON

THERE was once a Duke of Athens named Theseus, who was betrothed to Hippolyta, Queen of the Amazons. It happened that when they were talking of their coming marriage, an elderly courtier named Egeus came to them with his daughter Hermia and her two rival lovers, asking for the help of the Duke. It was her father's wish that Hermia should wed Demetrius, and she would have none but Lysander. On hearing this Theseus told her that, by the law of Athens, she must do as her father wished, else she could be put to death or condemned to remain unmarried all her life.

Hermia was fain to profess she preferred to remain unmarried. But when she had drawn apart with Lysander they agreed to meet the next day in a wood a mile distant and escape from Athens together. They took another into their secret, however, and told their plans to Helena, a friend of Hermia. As Helena was in love with Demetrius, she thought that by telling him of Hermia's purpose he would follow the lovers, and poor Helena herself would go after them so that she might have the happiness of being near Demetrius, although he was not fond of her.

About this very time, Oberon, the king of the fairies, had quarrelled with his queen, Titania, because she would not give him a little negro boy, of whose mother she had been very fond.

Oberon decided to play a trick on Titania for this, and so he told Puck, his mischief-loving fairy servant, to put the magic juice of love-in-idleness into Titania's eyes as she slept, that when she awoke she would fall in love with the first living creature she might see.

It so chanced that a company of rough workmen were rehearsing in that wood a little play which they were to perform at the wedding festivities of Duke Theseus, and by a magic touch Puck changed the head of one named Bottom, a weaver, into that of an ass ! This fat, ungainly man with the ass's head was the first thing Titania, the lovely queen of the fairies, saw when she had rubbed the sleep from her eyes, and, thanks to the juice of love-in-idleness, she straightway fell in love with Bottom, wound her arms about his hairy neck, bound flowers around his flapping ears, and bade her fairy attendants obey his every wish.

Puck had also been told by Oberon that an Athenian who was lost in the wood was neglecting his true love for a maiden who shunned him, and he bade the mischief-making fairy change the heart of this misguided Demetrius. But Lysander and Hermia, wearied with their walk from Athens, were lying down to rest when Puck came flying past, and, mistaking Lysander for Demetrius, the fairy squeezed the magic

10. FAMOUS BOOKS

This compilation was made by John (later Sir John) **Hammerton** (1871-1949), who has already been mentioned several times in the present work – see also the summary of his biography of Arthur Mee in the Appendix. He was to become the most eminent of the *Encyclopædia* contributors, being described in the *Dictionary of National Biography* as 'the most successful creator of large-scale works of reference that Britain has known'.

As already mentioned, in 1895 he went to work on the *Nottingham Daily Express*, where he met Arthur Mee, the start of their lifelong friendship. In 1905 he joined Alfred Harmsworth's *Amalgamated Press*, where again he collaborated with Arthur in producing the *Harmsworth Self-Educator*.

His greatest achievement was *Harmsworth's Universal Encyclopædia*, which – like the *Children's Encyclopædia* – was published as a fortnightly series in 1920-22, and sold twelve million copies throughout the English-speaking world.

Among the numerous publications in his own name, one can mention a biography of J.M. Barrie and studies of Charles Dickens and Robert Louis Stevenson. He also wrote an autobiography, *Books and Myself* (1944).

He was knighted in 1932, and became a fellow of the Royal Society of Arts.

There is fuller information in the *Dictionary of National Biography*.

As the front page indicates, this series starts with Shakespeare, covering sixteen of his plays – in fact, all the major ones. Their plots are recounted in little more than a page each (considerably less than Lamb's *Tales from Shakespeare*, of which there is no mention). This does not convey much of the drama, and nothing of the poetry; and one has to admit that with some of Shakespeare's plays – particularly the comedies – the plots alone do not make much sense. However, these abstracts would have provided the readers with a useful introduction and no doubt stimulated their interest.

The classics were at the time an indispensable part of a gentleman's education: Homer's *Iliad* and *Odyssey*, and Virgil's *Aeneid*, are the next works to be retold, again drastically summarised to a couple of pages each. These, the writer says, may be called 'the first famous books'.

Chaucer comes next, with seven of the *Canterbury Tales*. These lend themselves better to being summarised, and the use of modern English makes them more accessible.

Bunyan's *Pilgrim's Progress* gets more extensive treatment, stretching over two of the *Encyclopædia*'s fortnightly issues. Introducing them, the writer says that:

'No book, except the Bible itself, has had greater influence for good on the minds of men than "The Pilgrim's Progress". Written in simple, straightforward English, by a plain, straightforward man, who, from being a poor tinker, became a powerful preacher of God's message to mankind, this immortal story is likely to be read as long as our literature endures.' (p. 1027)

Some of the selections would be little-known today (to adults or children). One such is Edmund Spenser's *Fairie Queene* (1590), a romantic tale of knights and ladies (accompanied by a very romantic illustration, in a style much favoured by the *Encyclopædia*).

The main episodes of Cervantes' *Don Quixote* are retold in two issues. This, the writer says, 'is one of the greatest works in literature, for its abounding humour, its wisdom, and its true humanity'. (p. 843)

After the great classics just mentioned, the attention turns to English works of the eighteenth century, in particular *Robinson Crusoe* by Daniel Defoe ('the father of English fiction') and *Gulliver's Travels* by Jonathan Swift. The latter, the author points out, had been 'a favourite among young folk for many generations', but it was also a satire on the England of its time: 'Lilliput' was meant for England, and the absurd conflict with 'Blefescu' over the right way to open a boiled egg 'was meant to ridicule the stupid reasons nations had for making war, even so near our own time as the reign of George I.' [1]

'The grandfather of the Emperor of Lilliput, when a boy, as he was going to eat and egg, broke it at the larger end, according to the ancient practice, and cut one of his fingers. Whereupon the Emperor, his father, published an edict commanding all this subjects, upon great penalties, to break the smaller end of their eggs. This led to rebellion and civil discord, which was fomented and encouraged by the Emperor of Blefescu, at whose court the Big-Endian exiles found much favour...'. (p. 1314)

The nineteenth century naturally gets the greatest coverage. Summaries of Sir Walter Scott's *Waverley* novels – 'wonderful tales of the past' – continue through four of the fortnightly issues (as we move through the *Encyclopædia*, the abstracts tend to get longer and more satisfying).

Charles Dickens gets even more attention: all his major works are summarised, covering seven articles. The writer observes that:

'Most of the great novels of Charles Dickens were written "with a purpose". While they were first of all intended to amuse the reader, they were also meant to draw attention to some unhappy state of things which the author, in his warm love of humanity, sought to have abolished. Thus in "Oliver Twist" he exposes the shameful state of the public workhouses at the time of which he wrote, the early years of last century.' (p. 2551)

---

[1] This explanation is too brief. For Lilliput read 'England' and for 'Blefescu' read 'France'. The ridiculous conflict over the eggs refers to quarrels between Protestants and Catholics.

'So did "Nicholas Nickleby" expose the terrible state of boarding-school
life about the time when the story was written, 1836.' (p. 2651)

These abstracts from Dickens are accompanied by some of the original
illustrations: a sample of those for *Oliver Twist*, by the famous illustrator
Cruickshank, is reproduced here.

Thackeray's novels are recounted in four issues; *Henry Esmond* (1852) was 'the
finest historical novel ever written' (p. 3265). The works of Trollope, George Eliot,
Thomas Hardy and the Brontë sisters are not covered here, though there is
mention of these authors in other parts of the *Encyclopædia*; perhaps their work was
considered too adult.

Some recent works are omitted, perhaps on copyright grounds, perhaps
because the *Encyclopædia* authors thought them recent enough to be well known
anyway. Thus we do not find Robert Louis Stevenson's *Treasure Island* (1883) nor
Kidnapped (1886), which otherwise would have seemed obvious choices. (Some of
his poems are given in another section.) Nor are any of Kipling's books included
(again, a few of his poems appear later): *Jungle Book, Stalky & Co., Just So Stories* and
Puck of Pook's Hill had been published between 1894 and 1906. [2]

UNCLE TOM TAKEN AWAY FROM HIS CABIN AND HIS FRIENDS

His kind master having fallen into debt, Uncle Tom, the Christian slave, was sold to a hard-hearted slave-dealer,
who took him away to the Southern States, where he died of ill-usage, and he never saw his old cabin again.

---

[2] Copyright protection at the time lasted for forty-two years after publication or seven years
after the death of the author, whichever should prove the longest. The 1911 Act, implementing
the Berne Convention 1886, extended this to fifty years after death.

Some of the choices would not get priority today, such as Charles Kingsley's *Westward Ho* and *Water-Babies*, Thomas Hughes' *Tom Browne's Schooldays*, Charles Reade's *The Cloister and the Hearth*.

An interesting choice, on the other hand, is *Uncle Tom's Cabin*, by Harriet Beecher Stowe (1851). This, the writer observes, was 'a great book against slavery'. Other American works are Fenimore Cooper's *The Last of the Mohicans*, Louisa May Alcott's *Little Women* and *Good Wives*, and General Lewis Wallace's *Ben Hur*.

Several French works are covered: Jules Verne's *Round the World in 80 Days* and *20,000 Leagues under the Sea*, Alexandre Dumas's *Count of Monte Cristo*, and Victor Hugo's *Toilers of the Sea* (*The Hunchback of Notre-Dame* is better known but was perhaps considered unsuitable for children).

These résumés – with the main exception of the shorter ones on Shakespeare, Homer, etc. early in the work – convey a good idea of the original works. They are interesting and enjoyable; the emphasis is on adventure stories, particularly those involving young heroes or heroines. They pre-suppose quite a high level of reading ability. A young reader who had assimilated these abstracts would have acquired a very extensive literary knowledge, and would have been well equipped to tackle the original works.

SCENES FROM THE STORY OF OLIVER TWIST

Oliver Twist was an orphan, who was brought up by the parish until he was ten. They were so badly fed in the workhouse, getting little more than a small basin of thin gruel for each meal, that the boys drew lots for one of them to ask for more. It fell to Oliver to make this request. His boldness resulted in his being sent out of the workhouse as an apprentice to a coffin-maker, from whom he ran away, and fell in with a gang of young thieves in London. One of them, the "Artful Dodger," robbed an old gentleman at a bookstall, but Oliver was captured. The bookseller proved Oliver was not the thief, and the gentleman took him to live with him.

But Oliver was recaptured by Fagin, the leader of the thieves, and was handed over to Bill Sikes, to assist that villain in the burglary of Mrs. Maylie's house. Oliver made up his mind that when he was put through the window he would alarm the household, but before he had a chance of doing so he was shot in the arm by the butler. Here again he fell in with friends, as Mrs. Maylie adopted him, and educated him like a young gentleman. In the last picture we see Fagin and a man named Monks, who have an evil plot against Oliver, watching him while he has fallen asleep at his books on a summer day. But, happily for all, these scoundrels are punished at last.

These pictures are from the famous original engravings by George Cruikshank in the first edition of "Oliver Twist."

THE TALES OF LONG AGO

WE turn to this part of our book for our stories, the great stories that we all love to hear. And what wonderful tales they are—tales of fairies, and giants, and ogres, and goblins, and castles, and mysteries which no wise man could ever understand. We shall read them here together. We shall meet here friends and enemies. Brave Jack the Giant Killer, beautiful Little Red Riding Hood, sad little Cinderella—all these and a whole host of wonderful people come into this part of our book. Who wrote these tales we do not know; but we know that since the world began boys and girls in every country have sat by the fire listening to the tales which never make us tired, and we know, too, that children will sit listening to them patiently as long as the world lasts.

Aladdin and the Wonderful Lamp

ONCE upon a time an African magician came to China to find a wonderful lamp.

In order to get it he had to crawl through a passage leading to a fairy palace beneath the earth. The passage was very small, and anyone who let his dress touch the walls was killed by magic. The magician did not like to risk his own life, so he made friends with a little Chinese boy, called Aladdin, and took him to the fairy palace.

"In this place," said the magician, "a treasure is hidden. Do what I tell you and you will become the richest man on earth. Keep this ring on your finger, and do not let your clothes touch anything until you have put out the little lamp that burns in the garden, and placed it in your pocket. Then you can take away as much treasure as you wish."

Down jumped Aladdin into the passage leading to the palace. He found the lamp in a garden where diamonds and pearls and rubies grew upon the trees. Putting it under his vest, he filled his pockets with jewels and returned to the passage.

"Give me the lamp, and then I will help you out," said the magician.

"No," said Aladdin; "help me out and then I will give you the lamp."

This made the magician very angry, and he closed up the opening in the earth, and went back to Africa.

For two days Aladdin wandered about the fairy palace without finding anything to eat, or any way of escape. On the third day he happened to rub the ring which the magician had put on his finger. A spirit then appeared before him, and said:

"I am the slave of the ring. What do you wish me to do?"

"Please take me home," said Aladdin.

In the twinkling of an eye he found himself outside his mother's house. She was a poor widow, and had nothing for him to eat and no money to buy him anything. So he gave her the wonderful lamp, and asked her to sell it and get some bread.

"It is very dirty," she said, giving it a rub.

A spirit then appeared, and said:

"I am the slave of the lamp. What do you wish me to do?"

The widow was too frightened to reply, but Aladdin boldly said:

"Please bring us something nice to eat."

In the twinkling of an eye a table appeared on which there were all kinds of meat and wine, in dishes of gold and goblets of crystal.

Having dined in this manner, Aladdin went out for a walk, just as the daughter of the King was riding by. Princess Badroulboudour, as she was called, was a lovely girl, and Aladdin fell in love with her. He went indoors and rubbed the wonderful lamp, and said to the spirit:

"Please make me rich and build me the finest mansion in the world."

In the twinkling of an eye Aladdin and his mother found themselves in a palace of gold, with six hundred servants to wait upon them, and wealth enough to buy a kingdom. They sent forty basins of gold filled with diamonds

11. STORIES

This collection of stories is ascribed to **Edward Wright**, and others. It has not been possible to find out anything about Edward Wright, who is not mentioned in the *Dictionary of National Biography*, nor is there any trace of other writings by him.

Each fortnightly issue of the *Encyclopædia* included 8–10 pages of stories, some less than a page, others taking up two or three pages. Overall, the eight volumes contain around four hundred such tales.

These fall into several categories. Many are 'fairy tales'(a *genre* in which fairies, in fact, rarely appear: princes and princesses, giants, witches, talking animals are much more frequent characters).

The introductory page (reproduced) is not quite accurate in declaring: 'Who wrote these tales we do not know'. Indeed, the sources for the individual items are not cited. In fact, 'Sindbad the Sailor' comes from the *Arabian Nights*; the stories of 'Ali Baba' and 'Aladdin and the Wonderful Lamp' are often associated with that collection but may not have originated with it.

The favourite *Contes de ma mère l'Oye* by Charles Perrauld (1628–1703) are included: 'Cinderella', 'Sleeping Beauty', 'Tom Thumb' and 'Little Red Riding-Hood'.

A substantial number come from the Brothers Grimm (Jacob, 1785–1863 and Wilhelm, 1786–1859) who wrote nearly two hundred *Märchen*): these include such well-known stories as 'Hansel and Gretel', 'Rapunzel' and 'Rumpelstilskin'.

Hans Andersen is also well represented, with 'The Ugly Duckling', 'The Emperor's New Clothes" and 'The Tinder-box' and others; but not 'The Little Mermaid' nor 'The Princess and the Pea'.

These stories are given two or three pages (about half the original length). Each story gets an illustration, large or small.

Washington Irving (1783–1859) was the author of 'Rip van Winkle' under the pseudonym Diedrich Knickerbocker. (Rip van Winkle's long sleep took place during the American War of Independence, and he got into trouble on awakening by thinking he was still under the reign of King George.)

Less well-known in Britain today, perhaps, we also find from America the tales of 'Uncle Remus'. (In this case the author is named: he was Joel Chandler Harris, who died in 1908, when the *Encyclopædia* started appearing.) 'Uncle Remus' is supposed to be an old negro slave. Here is the first of his 'Brer Rabbit' stories (*Encyclopædia* p.3786); each story is accompanied by a small line drawing.

BRER RABBIT AND BRER FOX

Brer Rabbit was a naughty, cunning little creature, and as saucy as a jail-bird. He was always playing tricks on his neighbours, and they were always trying to catch him. But it wasn't by any means an easy task to catch Brer Rabbit. One day, Brer Wolf says to Brer Fox:

"If we don't get that little varmint for supper tonight", says he, "I'll give up being a wolf, and eat grass. You jus' run along home and get into bed, and make out you're dead," says he. "And don't you say anything till BR comes along and puts his hands on you. Then we'll get him right enough."

So Brer Fox went home and got into bed, and Brer Wolf he marched off to Brer Rabbit's house, and knocked at the door.

"Bad news, Brer Rabbit," says Brer Wolf. "Poor Brer Fox died this morning, and I'm off to arrange his funeral," says he.

Brer Wolf trotted away, and Brer Rabbit went round to Brer Fox's house to see what he could see. He peeped in, and there was Brer Fox stretched out on the bed stiff as a poker, looking just as if he was dead. But Brer Rabbit was always too wide-awake to be easily deceived, and he says out loud, as if talking to himself:

BRER FOX WAS STRETCHED ON THE BED

"Poor old Brer Fox! I hope he isn't dead; but I expect he is. I'd better sit here till the neighbours come round. But I wonder if he's really dead", says Brer Rabbit in a kind of doubtful way. "Doesn't look like it," says he. "You can always tell when a fox is dead by the way he keeps shaking his hind leg," says he.

When Brer Fox heard this, he thought he'd show he was really dead, and began shaking his hind leg, and as soon as Brer Rabbit saw it he tore out of the house as fast as he could, and did not stop till he reached the safety of his own home. Brer Fox and Brer Wolf had to go to bed without any supper that night.

Another category consists of folk-stories, some legendary. The tale of 'St. George and the Dragon' is one such item. The epic of 'King Arthur and his Knights' gets a lot of attention, appearing in several issues. 'Robin Hood' is perhaps semi-historical.

Among historical characters, we hear of the heroism of William Tell and his son. Also of the 'Little Princes in the Tower', imprisoned and assassinated by order of Richard Duke of Gloucester, to clear his way to the throne. More prosaically, there are several items on Napoleon – his escape from Elba, his campaign in Russia and his defeat at Waterloo – told dramatically though not altogether accurately.

A selection of Aesop's fables, with their morals, appears in almost every issue. These are mostly very short, just a few paragraphs; most are accompanied by a line drawing. An example, taken almost at random, is shown here.[1]

There are some special items. These include 'The Labours of Hercules', 'Tales from Greece and Rome' and 'Legends of the Stars'. There are some short stories from the Talmud; others entitled (dubiously) 'Fables of the Buddha'.

A number of short items concern 'holiday places', such as Brighton, Scarborough, Folkestone, Bath, Tunbridge Wells. The writer observes that it is good to know something about such places before going there.

THE ANT AND THE GRASSHOPPER

A NEST of ants had been busily occupied all through the summer and autumn in collecting food for the winter, and they had carefully stored it in the

wonderful underground chambers of their home. Thus, when the winter came, they had plenty of food to eat.

One cold day a grasshopper, who was almost starved with cold and hunger, came to the ant-hill and begged that the ants would give him a little food to save his life.

One of them asked him how he had spent his time during the summer, and whether he had not saved up anything for the winter. He replied: "Alas! gentlemen, I spent all my time in singing, playing, and dancing, and never once thought about the winter."

The ant answered: "Then we have nothing to give you; for people who play all the summer must expect that they will have to starve in the winter."

Lay by for a rainy day.

---

[1] Rev. Gregory Carlson at Berkeley has found in the American version (*The Book of Knowledge*) a valuable source of fables. On this, and much more on the subject, see:
http://aesop.creighton.edu/jcupub/default.htm

Many families would have possessed 'willow-pattern' crockery, and children would have wanted to know the meaning of the picture. The *Encyclopædia* recounts this Chinese story, with an illustration of a plate: this is reproduced here.

Whoever the *Encyclopædia* writers were, they knew how to tell a story. All these pieces, short or long, are vivid and memorable. Some, particularly the fables, would have been easy reading to start with, encouraging children to read from quite an early age, and they could have graduated to the longer stories. By the end, they would have acquired a valuable culture of folk-lore.

Volumes 6–8 include some short stories in French. These are not original French tales, but translations of items appearing in English earlier in the *Encyclopædia*. The linguistic level is far higher than the French of the **SCHOOL LESSONS** (see Chapter 13); whoever did these translations knew the language perfectly (although this is the occasion for one of the very few misprints in the *Encyclopædia*).

STORY OF THE WILLOW-PATTERN PLATE

ON certain old china there is a painting in blue which is known as the willow pattern, and willow-pattern plate is perhaps the most famous china in the world. And it really comes from China, or so did the first plate, for the story is Chinese. This is the story.

A beautiful Chinese girl, named Koong-Shee, fell in love with her father's secretary, Chang, who was a poor man. But the father of Koong-Shee wanted her to marry a rich man, and because she would not give up Chang his letter inside the shell, dropped it into the lake, and watched it sail across to where Koong-Shee sat watching. Koong-Shee read the letter and sent back her answer. She said she would go if her lover were brave enough to come and fetch her. Chang went boldly up to the little house and took her away. They had to cross the bridge to get out of the garden, and as they were half-way across Koong-Shee's father saw them, and hurried after them. Koong-Shee went first with her

her father sent her away to a little house at the end of the garden. Outside Koong-Shee's window was a willow tree, and just beyond a fruit tree, and Koong-Shee sat all day watching it bloom. She was very lonely and unhappy, until one day Chang wrote and asked her to fly with him.

Chang dared not post the letter lest it should fall into the hands of Koong-Shee's father, but he found a cocoa-nut shell, fixed a sail to it, and, putting distaff, Chang followed carrying her jewel-box, and behind them ran the father with a whip. But the father did not catch them, and they escaped to a little house on the other side of the lake, where they lived happily. But the rich man who had wanted to marry Koong-Shee was so angry that he found out where she lived, and one day he set fire to the pretty little house, and Koong-Shee and Chang were killed.

Two pigeons flying high,
Chinese vessel sailing by,
Weeping willow hanging o'er,
Bridge with three men, if not four.

Chinese temple, here it stands,
Seems to cover all the land,
Apple tree with apples on,
A pretty fence to end my song.

309

197

THE WORLD'S GREAT POEMS

IT is a splendid thing to be able to say something which the world will never forget, and many books that will never die have been made up of fine words spoken and written by great men and great women. Most of these never-to-be-forgotten words are in poems, because poems are much more easy to remember than ordinary reading, which we call prose. There are thousands of beautiful poems that everybody ought to read, and nobody who does not read them can really know how fine a thing reading is. True poetry is more precious than gold. It helps to make us good, and happy, and hopeful, and it is so pleasant to read that the words sound like music. We shall find in this part of our book some of the best of all these poems, which will make us anxious to read more and more poetry as time goes on.

POETRY THE MUSIC OF WORDS

By J. A. HAMMERTON

THERE are two ways of writing a story, or telling about a place or a thing or an event. The one way is to write it down in words like those we use in speaking one to another, but using the words more carefully, so that they will give as good an idea of what we have seen or thought as words can give. This kind of writing is called Prose. The words and sentences used by great writers are so well chosen and arranged that they give us a clear idea of what has been in the writer's mind, and in reading them aloud we find that they have a fine and pleasing sound.

But there is another kind of writing in which the words and sentences used by the writers sound far sweeter and more musical than the words of prose. This we call Poetry, and those who write it are called Poets.

Prose is used to tell almost any kind of story, or to describe anything; but there are grand things in history, beautiful scenes in the world, noble thoughts in the minds of men, that can be better described in poetry.

Poetry began, very likely, with the desire for singing, which comes when we are very happy or after a success of any kind. Long ages ago, when our far-off forefathers could not even read or write, they had poets who went with them into battle, and after the victory these poets, or bards, as they were called, would compose verses of fine-sounding words to celebrate the victory. These verses they sang while they played a harp. In this way poetry began, perhaps, men having their minds full of happy thoughts, and finding that they could best utter these thoughts by choosing words of musical sound. Homer, one of the greatest of poets, was a blind Greek who lived more than eight hundred years before Christ. He used to recite in public places in Greece his poetical descriptions of the wars of the Greeks.

There are three kinds of poetry. There is Dramatic Poetry, which is written in the form of people speaking to each other, as in the plays of Shakespeare. Then there is Epic Poetry, which is usually a description of some great event, a hero, or the history of a nation, told in grand, noble words. The third kind is called Lyric Poetry, from the fact that it was originally intended to be sung to the playing of a lyre, which is a very ancient musical instrument somewhat like a harp. All beautiful songs come into lyric poetry.

Another thing to know is that poetry is written sometimes in rhymed lines and sometimes without rhymes. A rhyme means that similar sounds occur at the ends of lines, though the words are different. Here is one, with the sound that makes the rhyme printed in different type:

The world is so full of a number of th*ings*,
I'm sure we should all be as happy as k*ings*.

If you count the syllables in these two lines you will find that both have

12. POETRY

Like the collection of **FAMOUS BOOKS**, the poems here were compiled by John Hammerton.

As the first page (opposite) says, poetry is 'far sweeter and more musical than the worlds of prose': in fact, it probably began with singing.

The writer explains the main genres:
- dramatic, as when people are speaking to each other (e.g. the plays of Shakespeare;
- epic, usually a description of some great event;
- lyric, which gets this name because it was originally intended to be sung to the accompaniment of a lyre.

He also explains the principles of rhyme, while pointing out that sometimes poetry does not rhyme (as in Shakespearean 'blank verse').

The final volume of the *Encyclopædia* includes a special index of poems. This covers twelve pages of small print: even allowing for the fact that most poems appear three times – under author, title and first line – this is a very substantial number.

Just over two hundred authors are cited (for comparison, The *Golden Treasury*, of approximately the same date, contained 124).[1] Some items are accounted for by the 'Little Verses for Very Little People' which occupied a page in each fortnightly issue, and which would not appear in an adult collection. Nevertheless, all major poets and all well-known poems are included, besides others of lesser significance.

Apart from providing such statistics, there is no obvious way of summarising the articles in this section. It seems preferable to give a sample of contents from one issue, taken more-or-less at random (this is on pages 2123–28, in Volume 4). Here we find, in the following order: [2]

---

[1] The *Golden Treasury* first appeared in the mid-nineteenth century; I am referring here to a later edition inherited from my mother. Like the *Encyclopædia*, this bears no date: it is however inscribed 'To Jeannie Renton [my mother's maiden name] for gaining Certificates in Welfare of Youth Class, U.F. Church, Arbroath 1909'. It had probably been re-issued at that time.

[2] I have inserted the dates: as usual, the *Encyclopædia* does not provide these, though each item is preceded by a useful short introduction about the poet and the poem.

- by Thomas Hood (1835–74): 'The Dream of Eugene Aram' (a longish ballad);
- by William Wordsworth (1770–1850): 'To the Skylark';
- by Robert Herrick (1591–1674): 'Fair Daffodils';
- by Robert Southey (1774–1843): 'The Inchcape Rock' and 'The Traveller's Return';
- by Ella Wheeler Wilcox (1850–1919): 'Wishing';
- by William Cowper (1731–1800): 'The Dog and the Water-Lily' and 'Epitaph on a Hare';
- by Mary Lamb (1764–1847): 'The Child and the Snake';
- by Lord Byron (1788–1824): 'The Vision of Belshazzar'.

Of these, the *Golden Treasury* included only 'To the Skylark' and 'Fair Daffodils' (though other pieces by each of these authors did appear, with the exception of the American writer Ella Wheeler Wilcox).

The article concludes with the usual page of 'Little Verses' (reproduced). As can be seen, these include one little song or nursery rhyme with a simple but pleasing piano accompaniment (composer not indicated).

LITTLE VERSES FOR VERY LITTLE PEOPLE

OLD Abram Brown is dead and gone,
  You'll never see him more ;
He used to wear a long brown coat,
  That button'd down before.

I'LL sing you a song,
  Though not very long,
Yet I think it as pretty as
  any.
Put your hand in your purse,
You'll never be worse,
And give the poor singer a
  penny.

IF ifs and ans
  Were pots and pans,
There would be no need for tinkers !

YOU shall have an apple,
  You shall have a plum ;
You shall have a rattle-basket,
  When your dad comes home.

THE cock doth crow,
  To let you know,
If you be wise,
'Tis time to rise.

THE man in the moon
  Came tumbling down,
And asked his way to
  Norwich ;
He went by the south,
And burnt his mouth,
With supping cold pease-porridge.

DANCE A BABY

Dance a ba - by did-dy....... What can mam-my do wid 'e ?........

Sit in a lap, Give it some pap, And dance a ba - by did-dy........

MY little old man and I fell out ;
  I'll tell you what 'twas all about :
I had money and he had none,
  And that's the way the noise begun.

THE King of France went up the hill,
  With twenty thousand men ;
The King of France came down the hill,
  And ne'er went up again.

THERE was a little boy and
  a little girl,
  Lived in an alley ;
Says the little boy to the
  little girl,
  " Shall I, oh, shall I ? "

Says the little girl to the
  little boy,
  " What shall we do ? "
Says the little boy to the little girl,
  " I will kiss you ! "

WHEN little Fred was
  called to bed,
  He always acted right ;
He kissed Mamma, and then
  Papa,
  And wished them all good-
  night.

He made no noise, like
  naughty boys,
  But gently upstairs
Directly went, when he was sent,
  And always said his prayers.

A SUNSHINY shower
  Won't last half an hour.

AS the days lengthen,
  So the storms strengthen.

THE NEXT POETRY AND NURSERY RHYMES BEGIN ON PAGE 2175
2128

WHAT OUR LESSONS WILL TEACH US

WE shall not learn in our book all that we must know when we are grown up and go to school, but we shall begin to learn many things which will help us at school and help to make us useful when we grow up. Everything we read in the CHILDREN'S ENCYCLOPÆDIA will be useful to us and make our school life easier, but in this part we shall learn some special things. We shall learn what figures are, and the wonderful things that can be done with them. We shall try to draw pictures of the things we see at home and in the streets. We shall learn how to read and write, so that we can read the story-books ourselves and write letters to our friends. We shall find out all about music and what a beautiful thing it is, so that we can learn to play the piano and sing; and those who are learning French will find here little stories written in French which they will be able to read and understand. All these useful things we shall learn just as if this were our school, and we shall find them as interesting as real stories.

READING

HOW TO LEARN THE A B C

BEFORE we can read our story-books ourselves we must learn our letters. Then, when we have learned these, we shall be able to make words and read them, and when we can read we shall find that nothing in the world brings us more happiness than reading books.

There are twenty-six letters in the alphabet, and we can write them in two ways, because sometimes we want to write them big and sometimes little. Here they are all together, the little letters and the big letters side by side.

The Big and Little Letters of the Alphabet

A a	E e	I i	L l	P p	S s	W w
B b	F f	J j	M m	Q q	T t	X x
C c	G g		N n		U u	Y y
D d	H h	K k	O o	R r	V v	Z z

We must learn these letters until we know them as well as we know our names, and it will help us to remember our letters if we learn the Animal Alphabet on the next page. That is an easy way of learning A B C, and we must read the Animal Alphabet, and say it over and over again until we can say it through without a mistake. Here is another way of remembering where the letters come ; it is a little rhyme telling us the place of each letter :

A before B, C before D,
F after E, H after G,
I before J, L after K,

M before N, O and P then ;
R after Q, then S, T, U,
V and W next come to view ;

with X, Y, and Z, all the letters are said.

Now we must learn to put the letters together and make words, and we shall find it very interesting, as we get along with our lessons, to see how the letters come together to make the very words we know.

I F spells IF	O F spells OF	W E spells WE	G O spells GO
I N spells IN	O N spells ON	B E spells BE	N O spells NO
I S spells IS	O R spells OR	H E spells HE	S O spells SO
I T spells IT	O X spells OX	M E spells ME	T O spells TO

Pictures will help us to learn the words, and a clever artist has drawn some pictures to show us what the words below them mean.

13. SCHOOL LESSONS

The writers of these articles are given as:

Reading: Gerald K. Hibbert
Writing: Miss A.B. Barnard
Arithmetic: H.J. Allport
Drawing: Miss Marion Thomson
French: Miss Lois Mee

Of these, there is information only on **Lois Mee**. She was Arthur's sister – in fact, according to Hammerton's biography, his favourite sister. She accompanied him on a journey to Egypt, and another to Paris (Arthur did not travel much, and knew no languages except a little French).

The introduction to the first of this series (see first page) explains that the intention is to make school life easier, not to substitute for school lessons. Each of the fortnightly issues has articles covering reading, writing, arithmetic, music, drawing and French; different authors are responsible.

Reading

As can be seen from the front page, this begins at a very elementary level with the letters of the alphabet and, on the following pages, two- and three-letter words that can easily be recognised (BAT – CAT – HAT – RAT, etc). Subsequent articles introduce longer words.

From Volume 2 onwards, the basic elements of grammar are explained: first the concept of plurals, then the role of nouns, pronouns, adverbs and adjectives. By Volume 4 there are explanations of how to 'parse' a sentence into its grammatical components.

Volume 4 includes an interesting article on 'the story of words'. It explains that long ago there was a big group of people in the centre of Asia speaking one language (Sanskrit). Some of these went to India, others to Russia, some settled in the south of Europe, others in Germany. So most European languages, though they have grown apart, are part of the 'Indo-European' family. English is a brother to German, a first cousin to Latin, Greek and the languages that came from them, including French. Hence 'father' is like *Vater* in German, *pater* in Latin (*p* and *f* can change places), *padre* in Italian, *père* in French, and so on. (These are useful hints which I personally learnt only doing Modern Languages well into my secondary-school period.)

Volume 5 explains how words have changed over time. Thus:

– 'Idiot' was a Greek word for a person who took no part in public life: the Greeks thought that all such people were very foolish.

- 'Surgeon' was formerly 'chirurgeon', which was also from the Greek and meant 'a worker with the hand'.
- 'Villain' used to mean a slave attached to a farm: now it means a 'wicked wretch'.

There are also words made up from names, e.g.:
- 'Bayonet' gets its name from Bayonne in France, where bayonets were first made.
- 'Jovial' is called after Jove or Jupiter, whose name was given to a planet, and it is considered lucky to be born under that planet.
- 'Parchment' is called after Pergamon in Asia, where it originated.
- 'Sherry' is from Xeres in Spain.

The names of the days and months are explained:
- 'Sunday' is the day dedicated in old times to the sun and its worship;
- 'Monday', in the same way, to the moon.
- 'Tuesday' comes from Tiw, the Saxon god of war; etc.
- 'January was the month dedicated by the Romans to their god Janus, who had two faces: the first month of the year seemed to look back to the old year and forward to the new one.

There are also words that tell stories.
- 'Alphabet' is made up of the two first letters in Greek, Alpha and Beta.
- 'Encyclopædia', also from the Greek, means 'the circle of human instruction'.
- 'Umbrella' is from the Italian umbra, a shade, as umbrellas were first used as a shade from the sun: this has changed its meaning, in 'a sad tribute to the amount of rain we get in this country! '

There is more etymology in an article telling us how some animals got their names:
- 'Ass' is a word found in several languages: it is *assa* in Anglo-Saxon, *asilus* in Gothic and *asinus* in Latin; and is thought to be connected with the Hebrew *athon*.
- 'Bear' is the Anglo-Saxon word *bera*; in German this appears as *bär* and in Latin as *fera*, meaning 'wild beast' (b and f can change places).
- 'Cat' is also a word found in many languages in almost the same form.
- 'Dog' is from the Middle English *doggë*.
- 'Giraffe' is from the Arabic *zaraf*, via the Spanish *girafa*.
- 'Rhinocerus' comes from two Greek words – rhinos meaning 'of a nose', and *keras*, 'horn'.
- 'Tiger' is from the Latin *tigris*, and that comes from a Persian word meaning an arrow: this name was given because the Tigris river was so swift-running.

Volume 6 (where these lessons end) gives derivations of a number of place names:
- 'Buckingham' comes from the Anglo-Saxon *boc*, a beech-tree, because there used to be fine beech trees on this county.
- 'Chester' comes from the Roman *castra*, a camp; similarly Doncaster and other names.
- Dublin is the Irish *Dubb-lin*, meaning black pool.
- 'London' is probably a corruption of *Llyn-dun*, meaning a fort by a pool, which was the name given by the Britons to their settlement on the banks of the Thames.

We are also told the meanings of phrases. Some of the most common are:
- 'Baker's dozen' means thirteen: bakers used to be heavily fined for giving short weight, so to be on the safe side they gave an extra loaf to every dozen.
- 'Carry coals to Newcastle' means to do something unnecessary: Newcastle was one of the greatest coalfields in the world.
- 'To put a thing off until the Greek kalends' means that it will never be done, for there were no 'kalends' – the first day of the Roman month – among the Greeks.
- 'To cross the Rubicon', i.e. to take some action from which there is no going back, refers to a stream between Italy and Gaul: when Julius Caesar crossed the Rubicon, he had passed from his own province of Gaul and had begun to invade Italy.

Another article gives a long list of abbreviations, covering six pages. These include some in frequent use, such as c/o, e.g., i.e., U.K., U.S.A. Others seem unlikely to be encountered by young children: F.R.C.S. (Fellow of the Royal College of Surgeons), H.M.I.S. (His or Her Majesty's Inspector of Schools); S.P.C.K. (Society for the Promotion of Christian Knowledge), etc.; these would be useful only for reference. Some explanations, however, are interesting:
- A.D. is the Latin *Anno Domini*, in the year of Our Lord, reckoning the year of Christ's birth as 1; B.C. is 'Before Christ'.
- A.M., however, is *Anno Mundi*, in the year of the world: the Jews reckon the years from the time the world was supposed to have been created, which was 3760 B.C.
- I.H.S., according to the *Encyclopædia*, is from the first three letters of the name Jesus when written in Greek capitals, and does not, as often supposed, represent *Jesus Hominum Salvator*, Jesus Saviour of Men. [1]

---

[1] An abstruse point for young readers! The *Encyclopædia*'s interpretation is almost correct: IHS is a Latinised form of the Greek monograms for *Iesous Christos*. As a representation of the 'Most Holy Name' it was promoted by Saint Bernardino and others, and is used by the Jesuits. See *Wikipedia* entry and other Internet sources.

The last article in the series on 'Reading' gives a list of foreign words and phrases, mostly French and Latin. The introduction explains that some of these are used because they express better than any English words what the speaker means: examples given are *chic, de trop, ad nauseum*. Others are legacies from the time when British laws were composed in Latin, such as *ad referendum*, and many Church phrases – such as *Deo gratia* – have also come from the time when Latin was the language of the Church.

The overall concept of this series is puzzling. For a start, a small child just beginning to learn letters and simple worlds could certainly not read the texts of the articles: so the intervention of an adult – parent or perhaps nurse-maid? – would have been required. This seems a cumbersome approach: there are today many more attractive means (such as alphabetic tiles or bricks) whereby a child can start learning to read – surely such games were available to the Edwardian child?

The grammar lessons which follow would have been appropriate for a child several years older: not one who had started elementary reading just a few months previously.

By Volume 5, the series becomes very interesting indeed, with the articles on etymology and other subjects outlined above. This now seems aimed at the teenage level, where the explanations could spark a lively interest into the origins of the language – in fact many grown-ups could profit from this knowledge!

So the series could not have worked as progressive teaching for an individual child over the two-year duration of the *Encyclopædia*'s publication. On the other hand, the later volumes would have appealed to older children in the family, or remained to be read with profit in later years.

Writing

This series too begins at a very elementary level. The articles in Volumes 1 and 2 are taken up with instructions how to form the characters; clearly, the pupils could not have understood these instructions unless they were helped by an adult, who could probably have taught them in any case.

By Volume 3 capitals are introduced; then figures. Then, rather improbably, the children are apparently considered able to write a model letter to a friend. The final article comes already in Volume 4, with warnings as to how not to write – i.e. examples of common mistakes.

This is probably the least satisfactory series in the *Encyclopædia*; maybe this was apparent to the Editor and explains why it fizzled out so soon.

Arithmetic

This is much more challenging. It starts in the form of a story about children visiting a farm and counting the animals (up to six); there are illustrations to help. Larger numbers are gradually introduced; then addition and subtraction, multiplication and division. By Volume 4 we get to long division – e.g. 1255629 divided by 571 ...

Then money is introduced, and we are reminded of the pre-decimal complications of British currency. The coinage had sovereigns (pounds), half-sovereigns, crowns (five shillings) half-crowns, florins (two shillings), shillings, sixpenny pieces, threepenny pieces, pennies, half-pennies and farthings. To make calculations one needed to know that there were four farthings to a penny; twelve pennies to a shilling, twenty shillings to a pound. 'How many farthings are there in £37 5s 9½ ?' is a question that would cause modern children to give up in despair (the answer is 35,798).

An extract from Volume 5 is reproduced to show some of the complications of working with amounts of money. Adding and subtracting was bad enough; multiplication and division even worse!

This series ends in Volume 6 with instructions on how to work with fractions. One of the 'simple' examples given is how to find the value of seven and two-ninths less three and eleven-fifteenths (these fractions defeat the keyboard of a modern computer). There is no hint here that decimalisation might make things easier (though in answer to a question in **WONDER** the general advantages of the decimal system had been pointed out). These lessons do not go on to deal with measures of length, weight and capacity, which would have raised still more problems...

MULTIPLYING SUMS OF MONEY

WE know how to take away several simple numbers from another number all at the same time. We can use the same method for compound quantities. For example, if we have a sum of money and wish to know how much will be left if we spend several stated amounts out of it, we need not add together the several amounts and then subtract the total from our sum of money. We proceed instead in the following way :

Example 1. A lady pays £1 3s. 5d. to the butcher, 14s. 7½d. to the baker, £2 1s. 8½d. to the grocer, and £1 5s. 6½d. to the dairy. How much will she have left out of £8 5s. 4d. ?

£	s.	d.	
8	5	4	Write down first the amount she has, and separate it by a line from what fol-
1	3	5	lows. Then write down the
	14	7½	various amounts she pays
2	1	8½	away. We have now to find
1	5	6½	what must be added to these various amounts in order to
3	0	0½	make £8 5s. 4d. We there-fore add them together, and

make up the total to the required amount. Thus :

½d., 1d., 1½d., and ½d. make 2d. Put down ½d. Carry 2d. 2d., 8d., 16d.,

23d., 28d., and 0d. make 2s. 4d. Put down 0d. Carry 2s. Now add the shillings. 2s., 7s., 8s., 12s., 15s., and 0s. make 15s. ; carry 10s. Then 10s., 20s., make £1. Carry £1. £1, £2, £4, £5, and £3 make £8.

Hence, the amount left is £3 0s. 0½d.

Example 2. From £17 4s. 2½d. take the sum of £3 6s. 2¼d., £5 1s. 4½d., and £7 18s. 9¾d.

£	s.	d.	
17	4	2½	Say, 3 farthings, 5, 6, make 1½d. Carry 1d. 1d., 10d.,
			14d., 16d., and 10d. make
3	6	2¼	2s. 2d. Carry 2s. 2s.,
5	1	4½	10s., 11s., 17s., and 7s.
7	18	9¾	make 24s. Carry 20s. 20s.,
			30s., and 10s. make £2.
	17	10	Carry £2. 2, 9, 14, 17,
			make £17.

Hence, the result is 17s. 10d.

Now let us set a few examples of these money sums to be worked :

1. Add together £212 14s. 8½d., £19 1s. 2d., £48 11s. 10¾d., and £101 2s. 8d.

2. Subtract (i.) 14s. 10½d. from £1. (ii.) £3 5s. 6d. from £11 8s. 4d. (iii.) £129 13s. 9½d. from £201 6s. 3d.

3. Add together £3 16s. 10d., £11 19s. 8d., and £6 12s. 9d., and take £19 11s. 4d. from the result.

Music

The tone of this series is set from the start, and is best rendered by quoting the opening paragraphs:

> 'I want to take you to the wonderful land of Sound, a country so beautiful that we will call it our Magic Kingdom. In this Kingdom there are Fairies who will sing to us, and when we know them, and can understand their language, they will tell us stories of the winds, they will bring to us the songs of the birds, the murmur of the brook, and all the beautiful sounds in the world.
>
> 'In this wonderful Fairyland, also, we shall find little black Goblins; but they are good-hearted Goblins, as kind as they are black; for in this beautiful land, Fairies and Goblins help one another, and join together to tell us the most delightful stories. We have all seen this Magic Kingdom, which is in nearly all our homes. We call it the Piano.' (p. 97)

The seven fairies are called A through G; illustrations show where they lie on the keyboard. 'Roads the Fairies travel on' are the lines of the staves on a sheet of music, and the position of each 'fairy' on the stave is shown. The writer is clearly anxious to make the first steps as attractive as possible to a small beginner. Perhaps she succeeded; a modern child might find this talk of Fairies and Goblins just soppy!

However that may be, the teaching is systematic and thorough. After the treble clef, the bass clef is introduced; and we come to 'King Semibreve, Lords Minim, Masters Crochet...' By Volume 3 there are instructions about how to play the notes on the piano; Volume 4 gives finger exercises. Volume 5 introduces scales ('Fairy Ladders'), both major and minor: in fact it shows the relationship between a major key and its tonic minor, and Volume 6 explains the difference between a tonic minor and a relative minor: this is becoming quite sophisticated.

In fact, one would like more, on harmony, for example, or about other instruments; but the series concludes in Volume 6:

> 'If we continue to practise carefully, first very slowly, then gradually – but very gradually – quicker, we shall be well on the way to running up and down our ladders of tone as quickly and evenly as the music fairies want us to.' (p. 3405)

Again, a small child could not have used these lessons without the help of an adult, but they would have provided a useful guide. We should note the assumption that a piano would be available in almost every household, which also implies that many children were expected to learn to play. This may reflect middle-class bias – it would have been less true of working households – but it is a useful reminder to us of an important aspect of family life in pre-television days.

Drawing

This is another subject that is not easily taught via a book. The series begins with a simple guide to drawing or painting an orange or an apple, in chalk or paint. More complicated subjects follow – leaves, twigs, flowers, an open book, a house, animals, etc. The use of colours is described. There is a useful demonstration of the rules of perspective, using an open door as an example. This series ends in Volume 5, with instructions for using pen-and-ink.

French

It is pointed out that children will not be able to learn how to speak French from these lessons, as the different sounds cannot be made clear on paper, but will help if they are learning French at school.

The lessons take the form of a picture-story about a family going on a visit to France. Under each picture, the French text is first translated word-by-word (with curious results), then given in correct English.

The text and illustrations (the first part of the story is reproduced here) show us the type of family which the *Encyclopædia* presumably regarded as typical, and how they travelled.

There are three children: Louis, ten years old, Jenny, eight and a baby of two. They are clearly prosperous: the parents and children are well-dressed, and they have a nurse-maid who accompanies them on the journey. They take a cab to the station, a train to Dover, a steamer across the Channel to Calais. On the boat, Mamma is ill. They pass through customs. The train to Paris takes four hours. It is the maid who takes the children shopping for new boots and toys. Taking a motor-car to see Napoleon's tomb is an adventure; Louis wants to become a great soldier like Napoleon. (It is curious that this is the only Parisian monument mentioned: one might have expected at least the Eiffel Tower.) At a party the children dance 'Sir Roger de Coverley'.

Papa has business in Paris so they stay for a year. The children get a governess, who tells them stories in French, still with line-by-line English translation. These take up most of the remaining articles, till in Volume 5 we move on to Aesop's fables and other stories, given here only in French though they appear in English in another section.

The picture-story approach to learning French is not the best method of language teaching: it is unlikely that these lessons alone would have enabled a child to read the stories which end this series. The subject-matter is, frankly, rather boring, but it does give us some idea how an Edwardian family might have travelled.

As has been seen above, these French lessons were written by Arthur Mee's sister, Lois. It is noteworthy that in this *Encyclopædia* which, in general, is remarkably free of typological or other mistakes, a list of corrections at the end of Volume 8 signals a disproportionate number of errors in these French lessons. Some of these are elementary grammatical faults, suggesting that Lois was not a professional French teacher.

LITTLE PICTURE-STORIES IN FRENCH

YOU will not be able to learn to speak French from these lessons. There are some sounds in French which cannot be made clear on paper, and you will only be able to understand these by hearing them spoken. But these lessons will help you very much if you are learning French at school, or if there is someone at home who can help you to understand how the words should be said. The French people say E just as we say A, and say I just as we say E. But there are some sounds which are not so easy to learn as these, and it will be better to ask someone to help you when reading these little lessons than to try to learn all these difficult things yourself, however hard we might try to make them easy for you. These lessons tell us the story of a visit to France and of the visitor's doings among the French people, and the pictures help to make the language quite clear. The first line under the picture is the French. The second line gives the English word for the French word above it. But the French people do not always put their words together in the same way as we do, and the third line shows how we make up the words into our own language.

Louis

Je m'appelle Louis, et   j'ai dix ans
I myself call Louis, and I have ten years
My name is Louis, and I am ten years old

Jeannette—Jenny

Ma sœur Jeannette a   huit ans
My sister Jenny   has eight years
My sister Jenny is eight years old

Bébé—Baby

Mon petit frère a deux ans
My little brother has two years
My little brother is two years old

On l'appelle Bébé
One him calls Baby
He is called Baby

L'école—The school

Jeannette et moi nous allons à l'école
Jenny   and I we   go to the school
Jenny and I go to school

Maintenant nous sommes en vacances
Now   we   are   in holidays
Now we have a holiday

Maman—Mamma   Papa

Nous allons en France
We are going in France
We are going to France

Nous allons avec papa et maman
We are going with papa and mamma
We are going with papa and mamma

La bonne—The nurserymaid

Bébé va   venir et la bonne aussi
Baby is going to come and the nurse also
Baby is going and nurse also

Nos malles—Our trunks

Notre bonne a fait toutes nos malles
Our nurse has made all our trunks
Our nurse has packed all our trunks

Nos jouets sont dans la grande malle
Our toys are in the large trunk
Our toys are in the large trunk

Nos jouets—Our toys

Nous avons beaucoup de jouets
We have many of toys
We have many toys

Bébé emporte son bateau à voiles
Baby is taking his sailing boat
Baby is taking his sailing boat

Le fiacre—The cab

Le fiacre est à la porte
The cab is at the door
The cab is at the door

Le cocher—The driver

Le cocher met les bagages sur le fiacre
The driver puts the luggage on the cab
The driver is putting the luggage on the cab

Dans le fiacre—In the cab

Nous sommes six dans le fiacre
We are six in the cab
There are six of us in the cab

1	**2**	**3**
Un	deux	trois
One	*two*	*three*
4	**5**	**6**
quatre	cinq	six
four	*five*	*six*

Le cheval—The horse

Le cheval marche très bien
The horse goes very well
The horse goes very well

Nous aimons aller en fiacre
We like to go in cab
We like riding in a cab

La gare—The station

Nous arriverons bientôt à la gare
We shall arrive soon at the station
We shall soon arrive at the station

The next picture stories in French are in that part of our book beginning on page 205.

211

These **SCHOOL LESSONS** show us what the authors of the *Encyclopædia* thought children should learn from an early age. The 'Reading' section in particular provides considerable intellectual stimulation; the 'Arithmetic' lessons remind us that in the pre-decimal and pre-electronic age, children had to cope with quite daunting problems. Though the author of the 'Music' section adopts a nauseatingly childish tone, the content of her lessons is thorough.

Still, these lessons seem the least satisfactory part of the *Encyclopædia*, which perhaps explains why they did not run throughout all the volumes. One might think that if the children were attending school, many of these articles would have been superfluous. However, in another part of the *Encyclopædia* (on **LIFE**), Dr. Saleeby has inveighed against the poor quality of most school education, with its teaching mainly by rote and enforced by corporal punishment.[2] We also know the importance attached to education by Arthur Mee: no doubt he and his colleagues wished to compensate for the failings of the system by providing a more inspiring and humanistic programme.

However, as has already been pointed out, there is ambiguity as to the age of the targeted audience. Each subject starts at a very elementary level, but some become quite challenging and indicate a much older readership. This is especially the case with the series on 'Reading', notably in its discussion of the origins of words and languages in Volumes 5 and 6. 'Arithmetic' comes to include calculations that look daunting, but were required in the pre-decimal age. The rate of progress needed would certainly have exceeded what was possible during the two-year period over which the *Encyclopædia* was initially serialised.

The younger children would have needed the help of an adult; and although one can imagine that the *Encyclopædia* itself would have stimulated the desire to learn to read, adults would still have been needed from time to time. This might have been the role of the mother, or, in well-off families, of a governess or tutor. It is difficult to imagine these lessons making any impact in working-class families, where the parents themselves would probably not have had the necessary education (even if such households had been able to afford the purchase of the *Encyclopædia*).

Indeed, the lessons provide us with useful glimpses into the type of family presumably considered to provide the typical readership: the picture-stories in French confirm that this is middle-class, with a father in business of some kind. The family is well-off: it can afford a house-maid, who looks after the children (though the wife presumably does not have a job) and it can travel.

---

[2] A judgement which is amply born out by many of the contributions to Arthur's *Lost Voices of the Edwardians*.

THE BOOK OF WORK AND PLAY

ALL work and no play makes Jack a dull boy and Jill a dull girl. Healthy play is natural and necessary for us all, and when school is over it is right that we should go merrily to our games. We shall learn here how to play them. We shall learn, also, many other things. It is remarkable what we can do at home when rain drives us indoors and the long winter evenings come, and we shall discover hundreds of ways of amusing ourselves and making use of our hands. We shall learn how to make wonderful things with cardboard and paper and other materials. The boy will learn what to do with his little box of tools, and the girl what to do with her needle and her clever fingers. Magical illusions, conjuring tricks, puzzles, problems, and simple scientific experiments will fill our pages and give us an entertainment of which we shall never grow tired.

HOW TO MAKE A MODEL TOWN

A Wonderful Work for Boys and Girls

IT is a very troublesome thing to build a real town, and it costs a great sum of money. There is the land to buy, streets to make, drains to lay, architects, builders, clerks, foremen, and workmen to pay. Then inspectors and surveyors come to see that the work is being done as they like. So that not many people have ever built a whole town alone. We will try to do so.

We shall be architects and builders as well. The ordinary builder does not make his plans. He may take the plans of the architect, and make his walls the sizes given him by the plans. But we must take the drawings given us and make new drawings for ourselves, the proper size of the houses we want to make.

We shall learn here how to build a town—let us name it Modeltown. We shall not start as grown-up builders do, and our town will not cost very much either. A very few pennies carefully spent will give us the materials for houses, churches, shops, railway-stations, fire-stations, bridges, a grand hall, and all the belongings of a go-ahead town. It may be possible to find in your home most of the things needed—some cardboard boxes, a penknife with a nice sharp point, which is better than scissors, a gluepot, a pencil, and a ruler marked in inches, and a pair of compasses or dividers.

But if you want to build the town very well indeed I will tell you what to get. For a foundation nothing is better than sheets of strawboard—the brown or yellow board which perhaps you would call cardboard. Our town can be made to stand upon a few imperial sheets of this, costing from twopence upwards. If you cut one of these in half you will have

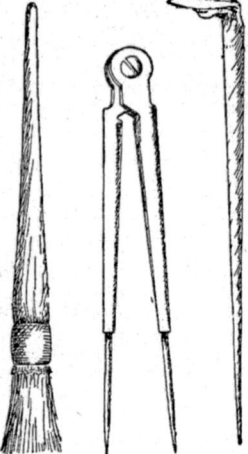

Brush   Compasses   Spill

a very nice plot on which to erect buildings. Some white cardboard, such as is used for mounts for pictures, will be the best material for the houses. Large sheets, enough to build a church or a museum and a few houses with, can be got for twopence, or it will cost more if a thick quality is used. You will want a rule marked in inches, with each inch divided into eight parts. You will also want a *scale* rule, which you can buy from most stationers or from any dealer in mathematical instruments. You will also be told the meaning of *scale* rules and how to use them. You must have a pair of dividers, or compasses, to measure up the lengths of your walls. A cheap pair was bought for threepence—here it is in the picture.

Two set-squares, which can be bought for a penny each, will save you a great deal of time and setting out by compasses. If we do not buy these, we can learn how to make a simple instrument of the same kind in that part of our book beginning on page 217.

Builders use mortar and nails and difficult joints in woodwork to stick the building together, but we shall not want any such troublesome materials. Stickphast, seccotine, or even gum will stick our house together. But far better than any of these is glue, and it is also cheaper. A penny will buy enough for our city. Put some pieces of glue, broken small, into a jampot with a little water. Put the jam-pot into an old saucepan with plenty of water in it, and let it get very hot on the side of the fire or on the stove. Soon the glue will melt, and it must then be used hot.

For the larger surfaces it will be necessary to have a brush. The brush shown in the

14. THINGS TO MAKE AND THINGS TO DO

There is great variety in these articles, ascribed to 'many writers'. Even more, perhaps, than other parts of the *Encyclopædia*, they bring home to us the reality of family life in an age before most of the modern 'conveniences'. Several of the suggested activities are for 'sitting around the fire': central heating is, in the literal sense of the word, less convivial. Some homes, but by no means all, had electric lighting, others might have had gas, but for many there would have been long winter evenings with only the relatively dim light of oil lamps and candles. Toys could of course be purchased, but there was nothing like the superabundance now available, so there was every incentive for children to make their own. [1]

Bearing in mind that the *Encyclopædia* originated as a series of fortnightly issues, the activities suggested have a seasonal flavour. Most of the issues – except those in mid-winter – had an item entitled 'What to do in the garden month-by-month'. For Christmas-time there were some special items: preparing 'a Christmas-tree for birds', making a toboggan, a party-game called 'a Christmas gymkhana', and advice on choosing presents for the family – bearing in mind that 'Men are not so easy to cater for, for after we have thought of pipe-stands, slippers, ash-trays and tobacco-boxes, there seems to be very little left' (p. 4882). For the summer months, outdoor activities and sports predominated.

A regular feature over numerous issues was the construction of 'Modeltown'. This was to be made mainly from stiff papers, matchsticks and glue, yet was remarkably ambitious: the designs appear complicated, but if the child – probably with parental assistance – had persisted, the result would have been a complete village with cottages, shops, a church and its vicarage, a farm, a railway station, a hotel and even gasworks.

---

[1] The delightful *Edwardian Scrapbook* (see Bibliography) covers many aspects of Edwardian life but includes no toys other than some board games.

6. The Doll's Little Frock

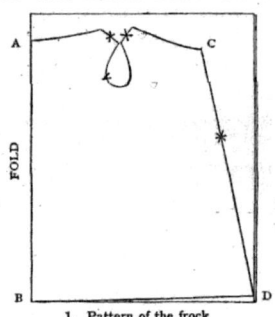

1. Pattern of the frock

2. Sleeve pattern

3. Back of the frock

Girls were taught how to make up a workbox, how to use needle and thread, how to knit and crochet, how to embroider, enabling them to make many useful items, such as dolls' clothes, tablecloths, cushion covers, socks, scarves and shawls; and how to patch and mend.

Using the square

Using a gimlet

Using the hammer

Taking out nails

Using a chisel

Straightening a bent nail

Using the plane

Using a screw-driver

Boys were encouraged to take up carpentry. Beginning with explanations of the necessary tools, and how to make basic joints, instructions were given for many items of domestic furniture – bookshelves, a chest of drawers, a flower-box – as well as outdoor items such as a wheelbarrow and a dog-kennel.

There were also many toys which children could make for themselves. These included a magic lantern, a simple camera, a field telephone. An interesting item was a submarine, made from a section of a round pole, bits of tin, a length of elastic and a lead weight.[2]

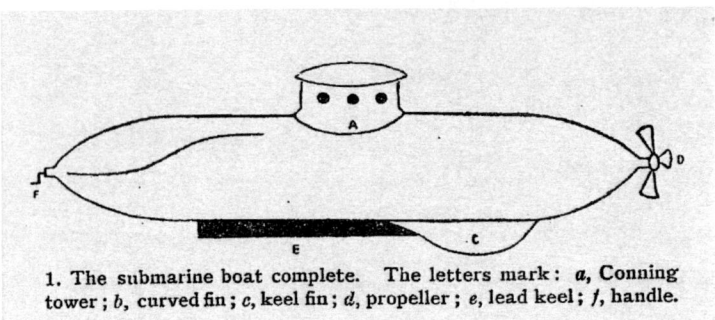

1. The submarine boat complete. The letters mark: *a*, Conning tower; *b*, curved fin; *c*, keel fin; *d*, propeller; *e*, lead keel; *f*, handle.

Many party games were described. Some – such as 'Consequences' or 'Simon says' – may have survived, but one fears that most would be found silly by children today.

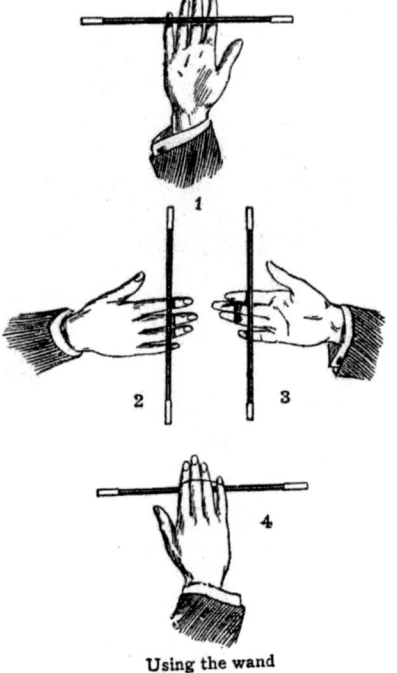

Conjuring tricks were very popular: they included tricks with coins, cards, matches, pieces of string, dominoes, etc. One was a 'self-suspending wand', the trick being to attach a loop of black thread through which the fingers could pass.

Using the wand

---

[2] I remember this submarine well, having made it as a boy with my father's help. Surprisingly, it worked. We sailed it (or rather, submerged it) successfully on a remote loch in the Scottish Highlands.

Secret codes have always fascinated children, and an example – looking rather like the Hebrew alphabet – is shown here, with its key. The Morse code was explained; so was the system of signalling with flags. There was even a list of some signs in deaf-and-dumb language.

a b c	d e f	g h i
j k l	m n o	p q r
s t u	v w x	y z

DEAR ELSIE,

I hope you can read this. Have you ever had a letter like it before? It is the first I have written in this way, but it does not seem very hard. When are you coming to see us? Father has bought me a beautiful pony, and I want you to ride him. With love from

EVA.

Some items were characteristic of Boy Scout practice (the movement was founded in 1907): how to tie knots, how to judge distances in the country, how to use one's watch as a compass, etc.

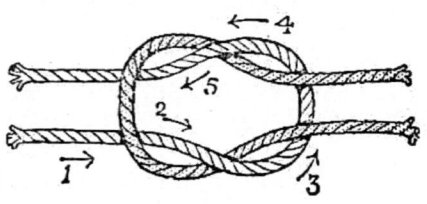

Reef knot

There was explanation too of how to calculate the height of a tree or a tower, using its shadow or, if there is no sunlight, by triangulation with a stick and something to measure its length and its distance from the base of the object.

The height of a tree shown by its shadow

Numerous out-door activities were suggested. One – a paper-chase on horseback – gives an idea of the social level of some at least of the readership. More modestly, there were instructions for building a sand-castle. A couple of simple Morris dances were explained. And there were explanations of all the major sports – rugby, 'association football', hockey, golf, croquet, tennis (see illustration – apparently a very lady-like occupation), baseball and its simpler form, 'rounders'), swimming – and some more obscure ones, such as 'stickerchief'. One can hardly learn to play these games from written instructions, but at least the rules were set out.

Finally, anyone wanting to know how to keep poultry, goats, rabbits, a tortoise, a guinea-pig or even a pet hedgehog could find instructions here.

THE RIGHT WAY TO PLAY LAWN-TENNIS

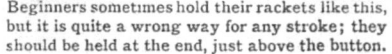

Beginners sometimes hold their rackets like this, but it is quite a wrong way for any stroke; they should be held at the end, just above the button.

This is the correct way to hold the racket to hit the ball when it comes to the right hand of the player. Note the position of thumb and fingers, and also of the head of the racket.

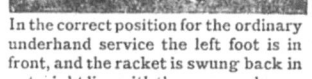

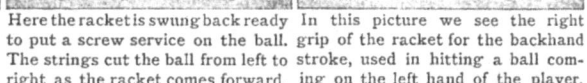

In the correct position for the ordinary underhand service the left foot is in front, and the racket is swung back in a straight line with the arm as shown.

Here the racket is swung back ready to put a screw service on the ball. The strings cut the ball from left to right as the racket comes forward.

In this picture we see the right grip of the racket for the backhand stroke, used in hitting a ball coming on the left hand of the player.

This is how to perform the "round-arm smash," a useful stroke with which to "kill" weak balls just over the net. Notice the free action, which should always be striven after in hitting.

This is the wrong way to hold the racket for a backhand stroke. The position is cramped, and the thumb should not be in front of the handle.

ARTHUR MEE'S FAREWELL

Over the five thousand and more pages since Arthur Mee's greeting to his readers, his name has not appeared. Of course, in his role as editor he would have been present throughout. We can guess that he wrote some of the replies under **WONDER** and perhaps some of the introductory passages to individual articles; but the bulk of the writing has been done by his contributors, several of whom have been named.

At the end of the last volume, however, he reappears with an emotional farewell, **'Goodbye to the Book of My Heart'**, addressed to 'My little travellers'.

His romantic view of childhood is again apparent in an illustration showing birds, butterflies, and flowers, at the centre of which stand prettily-dressed small children. (The original coloured picture is spread across two pages; it is reproduced here in on one). These children appear no older than those illustrated at the start of the *Encyclopædia*, although any who started with the first issue would now be two years older. Mee seems to have had a Peter Pan-like desire for children not to grow up...

However that may be, his final words (p. 5282) are typically eloquent and touching:

> 'Into a hundred thousand homes and more, fortnight by fortnight, this book of my heart has gone. From thousands and thousands of homes has come back to me the love that men count more precious than gold... We have learned together in this book the truth of Life... We know that the things that bind us in friendship are the things that last for ever...
>
> 'What has been written from the heart in this book, and what has come into your own heart from this book, will go on. It will go on in your own life, as long as you see with these eyes and feel with these hands. And when these eyes no longer see, and these hands no longer feel, all that this book has meant to you will go on working in the lives of those who remember you...'

GOOD-BYE TO THE

MY LITTLE TRAVELLERS

FOR we have been travelling together, you and I, two years. We have been companions on two journeys round the sun. Into a hundred thousand homes and more, fortnight by fortnight, this book of my heart has gone. From thousands and thousands of homes has come back to me the love that men count more precious than gold. And to-day I write this last page of all, the last note in the book that has made us friends.

BUT, though in these words there must be something of the sadness of good-bye, it is not the sadness that comes when friendship ends. For our book is to go on, and month by month we may still meet in the pages of the new *Children's Encyclopædia*. And have we not, in these years in which we have travelled through our lives together, been thinking the same thoughts, building up the same memories? It cannot be that the day will ever come when this book will be as nothing to you or to me.

THAT cannot, cannot be. We have learned together in this book the truth of Life. We have learned to count upon the things that matter. We know that the things that bind us in friendship are the things that last for ever.

BOOK OF MY HEART

AND, if we think of it deeply, we know that this book can never really end at all. For a book is made out of the hearts of men and women, and grows into other hearts and other lives. A book carries through the world the things that do not die, the things that move us to good or to evil, that make or spoil our lives.

THE *Children's Encyclopædia* may end in the form in which you hold this copy in your hand; the paper may perish, and all that the eye looks upon may cease to be. But what has been written from the heart in this book, and what has come into your own heart from this book, will go on. It will go on in your own life, as long as you see with these eyes and feel with these hands. And when these eyes no longer see, and these hands no longer feel, all that this book has meant to you will go on working in the lives of those who remember you; and after them, for ages after them, for ever and ever and ever, whatever is good in this book will live.

So now, to this book of my heart, Good-bye. To you who have helped me to make it, to those who have read it and loved it, to all who have read it and loved it—Good-bye. Good-bye, Good-bye.

Your affectionate Friend
ARTHUR MEE

223

Conclusions

The first point to make is the magnitude of this literary achievement. Over a period of two years, the authors of the *Children's Encyclopædia* covered all the significant fields of human knowledge. With very few exceptions, their treatment was thorough, and the presentation interesting. Some of the series were aimed at very small children: others would have been a challenge for intelligent teenagers (and perhaps their parents!).

The Editor, Arthur Mee, deserves the main credit for an overall plan which enabled so many topics to be covered in the fifty original, fortnightly issues, so consistently that the final bound eight-volume edition forms a coherent whole. Some of the writing must have been done in advance, but references to current events (e.g. the finding of the North Pole) show that the contributors were keeping abreast of their time.

We should also recognise the technical achievement: there are over five thousand pages, practically without spelling or typographical errors: a list of errata at the end covers less than a page. The alphabetical index, on the other hand, takes over eighty pages of small print: authors and publishers know how big a task that is!

There are no precise figures on the sales of this first edition, but in the Preface we have already referred to Sir John Hammerton's estimates. He reckoned that, together with the next edition published after the First World War and including complete sets bound by subscribers to the serial issues, the total would have been about 1.5 million volumes (approaching 200,000 sets).[1] And this, of course, was only the starting-point for successive editions, as well as for the American and foreign-language versions.

We have been able to learn a little about the main contributors. **Dr. Caleb Williams Saleeby** was a public and somewhat controversial figure because of his role in the eugenics movement, but this does not intrude too much on his writing here. More surprising is the fact that he was entrusted with the two major scientific series – **LIFE** and **THE EARTH** – although his own training was in medicine. Nevertheless, these articles are well-informed, and though sometimes verbose, are generally clear and readable. He does not hesitate to express strong views on

---

[1] The number of upper and middle-class households in Britain (i.e. England, Wales and Scotland) would not have exceeded the census figure of 2.6 million people in the categories of employers, proprietors and white-collar workers (cf. footnote in Introduction). Assuming that few copies would have been bought by working-class people, and disregarding sales to libraries, this could mean that by the 1920s about one in thirteen of such households would have possessed a set of the *Encyclopædia*. But this is only a rough estimate.

practical matters and moral issues, especially concerning health. Maybe it was his role in the temperance movement that caused Arthur Mee to recruit him, and on the whole that choice was justified.

We know much less about **Frances Epps**, who wrote the long series on **COUNTRIES**. One can only admire the knowledge she displays and the quality of her writing, and wonder just how much of the world she had visited herself. (The interest of this series has caused me to give it a disproportionate amount of space.) She is relatively open-minded, showing respect for other peoples, even those considered backward, and for other religions even though she does not agree with them. She remained extremely patriotic, proud of her nation and its Empire. Like other contributors, she steered clear of disagreeable topics: these included the Boer War, troubles in Ireland, the suffragette movement, and above all the implications of German rearmament and the dangers looming in the Balkans.

The most professional of the contributors was **Edward Step**, who had already written extensively on plant life, in the series on **NATURE**. It is not clear what were the professional qualifications of **Ernest Bryant**, who wrote the articles on animal life, but these too are comprehensive, detailed and interesting. Here, we have highlighted two themes which run throughout these articles: what we would now call 'ecological balance', and evolution – firmly Darwinian.

John Hammerton was to become the most distinguished of the contributors (being knighted in 1932). As a journalist, he had been a colleague of Arthur Mee and we have frequently referred to his biography of Mee. His tasks for the *Encyclopædia* were relatively simple: to collate lists of **FAMOUS BOOKS** and of **POETRY**.

We do not know anything about **Edward Wright**, one of those who put together the collection of **STORIES**.

For **BIBLE STORIES**, Mee selected a 'close friend', **Harold Begbie**, who was a committed Christian in the evangelical tradition. He wrote with enthusiasm and conviction: he could not be expected to take an objective view of his subject.

Among the contributors to **SCHOOL LESSONS**, we know only about **Lois Mee**, Arthur's sister. They had travelled together, including to Paris. Perhaps she did not know as much French as he imagined: her articles are distinctly weak. The other writers in this section were competent, although these 'Lessons' did not seem to work very well.

Other sections are attributed to 'Many writers'. It would be useful to know who wrote some of the **GREAT LIVES**. While these are generally enjoyable, despite the moralising tendency, we have noted, for example, the ignorant and prejudiced treatment of other religions – was this Harold Begbie?

What of Arthur Mee himself? The only pieces under his name were his introductory pages, his 'Greeting' and his 'Farewell'. It appears that, having established the overall scheme and chosen his contributors, he gave them a free rein. It is clear, however, that he took a special interest in the question-and-answer items in **WONDER**. This was attributed to 'The Wise Man': Arthur would no doubt have selected the questions to be answered and, if he did not deal with them himself, passed them on to the most appropriate of his colleagues. It is probable, for example, that Dr. Saleeby wrote the answers to many of the scientific questions.

Mee's signed pieces are rather a puzzle. As we have seen, both from the text and certain illustrations, he seems to have been targeting 'little children', pictured as small, sweet and very well-dressed. This is still the case with his 'Farewell', even though his original readers would by then have been two years older (as would his own daughter, Marjorie, born in 1901). Unlike other contributors (and despite what Hammerton says), he tends to 'talk down' to his readers. Mee was undoubtedly a romantic in his attitude to children: his ideal, the child in 'The Age of Innocence', reflected Wordsworth's vision. [2]

Yet, except for some of the stories, poems, songs and nursery rhymes, most of the articles targeted a considerably older age-group: this is the case with the items on science, literature, some of the school lessons, etc. It is also apparent from the photographs of children who had contributed questions to **WONDER**, and from those who appear in some of the illustrations there.

To sum up this review of the contributors, several points can be made:
- Several (if not all) were personally known to the Editor.
- They were not necessarily known as experts in their subject, though almost all handled their topic well. This was still an age when there was a role for the intelligent, well-educated amateur: it would be difficult now to imagine a medical man being asked to write on astronomy for an *Encyclopædia*.
- In general, they appear to have come from professional, middle-class backgrounds. The main exception was the Editor himself, who had working-class origins though this is not apparent from the contents of the *Encyclopædia* and is played down in Hammerton's biography.
- At least one contributor – Harold Begbie – was a committed Christian, of 'Nonconformist' tendency. Arthur Mee's background was also Nonconformist and he was certainly much influenced by the Bible, though it is not evident that he was a regular church-goer and his faith seems to have been rather vague. If others did not have strong religious views, they were careful not to let this appear, even in the scientific articles.

These points about the authors are important because we have to judge how representative they were of current knowledge and opinion. In fact, the descriptions above seem fairly characteristic of the educated gentry, except that many (in England) would have been Anglicans rather than Nonconformists. It is reasonable to conclude that the *Encyclopædia* was written by people similar in background and views to the families for whom the work was destined. This, of

---

[2] Cf. Cunningham, *The Invention of Childhood*, especially pages 132–6. Quoting Wordsworth's famous lines – 'Trailing clouds of glory do we come…' he points out that the poet's impact on thinking about childhood was 'deep and lasting'.

course, raises the question as to its relevance to the working classes, to which we must return.

Our aim with this review of the *Children's Encyclopædia* has been to bring out what it tells us of life, ideas and attitudes in the Edwardian, pre-World War I, era; and to assess its influence on its readers.

Given the vast scope of the work, many topics deserve further exploration. It would be interesting, for example, to describe more fully the toys which children were encouraged to make for themselves, or the party games which they could play – potentially useful antidotes, perhaps, to today's mass-manufactured goods, pre-packaged on-screen entertainment or computer games.

One could also investigate more fully the *Encyclopædia*'s attitude to art. The work of the great painters of previous centuries is adequately covered, though there are not many reproductions from the Italian Renaissance and none at all from the Flemish 'Primitives'. The great majority of illustrations are by English painters of the nineteenth century, some well-known, others less so; many pictures are unattributed and some may have been painted on commission for the *Encyclopædia*.

There is a distinct leaning towards romanticism, tending to sentimentality. The English 'pre-Raphaelite' school is represented in some illustrations, including a couple of pictures by Burne-Jones, but is not discussed. The attractive borders surrounding the initial pages of each section (reproduced here) are representative of the contemporary 'Arts and Crafts Movement' in Britain, though this is not explicitly referred to. ('Art Nouveau' was the name of a gallery opened in Paris in 1895, but this term – likewise 'Impressionism' – was not yet in general use).

In literature too, although there is some coverage of the Greek classics and of early English works, the emphasis is on the English nineteenth century, again leaning towards romanticism though adventure stories also figure prominently.

Choices of topic have had to be made, and these are bound to reflect my own priorities. My conclusions are set out below under some major themes, covering social, economic, political and religious issues. I have given in the Preface some indication of my own views on these matters. Here, while stating my opinion where appropriate, I have done my best to be objective: the reader can judge.

Education

Arthur Mee and his colleagues were clearly anxious to break new ground in their approach to children. In private schools, the quality of teaching varied greatly. In the state or 'Board' schools, which were free and which catered for the greater number, the system remained rigid and formal. Classes were large, with learning mostly by rote, enforced by frequent corporal punishment. The subject-matter did not extend much beyond the 'three Rs' (reading, writing and arithmetic). While English literature was taught quite thoroughly, as were Bible studies, history and geography were usually covered very superficially. Only a minority went on to secondary education; few of these came from working-class households.

The *Encyclopædia* reversed this attitude. Children were to be respected, listened to, their questions answered. The items in **WONDER** are significant in this regard.[3] We have also noted that the authors' admiration for Germany was largely motivated by that country's advances in education, as well as in science.

Not only did the *Encyclopædia* provide answers to children's questions: it also sought to stimulate their interest. The **SCHOOL LESSONS** reflect this aim, though we may query their usefulness in the absence of an adult to help the children. In the other series, the articles are always interesting. History is taught mainly in story form (mostly avoiding dates, which might have discouraged readers if they felt they had to learn them by heart, as would have been the rule in school). Likewise, the scientific articles – as in **LIFE** and **THE EARTH** – hardly ever use scientific terms such as Biology, Geology or Astronomy, which might have seemed off-putting; nevertheless they contain thorough explanations of the earth and the universe.

The articles on **COUNTRIES** provided a wide range of knowledge on the history and geography of all the countries of the world: given the lack of school teaching in this field, this series must have opened the eyes of young readers to the world beyond their immediate surroundings.

Children were also encouraged to think for themselves, and to observe what is around them. In **FAMILIAR THINGS** we find clear explanations, with pictures, of how household objects work, such as a clock or a camera. The articles on **NATURE** are not just a catalogue of animals and plants, but show how each is related to its environment and what may be found in which places.

A youngster who had grown up with the *Encyclopædia* and read most of the articles on **FAMOUS BOOKS** and **POETRY**, as well as the items on writers, artists and musicians under **GREAT LIVES**, would have emerged with an extent of cultural knowledge that we can only admire today. From **BIBLE STORIES** they would have gained a general idea of the purposes of the Old and New Testaments, though not an objective view.

Health education features occasionally in **THE CHILD'S OWN LIFE** – this was a favourite subject with Dr. Saleeby. We hear a good deal about unhealthy, stuffy conditions in schoolrooms, and in workplaces: the importance of fresh air is emphasised. Diet does not figure prominently; where it does we might not agree with all the recommendations. There is an interesting discourse on vegetarianism: do we really need to eat meat?

The authors' main wrath was directed at alcohol (we should remember that at least two – Mee and Saleeby – were active in the temperance movement). One

---

[3] Cunningham, in *Children and Childhood*, points out that by the late nineteenth century the concept had emerged among reformers and philanthropists that children were entitled to a 'happy childhood'. This fits well with the approach of the *Encyclopædia*.

might think this unnecessary in a book directed at children, but the problem – mainly in the urban slums – was serious enough to warrant legislation in the 1908 Children Act. The writers also discourage smoking, though the addictive nature of tobacco was not fully understood. Drugs were not an issue.

One item of education which is totally absent is sex. The word does not appear in the index; if any children submitted questions about where babies came from – as no doubt they did – these were disregarded. In fact, in the articles on **NATURE**, the process of reproduction is left vague even in discussing the animal kingdom. Though it is clear that females give birth, the reader could have wondered what was the role of the male.

Fundamentally, the *Encyclopædia* aimed at character-building. This is evident particularly in the examples of heroism, self-sacrifice and devotion to duty, presented as **GOLDEN DEEDS**. (One can see here a reflection of the 'public school' ethos.) The young readers were also taught civic duties and the importance of living together peaceably, both within the nation and as between countries.

Science and technology

The Edwardian era was an exciting time to grow up, and this is conveyed in the pages of the Encyclopædia. We have mentioned in the Introduction some of the main developments. The pages of the Encyclopædia capture these in text and pictures, and the optimism of the times is clearly reflected.

It was a charmed age, with no foreboding of the destructive uses to which these inventions would be put. (The Boer War was the last not to involve destructive machines such as tanks and airplanes.) There is even a dawning awareness of the power of atomic energy, seen here as a great potential benefit to mankind.

Knowledge of the nature of the earth and the universe had greatly expanded: the series on **THE EARTH** reflects recent and on-going discoveries, based on the ideas of Newton and the other great astronomers. The *Encyclopædia* had not caught up with Einstein, which is forgivable since he had only recently published his first theory of relativity; the concepts of the 'Big Bang' and the expanding universe were still several decades away. Still, the young reader would have formed a clear idea of the vastness of the universe, of the solar system and of the formation of the earth.

The nature of heat and light is explained, along with the vital principle of the conservation of energy. The *Encyclopædia* has greater difficulty over gravity – again forgivable – and its concept of the 'ether' as the medium in space through which energy travelled, though not illogical, was soon to be discarded by scientists. The movement of tectonic plates, and their role in provoking earthquakes, was another still unknown phenomenon.

The series on **NATURE** and **LIFE** are of interest because they would have left the readers in no doubt about evolution and the Darwinian principle of natural selection. Since this was a fairly recent and still controversial theory, this was quite a bold course to take. Man, of course, is presented as the highest form of life, though the *Encyclopædia* avoids asserting too clearly that he descended from the apes. [4]

Science and religion

This was a particularly sensitive area at the time of the *Encyclopædia*, especially following Darwin. As has been pointed out above, there is no hesitation in the scientific articles about presenting the Darwinian view of evolution, nor about presenting a view of the universe and the origins of the earth derived from Copernicus, Galileo, Newton and more recent discoveries.

Most if not all of the contributors, including Arthur Mee himself, would probably have called themselves Christians. Whether as a result of Mee's editorial control, or – more probably – of self-imposed restraint, no admission of conflict is allowed to creep in. Indeed, where scientific knowledge reaches its limits, as in dealing with the origins of the universe, of life itself, and of man's ultimate destiny, the scientific writers resort to some kind of *deus ex machina*, often using a circumlocution such as 'Nature', or 'the ultimate Author of all things', or 'Author of all the power in the Universe', rather than refer explicitly to 'God'.

This caution does not reflect the on-going debate at the time, and one may question the *Encyclopædia*'s policy in this respect. Should the young readers not have been offered a more balanced view of the issues involved? The probable answer is that, quite apart from the Editor's own beliefs, the *Encyclopædia* had to avoid controversy over this issue if it was to be widely accepted.

It should also be noted here that although Mee and at least one of the main authors were on the Protestant, Nonconformist wing, the *Encyclopædia* treads carefully in matters concerning Catholic-Protestant relationships. This is notable particularly under **GREAT LIVES** and **GOLDEN DEEDS**, where Catholic heroes and saints get as much attention as Protestant ones (the *Encyclopædia*, for example, is firmly on the side of Joan of Arc). Deliberate or not, this policy was successful:

---

[4] It was not so long since W.S. Gilbert, reflecting the furore provoked by Darwin, had parodied the thesis in *Princess Ida* (first performed in 1884*): 'A Lady fair, of lineage high, was lov'd by an Ape, in the days gone by... With a view to rise in the social scale, he shaved his bristles and he dock'd his tail... And to start his life on a brand-new plan, he christened himself Darwinian Man!'.* This would have been familiar to the Edwardians.

It is fair to point out that debate continues among scientists as to just how natural selection works. Moreover, the whole principle of evolution is again contested, particularly among fundamentalist Christian groups in the USA: a survey in 2005 found that two out of three Americans approved the teaching of 'creationism' (or its latest formulation 'intelligent design'), while 38% wanted Darwinism excluded from school programmes. 'Creationism' also seems to be gaining ground in Britain.

we know from Hammerton's biography that the *Encyclopædia* gained the approval of the Catholic hierarchy. [5]

Unfortunately, the *Encyclopædia* did not show the same open-mindedness with respect to other world religions. At best, it is mystified by Oriental religion and philosophy; at worst, it reflects ignorance and prejudice. No doubt is to be left in young minds that Christianity is far superior, in fact the only true religion. In this, of course, the *Encyclopædia* reflects the attitudes of the time, closely linked to the colonial experience; it does not, however, encourage its readers to seek fuller knowledge and display greater tolerance.

Society

We know from other sources that the conditions of the British working-class, though improved from Victorian times, still left much to be desired in terms of housing, working conditions, health and education. Reading the *Encyclopædia*, one has little inkling of this. There is brief mention of the bad working conditions in factories. But where the workers are presented, they appear as strong, healthy, willing (especially so in the coloured plate reproduced in Chapter 6).

A particularly telling demonstration of this attitude appears in the contrasting pictures in Chapter 1 of miners working at the coal-face and of a prosperous-looking family sitting comfortably at the fireside. That these pictures should be presented with apparently no sense of conflict suggests that the writer considered this a perfectly normal situation.

Many other indications, such as the well-dressed children shown in many other illustrations, or the clearly middle-class family of the French lessons written by Mee's sister Lois (who have a nurse, can afford to spend time in Paris, etc.), confirm not only that the *Encyclopædia* was aimed at the prosperous classes but also – more disturbingly – had no qualms in the matter. There is hardly any mention of child neglect and deprivation, though – as seen in our Introduction – this was a major issue at the time and was another target of the 1908 Children Act.

The class divide would have been conspicuous – and evident to children – in well-to-do families which could afford servants; and middle-class households would have had a least a maid. Yet, except for the nurse-maid in the French lessons, servants are nowhere mentioned: their subordinate role seems to be taken for granted, and nothing is said about their conditions of employment. [6]

---

[5] Hammerton writes (p.128 of his biography – see Annex) that 'Although its editor was well known for his strong Nonconformist principles, it had the endorsement of the leading Catholic churchmen. Cardinal Bourne, Father Bernard Vaughan, and the Archbishop of Liverpool, all gave it their blessing, and the Catholic Truth Society, after careful scrutiny, agreed that "it might safely be added to a school reference library".'

[6] The treatment of servants could be harsh or considerate, depending on the household. See Pamela Sambrook, *Keeping their Place: Domestic Service in the Country House* (2005).

So it has to be said, regrettably, that the *Encyclopædia* reflects the class-consciousness of its era, and did little to promote a more responsible social attitude. Indeed, expressions such as 'the lower classes' were used without hesitation, and there is even a hint of the 'social eugenics' prevalent at the time.

All this is odd when one considers that Arthur Mee himself came from a working-class background; he left school at the age of fourteen to go to work, and from then on was self-taught. Perhaps, like many others who had 'risen' through the social classes, he preferred to forget his origins. But this is a serious limitation on the educational role of the *Encyclopædia*. What did it do for working-class children? Did it even enter many working-class households? – this seems unlikely, and even Hammerton's biography has nothing to say on the matter. It was presumably taken up by public libraries, but would children from poor families have been likely to frequent such establishments? It would be good to think that it appeared in school libraries, but many Board schools did not possess libraries and when they did their stock was limited. [7]

On this important point it is difficult to find hard facts, but there is negative evidence to the extent that the memoirs of working-class people who were at school in the Edwardian era (cf. Arthur, Thompson and especially Rose) rarely mention the *Encyclopædia*, although they do refer to other reading material. [8]

The *Encyclopædia* is ambivalent about the role of women. Clearly, the work itself is aimed at girls as well as boys: among the **GOLDEN DEEDS** there are heroines as well as heroes; **THINGS TO MAKE AND DO** contains different tasks for boys and girls – carpentry for the former, dress-making etc. for the latter – but there are also many activities which they could do together, and girls are shown playing cricket as well as tennis and hockey.

However, considering that the suffragette movement was at its peak – or perhaps for this reason, given the *Encyclopædia* policy of avoiding controversial issues – it gives little or no guidance as to the adult role of women.

One main contributor, Saleeby, considered that girls should be educated so as to become good mothers. The main female contributor, Frances Epps, refers approvingly to other countries (there are not many: New Zealand and Finland) where women participate actively in political life; but even she avoids the issue when discussing Britain.

Imperialism

The *Encyclopædia* is proud of Britain's supremacy in the world and of its great Empire. It justifies Britain's rule over other peoples in terms of bringing them civilisation (railways

---

[7] According to Alec Ellis, *Educating our Masters: Influences on the Growth of Literacy in Victorian Working-Class Children* (1985) (quoted by Rose), 40% of inspected schools in 1900 had their own libraries, with an average stock of 221 volumes.

[8] Professor Rose helpfully informed me that he recollected some references to the *Encyclopædia* in the large mass of material he collected, but not enough to make any great impression.

playing an important role) and of converting them to Christianity (the work of missionaries is on the whole described with approval, though one can detect some doubts in this respect). The commercial motive is underplayed, and strategic considerations get only a brief mention.

The *Encyclopædia* is in no doubt that the white man is superior, and indeed clearly feels that among the whites, British is best. It was convenient that 'social Darwinism' provided a justification: if the white man was racially superior, it was right that he should take precedence. Here again we can see a reflection of the prevalent 'public school' mentality, preparing pupils to govern the Empire. [9]

In all this, the *Encyclopædia* reflects the assumptions of its time. Indeed, it is on the liberal side in that context, stressing that the 'lesser breeds' should be treated with respect and that white rule entails duties as well as privileges.

The *Encyclopædia* does not, however, notice that its criteria were those of white civilisation: basically, material progress and prosperity. It displays some regret over the fate of the American Indians, but on the whole does not consider that those other races – including the Australian aborigines, whom it puts at the bottom of the racial ladder – had a culture and life-style that were well adapted to their natural environment, until the arrival of the white man disrupted that equilibrium. [10]

Britain in the world

There is much to learn from the excellent series on **COUNTRIES**: a summary has been given at the end of that long chapter and it is not necessary to repeat all the points.

Above all, the *Encyclopædia* reflects Britain's confidence in its economic and military power. It acknowledges a rising challenge from Germany, particularly in the construction of battleships. It does not take this threat seriously, perhaps because in general it admires Germany for its scientific progress and its excellent education system; perhaps also because of misplaced confidence in the links between the Kaiser and the British royal family.

Again in line with its general tendency to avoid unpleasant facts which might distress its young readers, it fails to point out the dangers in the historic antagonism between France and Germany; though it explains well the complexities of the Balkans, it disregards the potential dangers there; and it is much too favourable to Franz Joseph of Austria-Hungary, whose misjudgements would subsequently precipitate the conflagration of 1914.

---

[9] Cf. Walvin. He also observes how stories for boys often revolved around the overseas adventures of ex-schoolboy heroes displaying the qualities learned in the classroom or on the playing-field; he writes (p. 179) that 'in the thirty years before 1914 children's books, magazines and comics rang with the tones of nationalism and imperialism'.
By the time I reached my 'public school' (in 1945) such attitudes had not much changed.

[10] On 13th February 2008, at the annual opening of the Australian Parliament, the recently-elected Prime Minister of Australia made a long-awaited public apology for the past treatment of the aborigines.

Consequently, the *Encyclopædia* gave no hint of the coming disaster, although in another context even Mee had expressed concern at German intentions. Some of its readers, and many of their fathers, uncles or elder brothers, would soon be called up to fight and die in the trenches of Flanders. There, the ideals of self-sacrifice and gallantry learnt from the *Encyclopædia* would be put to the ultimate test. Many would not return.

∽ঝ৵

My Introduction to this book was sub-titled 'The end of an era?'. Although some people were aware of the danger ahead, the spirit of the time was unquestioning confidence. Science and technology were progressing rapidly, and their fruits were to be seen all around. It was possible then to write in the *Encyclopædia*:

> 'The world is a beautiful place filled with living things, and men and women and boys and girls are the masters of creation.' (p. 17)

Moreover, Britain's supremacy in the world, with the immense wealth and power of its Empire, appeared to guarantee that its privileged position would last indefinitely. As Sir Geoffrey Keynes wrote in his autobiography:

> 'Young people of my age had lived through the Victorian and Edwardian times with a sense of complete physical security, and most of us had never given a thought to the possibility of our becoming involved in a European war.' [11]

Yet after 1914–18, nothing would be quite the same, for Britain or for other countries. True, Britain and its allies won that war, though with appalling losses among their soldiers. But a defeated Germany, mishandled by the victors, was to suffer social and economic trauma that provided the terrain for a still more dangerous threat as that country recovered its strength. The British Empire, despite growing tensions, survived to fight and win in the Second World War, but it emerged greatly weakened. The end of empire might be dated with the granting of independence to India in 1947, and the last attempted flourish of independent military power with the fiasco of the Anglo-French intervention in Suez in 1956.[12]

Subsequently, Britain – no longer a major power – has struggled to find its role in the world: above all, to define its relationship with the United States on the one hand, with Europe on the other. In this context, the assumption of supremacy conveyed by the *Encyclopædia* and many other influences may have been a hindrance, encouraging the persistence of 'Euro-sceptic' attitudes.

The United States, on the other hand, came out of the Second World War greatly reinforced, with the strength and will this time to aid the recovery of the European nations, including the defeated ones. After the collapse of the Soviet

---

[11] *The Gates of Memory* (1981), p.124.

[12] It is true that Margaret Thatcher successfully intervened in the Falklands Islands in 1982, the US remaining on the sidelines; but this was a campaign to reclaim the territory after it had been invaded by Argentina.

Union in 1991 it became the only world super-power. By the start of the twenty-first century, it was in a position not unlike that of Britain before the First World War: confident in its technological superiority, its domestic prosperity, its economic and military supremacy in the world, but – like Britain then – insensitive to changing needs and growing challenges.

Now, even that colossal American power finds itself challenged. Its high and rising levels of output and consumption contribute disproportionately to global environmental threats, and in the long run are unsustainable. Disparities in wealth and opportunity both within the country and as between the USA and the 'Third World', particularly its Latin American neighbours, are flagrant and invite hostility.

We know that empires come and go. Inevitably, in the twenty-first century, power will continue to shift to Asia, where the mass of the world population live and where economic growth is rapid. Already, without China no significant world issue can be resolved.

Britain justified its dominion over subject peoples on grounds of improving their lot, maybe too of Christianising them. The USA justifies its interventions abroad in terms of combating terrorism and promoting democracy. In both cases, an objective observer can easily discern more self-serving motives.

Confronting the rise of militant Islam, the USA has relied primarily on its military might. This power will no doubt remain dominant for some time to come; but if misused it makes more enemies than friends. American actions have pushed Russia, still a power to be reckoned with and a necessary ally in the 'war on terror', back into antagonism.

The world has become a more dangerous place, and needs wise leadership. Unfortunately, just as Britain was reluctant to give up her Empire, the USA now will not easily learn the lessons of history.

The Children Act, 1908

PART I: INFANT LIFE PROTECTION
– supervision of persons undertaking 'for reward' the nursing and maintenance of infants (under seven years).

PART II: PREVENTION OF CRUELTY TO CHILDREN AND YOUNG PERSONS
– punishment (fine or imprisonment for any person in charge who assaults, ill–treats, neglects or abandons his/her charges; includes failure to provide adequate food, clothing, medical aid, lodging, or if unable to do so, fails to take steps under provisions for relief of the poor.
– punishment also for permitting children in their charge to beg, to reside in or frequent brothels, or to practice prostitution.

PART III: JUVENILE SMOKING
– selling cigarettes to anyone under sixteen is an offence.
– a constable can seize cigarettes in the possession of anyone under sixteen in a public place.

PART IV: REFORMATORY AND INDUSTRIAL SCHOOLS
– provides for certification and inspection of such institutes, where offenders between twelve and sixteen can be placed.

PART V: JUVENILE OFFENDERS
– should not be sent to prison but to an approved 'place of detention'.
– abolishes penal servitude and the death penalty for young offenders (but whipping permitted).

PART VI: MISCELLANEOUS AND GENERAL
– giving 'intoxicating liquor' to children under five is an offence.
– children not allowed in licensed bars.
– medical officers can inspect children in school for vermin: parents/guardians to be notified where necessary, and in cases of non–compliance children can be taken to 'suitable premises' for cleansing.
– 'child' defined as under fourteen; 'young persons' as between fourteen and sixteen.

The Act was passed on 21st December 1908
and entered into force on 1st April 1909.

Bibliography

Only the most important books relevant to the main themes of this work are listed here; longer lists can be found in Hattersley (2004) and Cunningham (2006). Others cited in connection with specific points have their bibliographical details in footnotes.

Many of these works refer only to England (or England and Wales), even when this is not explicit. This is noticeable particularly in the books on education, where some comparison at least with the Scottish system (which was much better) would have been called for. Ireland is neglected, though it was part of 'British history'. The *Encyclopædia*, as has been seen, shares this anglo-centric bias.

General works
Chris COOK and John STEVENSON, *The Longman Handbook of Modern British History, 1714-1987* (second edition, 1988) contains useful facts and figures.
Eric HOBSBAWM, *The Age of Empire 1875–1914* (1987).
Ronald HYAM, *Britain's Imperial Century 1815–1914* (1976).
Andrew ROBERTS, *A History of the English-Speaking Peoples since 1900* (2006) – mentioned here for completeness, but this is a pretentious, biased and unreliable work.
Barbara TUCHMAN, *The Proud Tower – A portrait of the world before the war 1890 –1914* (1966) – this covers several countries, but her Chapter 7 is a readable account of the Edwardian period in England.

Contemporary sources cited in the Introduction:
Charles BOOTH, *Life and Labour of the People of London*, 1st series: Poverty (1902).
L.G. CHIOZZA MONEY, *Riches and Poverty* (1905).
C.F.G. MASTERMAN, *The Condition of England* (1909).
B. SEEBOHM ROWNTREE, *Poverty: A Study of Town Life* (1906).

Subsequent works on the Edwardian era:
Max ARTHUR, *Lost Voices of the Edwardians* (2006) – contains interviews with people from different walks of life.
Melvyn BRAGG, *The Hired Man* (1969) – a novel, but gives a vivid picture of the difficulties confronting a landless farm worker.
Roy HATTERSLEY, *The Edwardians* (2004) – provides a comprehensive survey while concentrating on the political aspects.
F.J.C. HEARNSHAW, *Edwardian England* (1933) – an interesting series of lectures first given at King's College, London on various aspects of Edwardian life.
Simon NOWELL-SMITH (ed.), *Edwardian England 1901-1914* (1964).
Robert OPIE (as compiler), *The Edwardian Scrapbook* (2002) – provides light-hearted relief in picture form.
Donald READ, *Documents from Edwardian England, 1901-1915* (1973) and *Edwardian England 1901-15 – Society and Politics* (1972).
Maisie ROBSON, *1906: Every Man for Himself!* (2002) – a collection of the requirements for different trades.
Paul THOMPSON, *The Edwardians – The Remaking of British Society* (1975) – includes accounts of the lives of twelve Edwardians ranging from the aristocratic to the working-class.

Issues relating to childhood:

Hugh CUNNINGHAM, *Children and Childhood in Western Society since 1500* (1994) and *The Invention of Childhood* (2006).

Anne DAVIN, *Growing Up Poor – Home, School and Street in London, 1870-1914* (1996).

Eric HOPKINS, *Childhood Transformed – Working-class Children in Nineteenth-Century England* (1994).

Pamela HORN, *The Victorian and Edwardian Schoolchild* (1989).

J.S. HURT, *Elementary Schooling and the Working Classes, 1860-1918* (1979).

Jonathan ROSE, *The Intellectual Life of the British Working* Classes – ch. 5 'Willingly to School' (2001).

James WALVIN, *A Child's World – A Social History of English Childhood 1800-1914* (1982).

On Scottish education, *Wikipedia* comes to the rescue.

Biographies of Arthur Mee:

Gillian ELIAS, *Arthur Mee – "Journalist in Chief to British Youth"* (1993) – a slight work, but contains some information from family archives in Nottinghamshire.

John HAMMERTON, *Child of Wonder – An intimate biography of Arthur Mee–* this is the basic work, by his life-long friend, also a contributor to the *Children's Encyclopædia*; written soon after Mee's death.

Maisie ROBSON, *Arthur Mee's Dream of England.* (2003) – often neglects to quote sources, and draws largely on Hammerton, but covers Mee's later life and works.

All three biographies tend to be laudatory, with little or no critical analysis.

Present-day encyclopedias for children

It is of interest to compare the *Children's Encyclopædia* of 1908–10 with current offerings. There are several works of a specialised nature, dealing for example with animals, or space, or the human body. Two of a general nature bear comparison.

The *Usborne Internet-linked Children's Encyclopedia* contains 320 small-format pages. Illustrations take up a large amount of space; text is short and simple. This work is clearly aimed at small children. Most topics are covered in two facing pages. The arrangement is not alphabetical: topics are grouped under broad headings, such as 'Animals and Plants' or 'How Your Body Works'; to find a particular item you need to look in an index at the end. The 'Internet link' is perhaps a selling-point, but in fact consists of the same reference on most pages to a Usborne web-site, and a further search – not easy – is needed to find specific information. Any child able to do this could also use one of the well-known search engines.

The *Doreen Kindersley Children's Illustrated Encyclopedia* is a much more serious affair: it has 800 large pages, with thorough textual explanations on each subject accompanied by helpful illustrations. Topics are arranged alphabetically and are easy to find; for most items there are useful cross-references to other items. There is a table of contents at the beginning and a detailed index at the end.

Any present-day encyclopedia can of course use technical possibilities of which the Edwardian authors could not only dream: above all, abundant colour illustrations. Both these works, particularly the second, provide information in an attractive and easily-assimilated form.

Keeping up-to-date is nowadays an important issue for any work of reference. The *Usborne* book does not clearly state its date of publication. My copy of the *Doreen Kindersley* work indicates 'Fifth Edition 2000'. Despite the quality of the latter work, children today are more likely to look for up-to-date information directly on the Internet.

Neither is really comparable with the *Children's Encyclopædia*. For a start, the latter has over five thousand pages; the treatment of scientific subjects is discursive and extensive; it includes stories, résumés of major literary works, poetry, etc. While the contemporary works provide succinct information, the authors of the *Children's Encyclopædia* aimed also to stimulate and respond to children's questioning on a wide range of subjects, including moral, religious and philosophical issues.

It is doubtful whether children of today, accustomed to getting well-packaged information, would have the patience to plough through the relatively lengthy articles of the Edwardian work. Is this progress? Or has something been lost?

Sir John Hammerton's biography of Arthur Mee

'CHILD OF WONDER' [1]

Sir John describes this work as 'an intimate biography. It was published in 1946, just two years after Arthur Mee's death. The two had been lifelong friends, in fact since 1895 when they were both on the staff of the *Nottingham Daily Express*; subsequently they had worked together on several projects, including the *Children's Encyclopædia*. He says the *Encyclopædia* was 'dedicated to the youth of two generations and of many races whose love of knowledge was nurtured and character enriched by works of Arthur Mee'. It was 'a life story full of human interest and the romance of life'.

In **Chapter I**, he describes Mee as 'a Christian romantic'. He was 'no deep thinker who set himself to ponder over the ways of the world in which he had come to life, but just a healthy-minded human being greatly gifted beyond the ordinary healthy-minded human being, and for that reason destined to leave his impression on his age'.

Arthur 'presented an enigma in holding fast to the sectarianism of his father while keeping in step with all advances of science from Evolution to the Splitting of the Atom'.

Chapter II describes Arthur's childhood. He was born in Stapleford, Nottinghamshire, in 1875, the second of ten children. His father, 'an engineer' (Sir John seems reluctant to admit Mee's working-class origin), was 'a man of strong political and religious views, a Radical, a militant Nonconformist, an upright, earnest citizen'. He devoted his life to the Baptist Church, of which he was a deacon.

Arthur attended an excellent school in Stapleford, where the headmaster, one George Byron, was a very different character: a Tory, believing firmly in the principle of 'The rich man in his castle, the poor man at the gate: God made them high and lowly and ordered their estate.'

Such an upbringing no doubt contributed to three commanding interests throughout Mee's life: unshakeable faith in Christian ethic as based on the Scriptures, love of his native land, and belief that the British Empire was the greatest force for world welfare.

Chapter III relates how in 1889, when Arthur was fourteen, the family moved to Nottingham. Then there was no more schooling for him: he went to work in a bakery.

At this point Sir John makes an interesting comment. Arthur had said at some point: 'I know nothing about children'. In fact, 'Arthur did not assume a pedagogic pose in addressing them, but in the most natural way wrote and planned for them to their complete understanding: he was always a child himself in his cast of mind but

---

[1] This interesting though uncritical work has unfortunately been out-of-print for some time and second-hand copies are not to be found. I was able to consult it in the Cambridge University Library.

Sir John's own career – a prominent one – has been briefly noted above in relation to the series on **BOOKS**, which he compiled.

gifted with a power of forthright expression which endowed his thoughts, even when they concerned the simplest things, with some essence of the wonder that possesses all young persons in their early contacts with life and the realities of nature'.

Chapter IV explains how Arthur entered journalism by 'the lowliest door', being apprenticed in 1891 to the *Nottingham Daily Express*. He became sub-editor of its evening edition, but that amounted to little more than collating items from the morning edition with the main events of the day.

Chapter V observes that Arthur avoided the pub-frequenting and beer-drinking that was habitual among other young men (especially journalists).

He was writing increasingly in his own right, and his views began to emerge. Sir John refers at length to a paper he gave to the Baptist Literary Society in 1895. In this, he had criticised those who held too narrow views of their responsibilities: 'We convince ourselves that we owe no duty to the Chinaman because he is so far away, while we acknowledge a brotherhood with the citizens of other foreign countries near our own… It gives us a mean conception of mankind that Christianity cannot recognise…' He encouraged his listeners (other young people, apparently) to accept that they had 'a share in the building up of the new world… You cannot exaggerate the power of a single man with a great purpose. Nothing is so contagious as real, thorough, honest Christianity…'

Chapters VI and VII recount how, from 1896 onwards, Arthur was in London, writing constantly, mainly as a free-lance journalist but also with posts on the *Home Magazine*, the *Daily Mail*, and other periodicals. He learned a little French at this time; he did not know any other language. He married in 1897, and bought a house in West Norwood; his daughter Marjorie was born in 1901.

Chapter VIII describes 'The Wonderful Years', when Arthur asked John Hammerton to work with him on the *Harmsworth Self-Educator*, successfully published in fortnightly issues from 1906 onwards: the publisher was the proprietor of the *Daily Mail*, Lord Northcliffe. This was followed by the *Harmsworth History of the World*, again with Arthur and John as joint editors. At this point Sir John quotes from a letter Arthur wrote to Lord Northcliffe in 1908 about the growing sense of danger from Germany, particularly arising from their airships:

> 'As a reasonable human being I do think it is a great pity that the moment Zeppelin learns how to fly his genius should be turned to the uses of war instead of peace… I have a little girl, and I am very anxious about the sort of world she is going to grow up in… I am told that the German papers often say the most extraordinary things, and speak almost as if war had been declared with England; but surely this cannot be so (underlined)… It really is absurd that wars should be allowed to grow in these days out of misunderstandings, and certainly nobody wants war between England and Germany.'

As we have seen, there is no reflection of these concerns in the content of the *Encyclopædia*.

About this time, Arthur had the idea which grew into the *Children's Encyclopædia*. John himself thought this a forbidding name, and in any case it was to be really a collection of books for children 'rather arbitrarily grouped within the compass of one continuous work'. But Arthur 'was obsessed with the idea of providing for the young folk of his time a book which would bring to them all the essentials of useful, scientific, and practical knowledge, and also the endless entertainment that books could convey'. So he had his way, and his faith was justified by results.

Chapter IX is entitled **'Romance of the Children's Encyclopædia'** and deserves special attention here. Sir John stresses how the first of the fortnightly series, on 17th March 1908, was an immediate success – despite his own doubts about calling it an 'Encyclopædia' – and how the circulation increased with each issue up to the last, on 1st February 1910. It began to be sold in eight-volume form even before that date, and became 'the wonder book of the twentieth century ... the modern classic of the children's world'.

Subsequently, there had been twenty-six large editions (he must be counting reprints); from 1923 onwards it appeared in twelve-volume form. Sir John calculated that total sales throughout the Empire had amounted to 5,380,000, to which could be added some 1,500,000 bound by subscribers to the serial issues.

He emphasises the importance of the Index: nearly a hundred pages in the first edition, and greatly extended subsequently when it became in itself 'A Little Guide to Knowledge', with about 90,000 entries.

He saw little need to describe these treasures to his readers, as they would almost certainly be familiar with them. Writing probably in 1948, he remarks that most people in the age range 25-50 had been 'brought up' on the *Encyclopædia* (Sir John probably did not consort much with the working class). It had brought relief to thousands of parents by providing answers to their children's questioning.

Its great secret, he says, was the absence of any 'writing down' to the child's mind. He does observe that Arthur Mee's 'Greeting' and 'Farewell' are exceptions to this. Oddly enough, he has nothing to say about the role of the other contributors (including himself), which has been emphasised in the present work. Nor does he enlighten us as to how the work was planned and produced, in particular how much editorial control was exercised by Mee himself.

An important factor in its success had been that, despite Mee's strong Non-conformist principles, it had obtained endorsement from leading Catholic churchmen. Arthur had the skill and the acumen to avoid any appearance of denominalisation. (This, as we have noted, is hardly true of the series on 'Bible Stories' by Harold Begbie.)

Sir John also describes the events which led to publication in the USA. A publisher called Walter M. Jackson had secured rights for an American edition by his firm, the Grolier Society, even before the initial series was complete. He imported plates of the English edition intercalated with new material more suited to an American readership. Under the title *The Book of Knowledge* (with the English name as a sub-title) it was an instant success. Later editions grew to twenty volumes, and it was claimed that more than 3.5 million sets had been sold over a 35-year period. Grolier also produced a special Canadian edition.

There were also editions in French (Larousse, up to the Second World War), Italian (Mondadori, in 1928, 'a beautiful edition', with patronage by Mussolini), Spanish (in 1923, covering also South America), Portuguese (popular also in Brazil) and even Chinese (in 1927).

*   *   *

Subsequent chapters in the biography deal with Arthur Mee's life following the first edition of the *Children's Encyclopædia*: they are therefore less relevant to our present purpose and only some salient points will be picked out.

Mee, writes Sir John, somewhat modified his fundamentalism in later years. He gained fuller comprehension of the nineteenth-century discoveries by Darwin, Huxley, Spencer and others; but his Christian faith remained unshaken. The English Bible was not only the source of his faith but also the main inspiration of his literary manner. (However, there is no indication here – nor in the subsequent biographies, which draw largely on Hammerton – as to whether Mee was a church-goer).

After the end of the war in 1918, in a book entitled *Who Giveth Us the Victory*, Mee declared that mankind had been saved from the loss of its faith in God. Scientific progress could resume; and Mee saw no contradiction between science and God:

> 'The child born in the Great War will live on into a world beyond imagination now... We have found that matter is a colossal reserve of energy... The mind that understands the past will shrink from no vision of the future that imagination can conceive... Man has no reason to be surprised if tomorrow the mighty atom should suddenly release its power and banish poverty and weariness for human kind...'

Previously (after quoting Mee's speech in 1895) Sir John had provided a fitting conclusion:

> 'No man of his time more nobly did his best to strive for the ideals of his youth than Arthur Mee. And although at the end he was still far from seeing these being realised, for he died when the War was at the very zenith of its horror,[2] he could look back to his twenty-first birthday without regret and on all his life-work with the joy of service in the cause of human progress.'

------

[2] i.e. in 1943, before the explosion of the first atomic bomb.

List of illustrations

_____
* In the text.
# In colour.

Index

Main entries in bold, footnote entries in italics

INDEX